We'd Like Your Comments!

Thanks for purchasing *How to Make Money Writing . . . Fillers*

We sincerely hope it will be helpful and enjoyable to you. While you're reading the book you can use this card as a bookmark. Then, we'd like your comments. Please fill out the card and return it to us.

Your reaction to this book: _____

_____

_____

Other books you'd like to see Writer's Digest Books publish: _____

_____

Where did you get this book?

☐ Bookstore ☐ Library ☐ Ordered by mail ☐ Book Club
☐ Other, specify: _____

Check if you would like to receive free information about:

☐ New Writer's Digest Books ☐ Writer's Digest School
☐ Writer's Digest Magazine ☐ Photographer's Market Newsletter

Name _____ Phone: _____

Address _____

City _____ State _____ Zip _____

HOW TO MAKE MONEY WRITING

Little Articles
Anecdotes   Hints
Recipes
Light Verse

AND OTHER

FILLERS

CONNIE EMERSON

Writer's Digest Books
Cincinnati, Ohio

Library of Congress Cataloging in Publication Data
Emerson, Connie, 1930-
    How to make money writing little articles, anecdotes, hints, recipes, light verse, and other fillers.

    Bibliography: p.
    Includes index.
    1. Authorship.   I. Title.
PN147.E45 1983   808'.02   83-3623
ISBN 0-89879-104-9

Design by Charleen Catt.

The Permissions Acknowledgments on the following two pages and on pages 265 and 266 constitute an extension of this copyright page.

✦✦✦✦ PERMISSIONS ACKNOWLEDGMENTS

"For the Birds" by Ruth Schiefen from *Friend*, May 1982 © 1982 by Corporation of the President of The Church of Jesus Christ of Latter-day Saints. All rights reserved.

"Batty Story" by Lakenan Barnes, Copyright 1972, *The American Legion Magazine*, reprinted by permission.

"My Thirst Saved Me from an Accident" by Homer Walker from *Grit*, July 4, 1982, reprinted by permission.

"Pin-up Girl" by Vivian L. Hall from *Grit*. Reprinted by permission.

Review of *Quest for Fire* by John Stickney from *Discover*, March 1982, reprinted by permission.

"KK Tei" by Loryn Yim reprinted with the permission of *ALOHA, The Magazine of Hawaii*.

"A Sleeping Bag Canopy" from *Field & Stream*, March 1982 © 1980 by Norma Gaffron, New Brighton MN.

Puzzle "Sprung from Spring" by Dee Lillegard, first printed in *Wee Wisdom Magazine*, April 1982. Reprinted by permission.

Book review "Monk reflects on simple lifestyle" by Mary Brooke Casad from *United Methodist Reporter*, April 9, 1982. Reprinted by permission.

"Bright Side of the Road" Department from *Discovery*, Spring 1982. Reprinted with permission from Louis F. Root and *Discovery*, the Allstate Motor Club magazine.

"Her Forth Mistake" by Carolyn B. Wilson reprinted by permission from the July 1981 issue of *The Lutheran*, magazine of the Lutheran Church in America.

"The Gracious Art of Taking—and Giving" by B. Keith Cossey. Reprinted by permission from *Guideposts Magazine*. Copyright © 1982 by Guideposts Associates, Inc., Carmel NY 10512. All rights reserved.

Quiz "Plants Around the World" from *Annals of St. Anne de Beaupré*, April 1982. Reprinted by permission.

"Catholic Quiz" from *Annals of St. Anne de Beaupré*, April 1982. Reprinted by permission.

Review "Chas Jenkel: Questionnaire" by Steven X. Rea from *High Fidelity*, March 1982. Reprinted by permission. All rights reserved.

"Home Is Where the Chili Is" by Marjorie Menzies from *Odyssey*, July/August 1979. Reprinted by permission.

"Helping Keep Neighborhoods Safe" by Anita Hunter from Gemco *Courier*, May 1982. Reprinted by permission.

"Just a Choke" reprinted by permission from the July 1981 issue of *The Lutheran*, magazine of the Lutheran Church in America.

Anecdote by Helen Livingston from "Grandparents' Brag Board" from *Mature Living* © Copyright 1982 The Sunday School Board of the Southern Baptist Convention. All rights reserved. Used by permission.

"For the Birds" by Jeanne Westerdale from *Good Housekeeping*. Reprinted by permission.

"This age bit really gets old" by Caroline Clark from *Kansas City Star*, August 8, 1982. Reprinted with permission of The Kansas City Star Company, Copyright 1982.

"Chilean Methane Gas" from *Americas*, January-February 1982. Reprinted by permission.

"Philadelphia Story" from *Black Enterprise*. Copyright 1982, The Earl G. Graves Publishing Co., Inc., 295 Madison Avenue, New York NY 10017. All rights reserved.

"Easy Recipes: Leprechaun Soup" and "Dinosaur Dot-to-Dot" from *Children's Playmate Magazine*, copyright © 1982 by the Benjamin Franklin Literary & Medical Society, Inc., Indianapolis IN. Reprinted by permission of the publisher.

"Scrambled Places" reprinted from Dell Pencil Puzzles and Word Games, November 1982. Used by permission of Dell Publishing Co., Inc. Copyright © 1982 by Dell Publishing Co., Inc.

To my son,
Ralph H. Emerson III

✿✿✿✿✿ ACKNOWLEDGMENTS

Books don't come about simply because a writer and publisher decide they ought to be put in print. Although it's the author who gets the raves (or boos), most books are the result of the input and efforts of many people. To all the people who helped provide information, especially Shirley DeSantis, Howard Doerr, George Emerson, Chuck Manley, Celia Scully, and Erin Townley; to Carol Cartaino, Howard I. Wells III, and the other people at Writer's Digest Books who worked on the project, and to my husband Ralph, who was always there when I needed encouragement, a special thank you.

TABLE OF CONTENTS

6. GIVING PEOPLE A PIECE OF YOUR MIND 69

Do you want to share, inspire, or sound off? Short personal experience and opinion articles let you tell about your chance encounter with the Princess of Wales, how you watched your housebound neighbor become the busiest man in town, why you think plastic containers ought to be outlawed. Since you wouldn't be speaking your mind unless you wanted people to listen, you'll want to learn the most effective ways of making yourself heard.

7. MINI-INFORMATIONALS 87

This short article, like a sprinter in the 50-yard dash, must get off to a fast start. You have to be good at flash finishes, too. And since not all articles can be written in a few paragraphs, you'll want to know how to test your article ideas. For more information, read this chapter.

8. PEOPLE PIECES 106

Projecting personalities onto paper in a few hundred words is undeniably a skill. But it's a skill you can learn right here, with the help of top freelancers, interviewers, and the editors of magazines who are doing the buying.

9. THE NEWS IN BRIEF 121

Newspapers aren't the only publications that print the latest. Trade journals and general circulation magazines are looking for freelancers with a nose for newsbreaks. They want writers who can deliver the facts in their publication's style, either as contributing editors or stringers, or just once in a while.

10. THE GREETING CARD MESSAGE 132

When you care enough to send the very best, you'll care enough to send your submissions to the right markets. And we're not just talking about greeting cards. The thousands of bumper stickers, buttons, plaques, posters, calendars, mini-books, and other products that the ever diversifying social-expression industry produces each year mean opportunities for you. The rewards are many and the words are few.

11. DABBLING IN DOGGEREL (OR IT COULD BE VERSE) 147

Light verse is often snickered at, but light versifiers laugh all the way to the bank. You'd like to cash in on perfectly metered couplets and quatrains that tickle everyman's funnybone, too? Then grab your rhyming dictionary and let's go!

12. BRAIN TEASERS 160

Puzzle making's a mind-twisting business. Quiz construction can be perplexing, too, unless you know the answers. But the techniques required to put together crossword puzzles, anagrams, word jumbles, crostics, and find-the-words aren't hard to master. This chapter leads you through the maze of finding ideas, researching, structuring, and marketing quizzes and puzzles.

13. AND THE WINNER IS . . . 179

Want to win a gourmet trip to Paris? A complete home workshop? A year's supply of food for Fido? Coming up with a prize entry calls for many of the same skills as putting together a salable manuscript. So it's no wonder that many freelancers are consistent contest winners. You can be, too, if you follow our rules.

14. THE ART OF RANTING OR RAVING (FOR PAY) 193

It pays to be critical. Your candid evaluations of books, dance, drama, music, art, motion pictures, and TV programs—if they're crafted to the publication's requirements—can make you an editorial office hit. This chapter's advice will put you front row center.

15. EAT AND TELL 205

The discriminating diner who knows his Bechamels and Bearnaises can eat his way around town and end up with more money than when he started. And without writing a lot of words. This chapter's bill of fare tells how to get restaurant review assignments, what to look for when you're on the scene and how to reheat the memories back at the typewriter.

16. PINT-SIZE PIECES

Articles in children's magazines are just like those in publications for adults—only they're shorter and the words are easier, right? Uh uh. It's true that most children's pieces are 600 words or less, and research on a subject can often do double duty for kiddies' and grown-ups' articles. But approach, tone, and structure aren't the same. Thanks to the growing number of children's markets, vive la difference.

17. KEEPING LITTLE BODIES BUSY

Consider the editor of a kiddie mag's activity page. Her day's been a dreary succession of bad jokes, bleach bottle craft projects and dot-to-dots with missing numbers. Then she opens your submission. You've read her magazine from cover to cover, come up with fresh ideas geared to her young readers' skill levels and interests, and presented them the way she likes them best. In short, you've brightened an editor's day—and made a sale.

INTRODUCTION

SHORT FORMS, LONG RETURNS

I never write metropolis for seven cents because I can get the same price for city. I never write policeman because I can get the same money for cop.

Mark Twain

 like the things money can buy. And I don't want to work any harder than I have to in order to get them. I'm a writer, and regardless of what anyone says, I know there isn't such a thing as easy money in the writing business. On rejection days, I'm convinced that scavenging aluminum cans would be much more lucrative.

But through the years I've discovered the secret of making maximum profits with a minimum of writing: Devote a good portion of your time to short articles and fillers, writing several short pieces instead of one full-length feature. The reason is simple: The more well-written pieces you can produce in a given number of hours, the greater your chances of acceptances, paychecks, and by-lines. Look at it this way. If you write six short articles, ten hints and tips, four recipes, and an anecdote instead of three feature articles—and market them intelligently—you have seven times the chance of acceptance.

Why is it, then, that many writers don't recognize the potential for reward—both monetary and psychic—that lies in the market for short pieces? Perhaps it's because writing a cover story or a four-page article illustrated with half a dozen color photos promises more ego gratification. More likely, however, it's due to the misconception that there's not as much money in writing shorter pieces.

Let's put that myth to rest right now.

Once upon a two-week period I wrote four 500-word pieces and one 2,500-word feature article. I was paid $75 for each of the short pieces and $250 for the long one. It took three eight-hour days to write the feature but only two hours to write each of the little pieces. However you do your bookkeeping, $37.50 an hour beats $10.41 any day of the week. I've been paid as much as $1 a word for greeting cards, and I won $625 for a 100-word recipe.

Not that it always happens that way. Occasionally, you'll find that the "right" word you're missing in two lines of light verse will elude you for days, while a major piece may come tumbling out of your typewriter as quickly as you can punch the keys. But as a general rule, the ratio between time spent and money earned yields more profit when you write short forms.

I've received rejections on writing efforts of all lengths, too. But I have found rejection a lot easier to take when it's for a piece in which I haven't invested hours and hours of blood, sweat, and research.

There are other reasons for keeping your words to a minimum. Beginning writers will find that fillers and short articles open editorial office doors. It's often the only way a writer who hasn't written for a publication can make that initial sale. The editors' reasoning makes a lot of sense, once you've thought about it. A new writer is an unknown quantity.

Will she deliver what she has promised in her query?

His idea is great, but will he be able to sustain the reader's interest for 2,000 words?

Will she meet the deadline?

Will he send the piece at all?

By first purchasing a short piece or filler, the editor can allay these fears, risking a minimum of money and editorial space.

Writing short articles and fillers is also ideal for people who don't have large segments of uninterrupted time to devote to writing or who would like to become full-time freelancers but currently have other jobs that demand most of their energies. For people who want to make money in their spare time, short articles and fillers can be a winner—*if* they use part of that spare time to learn how to write and market their work effectively.

Half a short article can be rough-drafted while the wash is swishing around at the corner Laundromat. An entire joke, hint, or anecdote can take shape in scraps of time—while the baby's strained vegetables are warming, while you're in line at the post office, or as you wait for a traffic light to change. Many fillers take only minutes to write. Others, such as quotes, quips, and bloopers, require no writing at all.

Then there are the psychological advantages. For novices, composing a full-blown feature may look like as big a job as washing all the windows in the Empire State Building; a smaller bit of prose seems more possible to complete. For established writers, creating fillers and short articles is a refreshing change of pace. For any writer, payment for fillers, however small, can be a marvelously effective antidote to the "rejection slip blues."

Since life's experiences provide the stuff from which many short forms are crafted, you often don't have to do any research, or at least you don't have to leave home to do it. Moreover, research for longer articles can often provide information for several short pieces.

But the best argument in favor of short-form writing is this: the market is growing rapidly. Not too many years ago, magazine articles were more likely to run 5,000 words than 500. Because of a more hectic lifestyle, easy access to information through television, and competition from an explosion of leisure-time activities, people rarely sit still long enough to read a ten-page article. Though the majority of pieces in most magazines are in the 1,500-2,000-word range, pieces of 750 words and fewer are rapidly gaining popularity.

It also wasn't long ago that editors looked upon short forms as nothing more than convenient blocks of type to fill the gaps in their columns. Fillers sometimes perform that function today. But editors have found that their readers like short items so well that many magazines now have regular departments made up of them.

Fillers come in a variety of guises: jokes, quotes, quips, anecdotes, puzzles, recipes, quizzes, puns, cartoons, bloopers, news clips, and amazing facts, among others. Short on words (usually no more than 300), they are long on entertainment—they either stimulate the reader's curiosity or evoke emotional responses such as laughter.

In addition to magazine markets, there is the realm of greeting cards. Hundreds of thousands of card designs and greeting-related items are produced each year, and most staffs are not big enough to provide all the messages that are needed.

Consider, too, the contests. Many focus on short forms that require few words. If they are the right words, however, there is cash, a car, or any number of other prizes waiting at the end of the entry blank.

As a result of this trend toward shorter material, I'm convinced that writers who make the most of short-item markets will bring bigger deposits to the bank.

Enough of the sales talk. Start reading and learn how you can make more money by writing less.

CHAPTER ONE

THE FILLER WRITER'S BASICS

It takes twenty years to make an overnight success.
Eddie Cantor

ll of us have writing dreams—doing a cover story for *Sports Illustrated*, becoming a contributing editor to *Gourmet*, traveling to the Orkney Islands on assignment for *National Geographic*.

Writers who have just begun putting words on paper may look on these as impossible dreams, yearning only for that elusive first sale. Some of them will trade in their typewriters without ever attaining that goal. But for those who are willing to work diligently to develop the skills required to put together salable pieces, success *will* come.

The big dreams only take more time. Those by-lines in the large-circulation magazines represent years of apprenticeship. Sure, there's an occasional overnight wonder, but most successful writers started with a small sale and worked their way to the top.

Though getting there usually takes years, there are tricks of the trade that will speed you along the way. Every consistently successful writer I've known has had a marketing plan. I also know writers who don't, and their sales come far less frequently. Though they've laughed at the story about selling iceboxes to Eskimos, they haven't applied its message to their own careers. They continue to submit their work to publications whose editors are no more likely to buy their pieces than a confirmed vegetarian is to order rare roast beef.

If you're determined to be a successful seller of short items (or long, for that matter), you must have a marketing plan, which means knowing what the markets are and what their editors are buying.

KNOW YOUR MARKETS

My primary source of basic market information is *Writer's Market*, which is published and updated annually. It lists more than 4,000 markets for freelancers and tells what each of those publications' editors want.

There are so many filler markets that you have to develop a system of keeping track of them. Work your way through the listings in *Writer's Market*, noting in the margins the kinds of short material in which each publication specializes. I've found the following codes useful:

F = fillers
S = short articles
GV = greeting card verse
GI = greeting company product ideas
LV = light verse
A = anecdotes
RA = reviews of the arts
RR = restaurant reviews
H/T = hints and tips
C = children's material
R = recipes
PQG = puzzles, quizzes, games
NB = newsbreaks

When a publication sounds like it has great potential—when what they need is what you're good at producing and/or the pay is very good—add an asterisk. If it seems ideal, a couple of exclamation points are in order.

Other sources of marketing information include *Ayer's Directory of Publications; Business Publications, Rates, and Data;* the *Standard Periodical Directory; Ulrich's International Periodical Directory*, and *Working Press of the Nation*. These directories are found in the reference departments of most libraries. Since they're too expensive for most writers to purchase, you may wish to photocopy the most interesting listings.

These volumes contain many of the same listings as *Writer's Market*, but you will also come across information about other publications. *Working Press of the Nation*, for example, focuses on house magazines and trade journals and includes thousands of listings.

Your best sources of marketing information are the magazines themselves. Their pages contain the articles and fillers that editors have purchased in the past and will tell you what kinds of material they will buy in the future.

FORMS TO FIT YOUR LIFESTYLE

It's important to know not only where the buyers are but also what kinds of material you want most to write. You'll find that some short forms flow from your pen more easily than others. There are so many kinds of shorts that being master of them all isn't highly probable—or necessary.

Your evaluation should be based on your interests and abilities. If you travel a lot and love to explore new places, short travel pieces will be a natural. If you're a craftsperson, project how-tos will interest you. Even if you're housebound, your horizons needn't be limited. Hints and tips, light verse, book and record reviews, puzzles and quizzes, and contest entries can all be written without going out your front door.

Chances are, the kinds of short forms you'll enjoy crafting will be the same that you like reading. And you can try your typewriter at them all—quips today, Op Eds tomorrow; contests in the morning, greeting-card verse at night—without a big investment of energy.

Time will be a factor, too. Would-be writers juggling two jobs or wrestling with one job that's demanding may have loads of experiences but only minutes here and there to write about them. The key is to choose the short forms that can be written in the squidges of time you have during breaks, lunch hours, or bus trips to and from work.

Then there's the matter of your enthusiasm span. When, as a beginner, you're writing the longest of the short items—900 words or less—the process may take a longer time than your psyche can cope with. You may find that you're more successful with one-liners and anecdotes.

This doesn't mean you won't be able to turn your attention to other forms in the future. No writer's career is cast in concrete. But for those first ventures, concentrate on the forms with which you feel most comfortable.

TEARING SUBJECTS APART

After you've studied the markets and conducted your self-analysis, gather copies of 100 or more different publications that you have identified as potential markets. It won't be as hard as you think. You'll find them in exchange piles at libraries, Laundromats, and mobile home parks. Collect discards from doctors' offices, recycling centers, and friends.

You can also send for sample copies of those of your chosen publications that you can't find elsewhere. Many sample copies are free. Others cost their cover price or less.

Go through the magazines with scissors and a sharp eye. Organize by type, the short items you're interested in writing, making sure that they're identified by magazine and date. Though it may sound to you like a lifetime job, it takes only a few minutes to dissect each magazine. If you want to be a writer, magazine dissection is not only an invaluable education—it's fun.

Put clips from each category in their own file folders (marked "fillers," "short profiles," "anecdotes," "book reviews," and so on). If there are several items of the same type from one magazine, clip them together, along with a photocopy of the *Writer's Market* listing as well as any other information you may have gleaned from writers' magazines (such as editors leaving or arriving, which magazines aren't paying promptly, and any format changes in the offing). That way, you'll have an instant referral system. Keep adding examples to your file as you come across them.

MAGAZINE MATCH-UP

We will talk about ideas for specific kinds of short items in the following chapters. But whatever the idea, it must be suitable to the intended publication.

Research for my book, *Write on Target* (Writer's Digest Books 1981), convinced me that just as all of us have our own ways of ex pressing ourselves, each magazine does, too. Therefore, the freelancer must fashion material to fit a publication's distinctive personality in order to make sales. You must analyze each magazine for which you hope to write. Read the cover blurbs, the table of contents, letters to the editor, and the ads, so that you can form a precise image of the readers the editor is working to please—their interests, age range, likely occupations, and so on.

It is imperative that you study prospective publications in terms of their readership, style, and subject preferences. By reaching a clear understanding of the kinds of people who read a magazine, by paying close attention to the publication's way of saying things, and by zeroing in on the subjects the editor likes (and noticing any topics that are conspicuous by their absence), you'll learn how to tailor your writing to your audience and boost your chances of acceptance.

If a magazine uses quizzes about personal relationships only ("How Well Do You Know Your Husband?" 'What's Your Interference Quotient?" and the like) don't submit one about great historical figures. An editor who never uses anecdotes about children won't buy yours, no matter how cleverly it's written. The editor whose publication hasn't printed a how-to project in five years (unless that editor has just become the magazine's chief and plans a complete change of format) won't be interested in a piece on making stained-glass wind chimes.

THE QUESTION OF QUERIES

The query is one of the writer's most valuable sales tools. It is a short letter—usually no longer than a page—telling the editor about the piece you propose to write. My queries usually start with two or three paragraphs about the subject, followed by information on such things as research sources, availability of photos, and my qualifications for writing the piece.

Whether you should query before submitting short articles, reviews, or children's pieces can be perplexing. Since I don't write anything unless I know it has a very good chance of selling, I query whenever possible.

Queries, however, don t work for such short forms as anecdotes, fillers, greeting-card and light verse, hints, tips, recipes, puzzles, quizzes, and children's activities. An editor will have no basis for judgment until she sees the completed item.

PACKAGING YOUR PRODUCT

Any short forms you decide to write demand a professional presentation if they're going to make it without a return trip in your SASE (the self-addressed, stamped envelope you must enclose with every submission).

Your paper should be standard-sized typing paper (8½"x11"), preferably 20-pound bond. Never use the erasable kind; it smudges and is difficult to read. Your typewriter ribbon must be new so that the print is clear.

In the upper left-hand corner of the first page, single-space your name, address, and *telephone number with area code*. The phone number is imperative. Many editors detest dictating letters (or writing them themselves), and they often don't have time to wait for correspondence to make a round trip. If those editors have a telephone number that enables them to finish their business in minutes, you increase your chances of a sale.

In the upper right-hand corner, type "about" or "approximately," followed by your word count (rounded off to the nearest ten). There are all sorts of systems for counting words. The easiest one for me is to count the number of lines of type on each page and multiply by 11 (the average of words I type per line). You may average 10 or 12, depending on size (pica or elite) of your type and the width of your margins.

One-third of the way down the page, center your title in capital letters. Just as double- and triple-spacing allows room for editing, the white space at the beginning of a submission leaves room for the editor to write type specifications for the typesetter and a new title if yours isn't the editor's choice.

If your submission is one that doesn't require a title (certain anecdotes, for example, don't have them), go down a third of a page nonetheless. Where you place your by-line depends on the particular publication's format. Contributors' names usually appear at the ends of anecdotes and some short articles. Generally, when typing the short article, you'll place your name (as you want it to appear in the publication) two spaces below the title. The article or item should begin three spaces below that.

The general rule in typing manuscripts is to double-space. However, check the writer's guidelines from your intended publication to make sure. Some magazines specify triple-spacing, three spaces between paragraphs, or a certain number of characters per line. Whatever an editor wants, see that she gets it. By giving her exactly what she's requested, in the form she prefers, you will save her editing time. Don't forget that satisfied editors become repeat customers.

Although left-hand margins of 1 inch and right-hand and bottom margins of 1½ inches are suggested in most instructions for manuscript preparation, editors I've talked with say that they prefer more white space. When you're typing, set up your margins so that they are at least half an inch wider than the rules prescribe. In short, produce pages of copy that are as easy as possible for the editor to read, edit, and mark for typesetters.

On succeeding pages of your manucript, type your name in the upper left-hand corner. On the next line under that, type an identifying word, or *slug*—say, *Shoestring* for a piece called "How to Shop on a Shoestring." You wouldn't want to use *How to* as your slug, because the magazine might well have other articles in the works with that phrase in their titles.

If your submission is untitled, use the first three words of the submission or else a short identifying description. Following the slug, type a dash and the page number.

Move down at least four more spaces before you begin typing the copy on these pages. Two or three spaces below the final line of your submission, use some symbol to indicate that there is no more. I use a series of three centered and spaced asterisks. You can write *The End* if you wish, or - *30* - (newspaper shorthand for "end of copy").

Package any accompanying color slides in plastic pocketed sheets, available at camera shops or photo supply departments. Protect black-and-white glossies with sheets of cardboard. Be sure to include a keyed caption sheet with the slides and attach typed captions to the backs of each black-and-white with tape. On the manila envelope containing your photos, write in impossible-to-miss, large, legible printing, PHOTOS—PLEASE DO NOT BEND.

Whether you include a cover letter with any submission depends on the situation. In the case of short articles and reviews, it's usually a good idea. You can use typewriter paper, but your letters will look more professional if they're typed on business letterhead. The cover letter can be a short paragraph and should not be longer than three, unless your subject is unusually technical and warrants additional information on sources of your research. Refer to the contents and why you are sending them if the submission is the result of a query go-ahead. If you are sending your piece "over the transom" (without querying in advance), you might want to include your appropriate credits and your special qualifications for writing the piece. My cover letters are almost always of the first kind and go something like this:

Dear Ms. Bluepencil:

In response to your request of June 10, that I submit "America's First Shopping Center" to you for consideration, I have enclosed the manuscript along with a selection of color transparencies. If you would like further information, please don't hesitate to phone me at the number above.

Sincerely,

Be sure to spell the editor's name correctly. Many editors say they will reject an article automatically if their names aren't spelled right. This isn't as egotistical or arbitrary as it may seem. After all, if a writer hasn't taken the pains to find out exactly how the editor's name is spelled, there's good reason to assume that other information—names, dates, statistics, directions—won't be accurate either.

MONITORING PRODUCTION

Now that you've gone through the mechanics of manuscript preparation and mailing, put yourself on "fast forward" to the day when you're a short-form success. How will you cope with keeping tabs on your business?

Since recordkeeping is vital to even the part-time writer's survival, you'll want to institute efficient bookkeeping procedures. Not only income and expenses must be recorded; you have to keep track of what you've submitted and where you have sent it as well. Your writing job will be much easier too if you do a good job of organizing your research files.

Time is money when you are self-employed, so you'll want the system that works best for you. It may not be the one the freelancer across town uses. It might be one nobody else in the world is comfortable with. But if it suits your working habits and does the job quickly, that's enough.

Many writers use ledgers, entering submission dates and results, expenses, and income in the columns. One writer I know uses a daybook, making entries daily and attaching receipts to the appropriate pages. Those systems simply do not work for me. My method may not be right for you, but some variation of it might.

I prefer a filing system that allows me to keep all my records in two metal recipe card files and a larger accordion file. (If you go into greeting-card writing, you may want a third card file; see Chapter 11.)

One of the recipe card files has dividers that read QUERIES, WORK IN PROGRESS, SUBMITTED MANUSCRIPTS, and IDEAS. Most of my submissions start with idea cards. Whenever I have an idea for a short article, one-liner, light verse, or whatever, I jot down the idea and any snippets of contributing information I may have on a 3x5-inch card.

This is especially important when your idea-generating skills increase and you're bombarded with article and filler possibilities. Two weeks (or even two hours) later, you won't be able to remember that marvelous idea unless you've written it down, because dozens of others will have taken its place.

Whenever I decide to develop article ideas contained in the card file, I set up clearly labeled folders for each of them. After I have collected enough material on a topic to know that it can be developed into an article, I write the query.

The name of the article appears at the top of a 3x5 card that I place in the query portion of the file. Under the title, I write the name of the publication submitted to and the date, leaving room for the date that I receive word of any action (acceptance, go-ahead on spec, rejection) on the piece. If the query is rejected, I submit it to another editor, making appropriate entries on the next line of the card.

As the article idea progresses from query to acceptance on assignment or speculation, the due date is added and the card is moved to the work-in-progress section. Also in this portion of my card file are those ideas for submissions where queries are not appropriate, but the ideas have been developed to the point where I think they are salable. This development may range from the outline of an anecdote to a really good punch line for a piece of light verse to a half-dozen questions for a quiz.

When any piece of work goes into the mail, I put its card into the submitted section, recording the date of submission. When I am notified by the editor of an acceptance requiring no rewriting or other changes, I write that date midway down the card, along with the amount I'm supposed to be paid. When I receive the check, I mark "paid" next to that figure, along with the date.

Then I move to the part of the bookkeeping process I like best: putting the card for the sold submission into the second card file. My success file is separated into sections by alphabet divider cards, under which I file my sales by title.

My larger, accordion file measures about 8x10 inches and has twelve compartments. Originally, the tabs between compartments were labeled "dental bills," "utility receipts," "car maintenance" and the like. I covered them over with self-adhesive labels and wrote in my own categories: POSTAGE, OFFICE SUPPLIES, RESEARCH MATERIALS, TRAVEL, GASOLINE, PHOTOGRAPHY, TELEPHONE, ADMISSIONS, LODGING, DINING, PHOTOCOPIES, and INCOME RECEIPTS. Whenever the spirit moves me (usually when the pile is so huge that my desk becomes inoperative), I file all my receipts in the appropriate slots. It makes the job of recapitulating income and expenses an easy one at income tax time (I file a 3x5 card listing publication, date, and amount in the income compartment for any sales whose checks don't have a receipt portion).

The expenses you can write off are a matter for you and your accountant to decide, and your labels might differ from mine. Whatever they are, be scrupulous about keeping receipts for every expense that might be tax-deductible. At year's end you can put the file's contents into a manila envelope, label it with the year, and start filling the file again. Books you may find helpful are *The Complete Handbook for Freelance Writers* by Kay Cassill (for business affairs) and *The Writer's Legal Guide* by Tad Crawford and *Law and the Writer* by Kirk Polking and Leonard S. Meranus (for taxes).

RECYCLING REJECTS

Into each writer's life some rejection slips must fall. To oversensitive souls, the results can be devastating. But those of us who manage to keep several items circulating at the same time don't take it nearly so hard. For us, there's always tomorrow's mail. Another antidote to rejection dejection is to send the rejected piece (or a query regarding it)—immediately—to another appropriate market.

Some of the items may need a few minor changes here and there in order to fit the new market, and many of them will require retyping. If they do, get the job done quickly and send them flying again.

There's a good chance that you won't have to spend much of your writing time dealing with rejects. If your ideas are on target, your markets well chosen, and your style and structure compatible with the intended publications, you won't often suffer from the bounce-back blues. (Do plan to set aside some time, though, for making those trips to the bank.)

CHAPTER TWO

SNIP-ITS, CHUCKLES, AND BLOOPERS

*The mind ought sometimes to be amused, that it
may the better return to thought, and to itself.*
                    Phaedrus (5th century B.C.)

 used to crawl the walls when people were late for appointments or I had to wait what seemed like hours with drops in my eyes in the ophthalmologist's holding room.

Not anymore.

I now spend that time dreaming up bits of whimsy and pieces of pithy prose—the "one-liners" that are fun to write and put money in the pockets.

Although one-liners aren't always only a line long, they are invariably short. They are *fillers* in the true sense of the word: little blocks of type that fill gaps in the pages of newspapers and magazines.

You will discover the traditional form—jokes, quips, quotes, puns, bloopers, news clips, epigrams, interesting/amazing facts—in at least half of the general interest and specialized magazines you read. Most publications pay about five dollars for each item; the "big pay" magazines can offer more than ten times that amount. Although joke writing takes a special talent, no extraordinary abilities are required to craft the other forms. In fact, you don't even have to be a writer to be a successful filler contributor. Although some of the material requires editing or the addition of a tag line, much of it needs only to be submitted in proper form. I'll cover that later in this chapter. First, let's look at the kinds of one-liners that are most salable today.

PUNS

Puns are plays on words that sound the same but have different meanings or on different meanings of a single word. Although they have been called the lowest form of wit, I agree with Oscar Levant, who said, "A pun is the lowest form of humor—when you don't think of it first."

These plays on words are accomplished in four basic ways:

1. By changing the spelling of a word in a definition to give it a second meaning:
   Window washing—Rx for dull *panes*.
2. By adding, deleting, or changing letters in a word of a familiar phrase to create a word with a different meaning:
   Madison Avenue is ruled by the law of the *jingle*
3. By substituting a word that rhymes with one in a common phrase:
   Ad promising results in rabbit raising—*Bunny* back guarantee.
4. By transposing words of a familiar phrase:

Party Favors

First Communist Official: The Commissar wishes to reward your services by giving you a dacha. Where would you like it to be?
Second Communist Official: On the Black Sea. I've always dreamed of seeing my *red sons in the sail set.*

The puns you most often find used as fillers are crazy definitions, proverbs, slogans, and titles in which some of the words have been changed. Here are two examples, both of which appeared in *Reader's Digest:*

Blithe Spirits

Witches—Hexperts

—Dan Small

Halloween treats—Ghoul Scout cookies

—Suzie Hillyer

Vampire—hemo goblin
—Lakenan Barnes in the *American Legion Magazine*
Halloween—Pranksgiving time

—Dell Crossword Puzzles

Leaf It Be

Remember, the family that rakes together aches together.
—Forester in the *Chicago Tribune*

There are times when puns serve as punch lines for jokes, as in this one from the *Saturday Evening Post:*

Just Pennies a Serving

A secretary was eating a diet salad in a quiet corner of a restaurant when her boss came by. "Trying to lose weight?" he chided her. "No," she replied, "I'm on a low-salary diet."

—Thomas E. Oetzel

Here's another, from *Modern Maturity:*

An accident victim was in the hospital recovering from a broken leg. "How are you being treated?" asked his concerned visitor. "Well," replied the patient, "I can't kick."

Some editors shun puns. Others adore them. It doesn't take long to gauge their reactions—just read the fillers they've bought in the past.

The easiest way to become a punster is to copy down oft-repeated phrases. The longer your lists, the better. Include well-known advertising slogans, proverbs, and names of movies, books, and songs.

Tailor your lists to the various markets for which you will be writing your one-liners. For general interest publications, don't include phrases the average person may not have heard. But when you're writing for special interest magazines—aimed at pilots, ham radio operators, or other groups whose hobbies or businesses involve specialized terminology—don't be afraid to use the jargon.

Then start playing with key words to place each phrase in a new context or call forth an unusual association.

Let's take a short list of phrases and try it out.

1. Variety is the spice of life.
2. law of the jungle
3. the right to happiness
4. A penny saved is a penny earned.

We'll start with the third phrase. There are lots of rhyming words for *right: bright, sight, plight, might, flight, cite, knight,* and thirty-two more, according to my rhyming dictionary. (A rhyming dictionary and a good dictionary of quotations are the only reference works the writer of one-liners really needs.) The word *right* itself has more than half a dozen meanings: correct, designed to be placed or worn outward, just, and so on. In addition, it sounds the same as three other words: *rite*, *write*, and *wright*.

After listing these possibilities, it's time to turn our attention to *happiness*. We find only six rhyming words: *gappiness*, *lappiness*, *nappiness*, *sappiness*, *scrappiness*, and *snappiness*—none of which seems particularly promising. All the dictionary definitions mean essentially the same thing, and there is no other word that sounds the same but is spelled differently.

What do we do now? We can change, add, or delete letters within the word, producing *hippiness* and *hoppiness*. When we look at the results of our mental gymnastics, we can see that we have at least one good possibility, especially if we devise a definition for it:

Overeating—the rite to hippiness

Spend some time with this method, playing with your own list. Chances are, your puns will be even better.

Another method is to start with a theme to trigger your imagination, then list all the words you can that are associated with that theme. Take "games people play," for example. The first step would be to write down names of games. Your list might contain the following:

Merry Widow	Space Invaders
Contract Bridge	Dominoes
Duplicate Bridge	Anagrams
Gin Rummy	Scrabble
Monopoly	Charades
Poker	Miniature Golf
Pac-Man	Croquet

After you've compiled the list, think consciously about plays on words. Then tuck the whole project into your subconscious, taking it out now and again.

Say, for example, you've focused on the phrase, "One good turn deserves another," and have concentrated on changing word order, spelling, and the like for several minutes without results. Turn your attention to other writing or unrelated chores. In other words, "forget about" the phrase you were working on. In reality, you won't really have forgotten. The matter will only have moved to another level of your consciousness and will surface at the most unlikely times—while you're walking the dog, sweeping the garage floor, canning peaches—as well as when you deliberately concentrate on it. If you can't come up with one or two items you think might be salable within a week or two, choose another theme and work with it.

QUOTES AND QUIPS

Quotes and quips include comments or statements made by people in the past or present. They can come from history, literature, speeches, ads, television programs, interviews, and other sources.

"Quotable Quotes" in *Reader's Digest* uses contemporary material as well as such oldies as this Italian proverb:

> Once the game is over, the king and the pawn go back into the same box.

Books of quotations are good places to start searching for quips and quotes, but don't stop with them. Listen for gems of wisdom from guests on interview shows. Be on the alert for profound or humorous statements in books you read. Scan quoted material in newspapers. Have your notepad ready whenever you attend a lecture or go to a political rally. I especially like a quip I heard while watching the television coverage of the 1980 elections:

> Those that live by the crystal ball learn to eat broken glass.
>
> —Dan Rather

Be sure that your quotes are accurate and that their sources are properly acknowledged. You may also need to seek permission from the original publisher and/or the author. When in doubt, inquire.

As you can see, you don't have to write a word in order to be a quote submitter. All you need do is analyze the kinds of quotes your intended publications use and then set about finding appropriate ones.

BLOOPERS

Bloopers are slips of the pen or tongue. Like quotes, they often need only be typed (double-spaced, please), with their sources, on a piece of plain typing paper and submitted. The form into which you put your bloopers will depend on the preferences of the publications to which they are submitted.

At times you may have to provide background material on where the blooper originally appeared. You may also need to create a clever title, as in the follow examples from *The Lutheran's* "A Little Salt" department:

Just a Choke

A bulletin announcement recently invited our bazaar work committee to "Please bring a gag lunch."

—Trinity Church, Towanda, Pa.

Her Forth Mistake

Our bulletin recently blooped this way: "Today's altar flowers are given by Cathy Gallop in honor of her 4th coming marriage to Bob Friedman. . . ."

—Carolyn B. Wilson, Bartlett, Ill.

People make mistakes—in writing and speaking—more often than we care to admit. In order to be a blooper submitter, you must be alert to these linguistic lapses. Keep your eyes open for typographical errors and misplaced phrases that change their messages' meanings. Listen closely to what speakers, disc jockeys, and television announcers say.

Amusing signs provide inspiration for other fillers that tickle editors' funny bones without your having to write an original word. All you need do to find them is to look around with a humorous eye. We've all seen unintentionally misspelled words on signs that make us chuckle: "Bird Food—Cheep," "For Sail—Boats," "Lenten Special—Filet of Soul." (Of course, sometimes these misspellings are intentional, in which case these bloopers are really puns—just as useful to the filler writer.)

While you're on the lookout for amusing signs, don't forget bumper stickers. Really funny bumper-sticker messages should make a hit with any editor who uses one-liners, and a few publications contain departments made up of them (*Reader's Digest*'s "Bumper Snickers," for one).

JOKES

Jokes are the only filler material that requires special talent. Gene Perret's book, *How to Write and Sell (Your Sense of) Humor* (Writer's Digest Books, 1982) is a good source of information if you're interested in producing material that makes people laugh.

I'll be the first to admit that I can't even remember jokes, let alone make them up. Unless you have gag-writing ability—and you'll know after a few tries—you'll probably want to stick to other filler forms or adapt jokes that someone else has created. You can redesign dozens of jokes that you hear as well as standard jokebook stories.

Be careful, though, to change the joke sufficiently not to infringe on copyrights. To make the adaptation work, you must change or rearrange the characters and dialogue enough that a joke different from the original results. For example, priests at the Vatican become missionaries in Zaire; the game is football instead of baseball. To find out more about the subject of copyright, see *Law and the Writer*, by Kirk Polking and Leonard S. Meranus (Writer's Digest Books, 1980).

As with other fillers, the kinds of jokes you submit will depend on the publication to which you are submitting them. Change the joke's central character to fit the magazine's readership (police officers for law enforcement journals, golfers for golf publications, and so on).

NEWS CLIPS

News clips are humorous, out-of-the-ordinary, or downright bizarre items you'll come across occasionally (frequently, if you're looking for them) in newspapers. Sometimes they can be submitted as they are, pasted on a piece of typing paper that bears your name and address as well as the source and date of the item.

If tag lines are customarily used in your publications, you'll have to provide them. They are required, for instance, by the *New Yorker*:

> "If you become seriously ill, injured or die in a foreign land, AIR-EVAC International will transport you back to the U.S. where you won't have to worry about communicating in a foreign language."
>
> —Flyer from AIR-EVAC International
>
> Or anything else.

> "Hawaii Pacific College's Career Center for Women starts free workshops on conflict resolution, assertive training, relationship enrichment and omelette making, for which you may begin registering today."
>
> —*Honolulu Advertiser*

If you can't resolve a conflict, break out the eggs.

The tag or twist, when it's added to a news clip, is actually a kind of quip—a phrase that reverses what has been said or makes a humorous comment on it. Prolific filler writer Louise Boggess says that the successful quip must contain the following ingredients: brevity, clarity, reader identity, and wit. Study the tag lines added to the news clips above and you'll see that they fulfill Boggess's requirements.

The more you read, the better your chances of finding news clips that will sell. Small-town newspapers, with room to print local news, are especially good news-clip sources.

Most of the time your news clips will come from copyrighted material. That's why you must acknowledge the item's source accurately upon submission. If, in the editor's judgment, permission to use the material must be secured, he or she will then know from whom to request permission.

Time is of the essence in submitting news clips, since really good material, especially that disseminated by the wire services, will come to the attention of lots of writers. In case of duplicate submissions, the first one received gets the paycheck if the submissions are identical.

THREE MORE FORMS

Three additional filler forms you will encounter, though not so often, are the **epigram, interesting or amazing fact,** and the **cartoon caption.**

Epigrams are witty, ingenious, or pointed sayings tersely expressed. They can be old sayings or proverbs that have been cleverly twisted, or they can be contemporary. I like this one by humorist Sam Levenson: "A sweater is a garment that a child wears because his mother is cold."

Amazing Facts

Though it was popular years ago, today you'll rarely find "the giant sequoia tree lives about 2,500 years" variety of amazing facts anywhere but in small-town newspapers and a few magazines. However, if you do discover markets for startling trivia, you will have no problem finding material to submit. Start with reference works like the *Guinness Book of World Records,* encyclopedias, and books devoted to nostalgia. Any fact that causes you to respond with interest is a candidate for submission.

Cartoon Captions

Most cartoons are purchased as a package including both drawing and punch line. There are a few magazines, however, that buy cartoon captions without the art. To supply them, you have to dream up topical or zany situations, describe how the cartoon should look, and provide the caption.

The "What if?" method is a good one for coming up with clever lines. Imagine various situations, such as a bird sitting on a telephone line, and ask yourself, "What if that bird were upside down?" Picture a woman putting bags of groceries on her kitchen counter and ask, "What if every inch of counter space were covered with bags?" Sound ridiculous? Not at all. Two creators of cartoon captions came up with lines for those situations: the first, "This always happens to me after a heavy meal," and the second, "I just remembered what it was that I went to the store to get."

Another technique is to make a list of "hot" topics—the fitness craze, the state of the economy, the video game mania—and look at them with a humorous eye. Thinking of your subject in terms of improbabilities (two very fat old ladies jogging, two dogs outside a butcher shop discussing the economy, an Einstein-type playing Pac-Man) will help you get started.

There's something to laugh about in almost every situation. It's the cartoon caption writer's job to find that something.

MARKETING YOUR FUNNIES

Some editors will do anything for laughs—even go so far as to devote whole departments to humorous one-liners and jokes. A few of the magazines with such departments are *High Adventure, Woodmen of the World Magazine, Modern Maturity,* and the *Saturday Evening Post.*

It will take a sharper eye to discover fillers in publications that use them in the traditional way—at the ends of articles. But by looking carefully, you'll discover that half to three-fourths of the magazines in your pile of a hundred or so use one-liners of some kind.

Fraternal magazines are among the best filler markets. The *Rotarian's* "Stripped Gears" department pays for jokes and what editors refer to as witticisms (in addition to anecdotes and light verse). The following quip illustrates the sort of wit they're looking for:

Costing Oil On

Troubled Waters

Thanks to the present price of gasoline, oil tankers should be called clipper ships.

—*The Bell*, East Hampton, Conn.

Material suitable for the *Rotarian* should also work for "Parting Shots" in the *American Legion Magazine* (which, incidentally, pays $5 more per item).

Tabloids are good markets, too. The *Star* pays $25 for its "Your Favorite Jokes" department. The *National Enquirer* pays $10 each for "Jokes Kids Tell." The *Star* and the *Enquirer* publish only one joke in each issue, but the *Globe*, though it pays less, uses about ten each week.

More than thirty markets for gags are listed under "Gag Writing" in *Writer's Market*. There's yet another outlet for one-liners: radio disc jockeys and announcers. Of the thousands of radio stations in the country, only a few can afford staff writers. Deejays and announcers, therefore, usually have to forage for and write their own material.

You, the freelancer, can come to their rescue. Start out by contacting the locals and sell them on your quick joke/one-line gag/funny quotes services. Then branch out. A disc jockey in Covington, Kentucky, can use the same material as his counterpart in Pendleton, Oregon, or New Braunfels, Texas. Compile a list of potential customers and send a sample of your witty wares to each of them. Even though such services already exist, if your material is clever, you keep your subscription price low, and you aim for volume business, you can be a show-biz whiz.

In all likelihood, however, most of your filler business will be with magazines and tabloids, simply because there are so many markets waiting there. Just as the articles you submit to a magazine must be tailored to fit the publication's personality, so must the fillers you send fit its image. Though few magazines spell out their specific filler requirements as completely as *Reader's Digest* (you'll find them on one of the first pages of each issue), you can find out for yourself exactly what *any* magazine's needs are by studying its content.

Most of today's publications are specialized—devoted to readers with a common interest, be it canoeing, cats, or conservative political theory. In order to sell fillers to their editors, the freelancer has to slant them toward the magazine's readership. By studying back issues, you will be able to determine just how strong that slant has to be.

For example, a department in *New Woman*, "Swap the Old Lady for a New Woman," has two columns of quotes under the heading "Sounds Like an Old Lady," two columns under "Sounds Like a New Woman," and two more under "A Thump on the Head To." The department editor's note (appearing on the same page) spells out contributor requirements: "Five dollars will be paid for quotes you find and *New Woman* uses. Send a tearsheet (from book, magazine or newspaper) that includes the quote and source, including date. Circle source and quote in red."

From reading heads and the blurbs you'll get some idea of what the editors want, but you should read several published quotes to get a complete "editor preference profile."

The "Sounds Like an Old Lady" quotes mirror the traditional "woman's place is in the home, double-standard" point of view. By contrast, submissions to "Sounds Like a New Woman" must echo the contemporary, nonchauvinistic philosophy. Quotes used in "A Thump on the Head To" have a tone similar to that of "Sounds Like an Old Lady," but are much more oriented toward the male macho philosophy.

Another example of filler specialization is illustrated by the cartoon caption requirements of *Trailer Life*. Each issue includes "It Never Fails," a cartoon department based on ideas contributed by readers. Contributors need not do any of the drawing; they are required only to describe an "it never fails" situation common to recreational vehicle owners, such as the driver who waits for two hours in a gas line only to find he's on the wrong side of the pump for his gas tank filler pipe and has no way to turn around.

To make it easier to remember magazines' preferences, you might want to compile an information sheet like this one for each of them:

Name of publication _____

Kinds of fillers used (jokes, bloopers, quips, etc.)

_____

Rate of pay _____

Specific submission requirements _____

_____

Age group _____

Special subject matter _____

Occupational/avocational interest slant _____

_____

Are items titled? _____

Clip examples from back issues to each information sheet, and you will have a handy reference whenever you're in a filler-writing mood.

FILLING YOUR FILLER ENVELOPES

To submit your bits and pieces, type them double-spaced with one item on each 8½"x11" sheet of plain white typing paper, unless manuscript guidelines specify otherwise. At the top of each page on the left-hand side, single-space your name, address, and telephone number.

Opinions are mixed on the number of fillers to submit in an envelope. One successful filler writer advises sending out only one item at a time to the highest-paying markets, two to the those paying medium rates, and half a dozen to the lowest-paying publications. That makes sense to me. Whatever you do, remember to enclose a self-addressed, stamped envelope.

Keep copies of your submissions by typing them on the backs of the index cards you use to record submissions. (If the item is short, it will be easier to copy it longhand). Be sure to keep your material moving through the mails. Even though one editor cannot use your joke or quip, the next one may decide it's perfect for filling in a gap.

CHAPTER THREE

LET ME TELL YOU A LITTLE STORY

The stories are the thing, no matter whence they sprang nor when.

The Arabian Nights

 ing Shahayar reclined against his pillows of silk and brocade, unable to sleep. Since his wife's betrayal, he had ordered his chief minister to bring him a virgin each night. Each morning he had ordered that same minister to slay his companion in order to ensure her fidelity. When there were no more maidens in the kingdom, his bride of the night was the daughter of the chief minister. She had persuaded her father to lay her virginity and life at the foot of the insatiable ruler, for she had a plan.

"I will tell you a little story," she said. And so strong was the spell she wove, that she was not killed on the morrow as more than a thousand of her predecessors had been. Nor did she die after the thousandth night, or after the thousandth and first.

The editor examined the chip in her nail polish and wondered why she had let her secretary book an appointment with this freelancer from Boondocksville. After all, she'd never bought an article from an unknown and she doubted she ever would. The freelancer was well aware of her policy. But he had a plan.

"Let me tell you a little story," he said.

The editor, heretofore known to her staff as the Great Stone Face, heard the story and erupted in laughter that shook the outer office filing cabinets and echoed down to the water cooler in the hall. The writer got his assignment—and another, and another.

ANECDOTES: LITTLE STORIES FOR LARGE SUMS

In writing full-length articles and books, writers use anecdotes as tools. These miniature stories can provide leads (as did the foregoing anecdote), offer glimpses into a personality, increase the credibility of informational articles, and dramatize points in problem-solving pieces.

For those of us who write short material, the anecdote is more than a device. It's an end in itself, and one worth pursuing. Anecdotes usually command more money per word than almost any other kind of short writing.

The anecdote is a brief story based on an actual happening—a short account or retelling of a single incident. To be successful, an anecdote must evoke a feeling on the part of the reader, be it laughter, surprise, sympathy, or some other emotional reaction.

All stories have unity—a beginning, a middle and an end, with well-developed characters and scenes. The anecdote is a mini-version of a story. We expect it to provide enough information to allow us to picture the event it describes, but we aren't looking for detailed explanations of how the principals look or why they behave as they do. The following anecdote by Bennett Cerf shows how a few well-chosen words can fulfill our expectations:

> The story goes that Mrs. Vanderbilt once demanded to know what Fritz Kreisler would charge to play at a private musicale, and was taken aback when he named a price of five thousand dollars. She agreed reluctantly, but added, "Please remember that I do not expect you to mingle with the guests." "In that case, Madam," Kreisler assured her, "my fee will be only two thousand."

Note the strong, descriptive verbs, *demanded, taken back, assured;* the adverb, *reluctantly;* the hauteur conveyed by word placement in "Please remember that I do not expect you. . ."; and the marvelous put-down expressed in the closing retort.

SOURCES AND RESOURCES

Ideas for anecdotes come from our experiences and those of others. Conversations are the most productive sources of ideas. I don't know about you, but friends are always telling me about the funny thing that happened on the way to work, the strange encounter a nephew had, or the cute remark a grandchild made.

To identify potential anecdotes, list the various jobs you've had, names of interesting/good/out-of-the-ordinary neighbors, friends and associates, places you've lived in and visited. Then use each item on your list to prompt your memory, recalling associated incidents: the neighbor who had a quip for every occasion; the funny story the plumber who fixed your disposal told you about his previous house call; what the Egyptian tourist said to you in the Amsterdam hotel lobby.

It's important to remember that the people who regularly sell anecdotes haven't had any more experiences than the average person. They have, however, learned to identify experiences that make good stories and to craft them professionally.

Not all incidents can be fashioned into anecdotes. In order to work, the incident must have at least one of the following attributes: humor (the biggest seller), drama/tension, teach a lesson, a surprise ending or twist, or conflict/complication. Most good anecdotes contain more than one of these ingredients.

By way of illustration, let's suppose that you lost a wallet containing $500. The billfold with all its contents was later returned to you by a charming little old lady. If that's all that happened, you don't have the raw material for an anecdote. People lose wallets and have them returned intact by charming little old ladies every day. There's nothing unusual about such an incident—no drama, no surprises.

Let's add a few details. That $500 was the money you had saved all year for Christmas presents. The little old lady was shabby and poor but refused to accept the reward you offered her. Instead, she asked if she might have one of the children's school pictures, explaining that she never had a family of her own and would like to pretend she had grandchildren, especially around Christmastime. You adopt her as your family's honorary grandma. Now you have makings of a little story with a surprise ending—one that evokes emotional response galore.

FACT OR FABRICATION?

A question prospective anecdote writers often ask is how faithfully they must relate the story. Must they set it down as it really happened? This question isn't easy to answer. Actual events, however dramatic or humorous or exciting they may be, don't always have the same qualities when transferred to paper. There are times when facts must be slightly altered or the time frame must be compressed to make the story work in print. Quotes may have to be rearranged for maximum impact, to clean up the language, or for a dozen other reasons.

Time frame problems usually occur when a story unfolds gradually over weeks, months, or even years. The story becomes too drawn out if each event is related in turn. Instead, you must condense some incidents so that the reader gets a clear picture of what happened without becoming bogged down in unnecessary detail: "During the weeks that followed, the neighborhood reeled from the terrible twins' treachery—raw eggs thrown at front doors, tacks set under tires, grafitti spray painted on sidewalks."

I know a writer whose children were twenty-two and twenty years old when she sold an anecdote based on an event that took place fifteen years before. In relating the event, she referred to her seven-year-old daughter and five-year-old son. If it didn't bother her kids, I can see no problem with that kind of fact-changing.

On the other hand, I do have trouble accepting completely fabricated anecdotes. Besides, if you have ever tried to create a story out of thin air, you know it's almost impossible.

Another problem is that people don't usually say things in a way that makes for sparkling anecdote dialogue. They leave out words, sprinkle their speech with *uhs* and *you knows*, dangle participles, and use plural verb forms with singular nouns. Then, too, they can emphasize words with their voices rather than the way they place them in sentences.

Therefore, a spoken sentence that brings laughs can be a dud on paper. It's up to you, the writer, to work with the words until they provide the zing your anecdote needs. Take these words, uttered by a feisty old gal after her ninety-fifth birthday party: "I was thinking about the people who didn't come and what dirty skunks they were." The words sounded awfully funny when she said them, but somehow a great deal is lost in their translation to paper. After moving the words around and adding a few for emphasis, you might come up with something like this: "I wasn't thinking about all the nice people who came to my party. I was figuring out which dirty skunks didn't show up."

However much you alter what really happened, you must succeed in making the story "read true." Readers, however unsophisticated, know when they are being put on. How much juggling you do depends, in the long run, on your code of journalism ethics and your ability to fabricate convincingly.

MEASURING THE MARKETS

Most writers are thinking of *Reader's Digest* when they talk about writing anecdotes. After all, that magazine has the most visibility and prestige of the publications that use the form. Moreover, the *Digest* uses a lot of the little stories in each issue and pays well for them (in some cases $4 to $5 per word).

But *Reader's Digest* is also the anecdote writer's Everest. According to its editors, approximately 35,000 contributions arrive monthly for the combined humor features ("Humor in Uniform," "Campus Comedy," "All in a Day's Work," and so on). Few can scale its $300 heights. I'm not here to discourage you from trying to snag that money. By all means submit if you have an anecdote idea that's strong enough to brave the competition and you've given the idea every possible chance by polishing each phrase so that it gleams like your company silver.

I do suggest, however, that while you're waiting in the wings to become one of the *Digest's* regular anecdote contributors, you also try other anecdote markets. They don't pay as well, to be sure, but your submissions won't be battling the horrendous odds of acceptance by *Reader's Digest*.

One very good market for fillers is "Bright Side of the Road" in *Discovery*, which prints travel anecdotes such as this one, by Louis F. Root:

> My cousin Bill and his wife travel all over the country in a large motor home.
>
> One day, while stopped for gas at a small, rural town, one of the local citizens sauntered up to the pump and asked, "What kind of mileage do you get on that thing?"
>
> "Oh, about eight miles per gallon," Bill answered.
>
> "Humph. That ain't much, is it?" snorted the old-timer.
>
> "Well," Bill chuckled, "I guess that wouldn't be too good for a car—but you can't beat it for a house."

To find out about other markets, scan the pages of *Writer's Market* and browse through the magazines you have collected. Tabloids, retirement magazines, and religious publications such as *Catholic Digest* and *Guideposts* are particularly good hunting grounds.

Taking the Measurements

Unlike articles, which must be tailored to their intended publications, anecdotes usually can fit the stylistic formats of any magazine that uses little stories, *provided the length and subject matter are appropriate.*

In order to estimate length, count the number of words in half a dozen anecdotes that have appeared in the magazine to which you're submitting. (If all the anecdotes are about the same length, you need count only one.) When it's impossible to tell your story in the prescribed number of words, save it for another magazine. Although an editor may like a story that's two hundred words too long, she will have to deviate from her format to buy it—and editors rarely stray from the tried and true.

Tailoring Your Topic

More important than length, however, is subject matter. *Reader's Digest* spells out its requirements for "Humor in Uniform," "Campus Comedy," "All in a Day's Work," and "Life in These United States" at the front of the magazine. To find out what editors of other publications are looking for, you'll have to study the material they have bought in the past and devise your own description of requirements.

You will probably be surprised to find out that many magazines don't use stories featuring youngsters. *Reader's Digest*, for example, doesn't solicit anecdotes revolving around children, although one occasionally appears in the magazine. Other publications, by contrast, dote on children's sayings. The *Star* has a "Things Kids Say" department that offers nominal payment for anecdotes like the following, by Felice Belcher:

> When my son turned two-and-a-half he hit the "What's that?" stage. I finally couldn't take it any more, so when he would ask "What's that?" I'd say, "You tell me!"
>
> One day I heard a loud bang from the room in which my son was playing and I yelled, "What's that?" and quietly my son answered, "You tell me!"

In *Mature Living*, "Grandparents' Brag Board" features anecdotes about grandchildren such as this one, by Helen Livingston:

> I had just put my young grandson to bed for the umpteenth time and my patience was worn thin. When I heard him cry 'Grandma' again, I yelled to him, "If you call 'Grandma' one more time, I'll spank you!"
>
> Afterwards there was quiet. Then, just as I sat down, I heard a wee whisper, "Mrs. Livingston, may I have a drink?"

These two anecdotes could have fit either publication's criteria as far as length and content are concerned (if "son" in the first one were changed to "grandson" for the second).

To quality for "Children's Corner" in *Supermarket Shopper*, however, little stories must have a couponing/refunding angle, as in this one, by Anna Pettyjohn:

> My 4½-year-old daughter Kristi is always asking why Daddy has to go to work. I've explained that he earns money to buy food and clothes and toys for her. Last week Kristi sat at the kitchen table with me as I opened the mail, which had just arrived. It was a particularly rewarding day for me. As I began totaling the cash and refund checks I'd received, Kristi's eyes grew wider. Suddenly she began jumping up and down, shouting excitedly, "Mommy, call Daddy quick and tell him he doesn't have to work any more! The mailman's giving us all his money!"

You won't make a sale to the "Happenings" department of *Expecting* unless your story has to do with pregnancy. This one is by Irene Valenti Kucinski:

> Our first childbirth class fell on the same evening as my husband's last softball game. He was player-coach and this final game was important to him. Since he wanted to get to the ball park as soon as possible after the class, he came dressed in his softball uniform. At the beginning of the class, the couples were asked to introduce themselves. When it came our turn, my husband stood up and said, "I heard my wife needed a coach for this, so I thought I'd dress the part!"

As you read anecdotes, notice not only length and subject matter but also the kinds of anecdotes an editor seems to prefer—whether they're humorous, tug at the heartstrings, point out a moral, or poke fun at customs or institutions.

ANECDOTE ANALYSIS

Anecdotes are written from two points of view: first person and third person, as you will note in the foregoing examples.

Two factors determine the point of view you should use: the style of your intended publication and the material with which you are working.

The principal devices employed in writing anecdotes are narration, description, imagery, and dialogue.

Narration

Narration is simply the act of telling, or narrating, the story. There are four basic rules of anecdote narration:

1. *Keep your events in natural sequence.* Don't backtrack.
If we were writing about the lost billfold incident discussed earlier,
we might start out with something like this:

> It was the Thursday morning before Christmas, and I'd finally saved
> up $500 for presents. When I dug into my purse to pay for some pur-
> chases at the drugstore, I discovered that my wallet was missing.
>
> For the next hour, I retraced my steps. Then, feeling that the Christ-
> mas lights had gone out in my world, I returned home.
>
> But the lights went on again when the phone rang.

To be sure you have the events in order, write the incident down
in chronological form:

saved money

went shopping

reached into purse

wallet missing

retraced steps

went home

phone rang

lady found wallet

went to her apartment

offered her reward

reward refused

she asked for picture

I asked her to be our grandma

2. *Don't overwrite or include extraneous details.* The checkout cashier
may have had punk-rock purple hair, the drugstore could have been
having a fabulous sale on electric can openers, or you might have
run into your friend, Alice Mae, while you were searching for the
wallet. But don't include that information if it is not vital to your anecdote.

3. *Keep explanations simple and uncomplicated.* Explain just enough

so the reader will catch the twist at the end. In the Fritz Kreisler/Mrs. Vanderbilt anecdote, the principals were so well known that Cerf didn't have to explain who they were. He didn't have to spell out in detail that even Mrs. Vanderbilt thought $5,000 was a lot to pay for a Kreisler performance. In the billfold anecdote, you don't have to explain that you aren't wealthy. The words "finally saved" tell the reader that.

4. *Write the last line so that it has punch.* Rearrange words to achieve the maximum impact, working with them until you achieve it. Though the meaning would have been the same, if Cerf's last line had read, "Well, if I don't have to talk to your guests I'll only charge you two thousand dollars for performing," its sparkle would have fizzled.

Description

Description, due to the brevity of the anecdotal form, must be used sparingly with short "tags" or descriptive adjectives telling about the people in the story or about its setting. Don't describe anything unessential to the story.

Imagery

Imagery is the use of words to paint verbal pictures, allowing the reader to "see" the action. One of the most touching anecdotes I've come across is "The Gracious Art of Taking—and Giving," by B. Keith Cossey which appeared in *Guideposts*. As you read it, study the effective use of imagery.

My Marine buddy and I were taking a lunch break, eating our rations on the steps of an improvised medical clinic that we were helping set up for Vietnamese civilians. Patients milled around us and we had almost finished our meal before we noticed the small, frail boy who was watching us intently.

He was about 11, and it was clear that he was being treated for malnutrition. We knew he was hungry. But he was not begging—just looking at us with friendly curiosity.

My partner and I glanced at each other, then walked over to the child and offered him the only food we had left, one of the round chocolate disks that fits in the bottom of a C-ration can.

Wordlessly, with narrow hands, the boy accepted the gift, then carefully broke it into three equal pieces. Placing one in my hand and one

in my buddy's, he bowed the impeccably gracious Vietnamese bow
and slipped away.

With each paragraph of this piece, I get a series of mental images. I
have been on enough military bases and watched sufficient television to picture the medical clinic. (In my mind's eye it's pale-green
concrete, but that doesn't matter—each of us can respond with images arising from our particular experiences.) I've never been to
Vietnam, but I have seen enough Vietnamese people and pictures to
visualize the setting.

The words, "small, frail boy," simple as they are, convey an image
that works on my visual senses, as does the description of the mal-
nourished child in the subsequent paragraph. I can see the two
marshmallow-tough Marines, the C-ration chocolate (I'm sure it's a
bit stale and slightly grey around the edges), the narrow hands, and
the child bowing. The anecdote wouldn't be so moving if it did not
prompt those mental pictures.

Dialogue: The Impact of Closing Statements

The easiest endings to write are those that involve dialogue, as illustrated by this story by Ruth M. Hube from "Hearts Are Trumps"
in *Catholic Digest*:

> During a terrible spring storm, I was up most of the night calming my
> small boy's fears and worrying about the house as huge limbs fell
> from the old elm tree. When the storm subsided, we fell into a long-
> awaited sleep.
>
> Much to my surprise, when I awoke the next morning I saw the last of
> the branches being cleared away from my yard by a neighbor boy I
> didn't even know. I quickly got dressed, but he was gone by the time I
> got outside.
>
> About an hour later my doorbell rang. It was the little boy who had
> cleaned my yard. He looked at me shyly and said, "My mother told
> me to ask if you minded my cleaning up your yard without your per-
> mission."
>
> "Of course not," I said, grateful for such efficient help. "Let me pay
> you for all your hard work."
>
> He quickly replied, "No thanks. Today is my birthday and I just want-
> ed to do something special."

In some anecdotes the final action must carry the wallop. To make this most effective, the ending should involve a reversal from what is expected, as in "The Real Mystery," by Jackee McNitt-Watson, from the "Facts of Life" department in *Savvy*. The writer works for a credit card center.

The world of credit cards is a mystery to the vast majority of consumers. It is for this reason we have opened our doors for pre-arranged tours.

Not long ago, I arranged a tour for what I assumed was a high-school group. When the group arrived, I realized my mistake. There before me were 30 seven-, eight- and nine-year-olds. How was I going to explain the complex workings of a credit card center to children?

What I hadn't realized was the phenomenon of our highly computerized operation was much more easily accepted and understood by this generation than by their adult counterparts. I had only one minor setback.

I had stopped the tour just outside the plastics department to explain the tight security measures taken to safeguard the more than a half a million blank credit cards housed there. I was taking great pains to describe the mantrap setup with its double-locked doors because I felt it would appeal to a child's love of cops and robbers. In the middle of my brilliant explanation, a small seven-year-old girl stopped me.

"Excuse me," she said. "Why do they call it a 'mantrap'?"

Slightly exasperated, I began my explanation again.

Again she stopped me.

"No, no," she came back. "I just wondered why they don't call it a 'people trap.' "

WRITING YOUR OWN: A SAMPLE

Let's write an anecdote to show how the process works. The idea for this one came from a conversation with my friend, Jean. She told me that she had given a plate of fudge to a neighbor's family for Christmas. Their six-year-old son David remarked that the candy would have been perfect if "Mrs. Mulroy could learn to make it without nuts."

Writing down the main points of the story is the first step:
1. Jean gave fudge to friends for Christmas.
2. Six-year-old David sampled a piece.
3. David reacted to the fudge.

Next, explore the possibilities of using description and imagery. In this case, only a few descriptive adjectives are necessary. Every reader can visualize the plate of fudge, so that needs no amplification. Likewise, readers need no further information about my friend or the family receiving the gift except that my friend's name is Mrs. Mulroy and the family's six-year-old is named David.

As to dialogue, quoting David's response rather than describing it passively ("David said that . . .") gives the piece its needed punch.
Here's the finished product:

> At Christmas, my friend gave a plate of homemade fudge to a neighbor's family. Upon sampling a piece, six-year-old David remarked, "You know, this candy would be perfect if only Mrs. Mulroy could learn to make it without nuts."

The marketing job for this anecdote should be easy. All it requires is submission to a publication that specifically asks for cute sayings by children.

A NOTE ON STRUCTURE

If you want to learn to craft first-rate anecdotes, those printed in *Reader's Digest* will serve you well as models. Most *Digest* anecdotes are composed of three parts. The first sentences introduce the characters and the situation or problem. The middle describes the action or expands on the conflict. The anecdote closes the action or expands on the conflict. The anecdote closes with a satisfying ending, usually a punch line or twist that catches the reader off balance. The following *Reader's Digest* anecdotes, divided into these three parts, illustrate this structure:

One

> To supplement my student grant, I spent a vacation working in a bakery in an English town. My job was to place slabs of cake in front of a long-time employee, who spread them with jam.

Two

> Three weeks had gone by, and still the jam-spreader hadn't spoken

one word to break the monotonous silence. Then on the morning of the fourth week, she suddenly asked,

"What do you do, love?"

"I'm studying politics and economics at Oxford," I replied.

Three

There was another long silence, then eventually she remarked, "Blimey, I bet that's boring, isn't it?"

N.F. West

One

A woman who works for the state of Louisana got a call from a man who paused when she told him the name of her agency.

Two

He then asked her to repeat it. "It's the Governor's Office for Elderly Affairs," she told him again. There was another pause.

Three

"For gosh sakes, sign me up," he said. "I didn't do too well when I was young."

Smiley Anders in the Baton Rouge *Morning Advocate*

One

As a cub reporter, I interviewed a woman on her 100th birthday.

Two

She proved to be a sparkling, intelligent person who delighted in recalling events from her colorful yesteryears. "I've lived from the covered wagon age to the airplane age and loved every minute of it," she exclaimed. Her blue eyes danced and her face was glowing. When I had exhausted all my prepared questions, she seemed reluctant to end the conversation, so I voiced one more inquiry.

Three

"Have you ever been bedridden?"
"Oh, honey," came the instant reply, "hundreds of times and twice in a haystack!"

Lucy Newman

As you can see, the first and third examples are written in first person and relate incidents experienced by the anecdotes' authors. The second anecdote describes what happened to someone other than the writer and is therefore cast in third person.

Whereas the first and third examples depend heavily on imagery (the picture of a never-ending procession of cake slabs to be spread with jam; the dancing blue eyes and glowing face reflecting a hundred years of living), the second is a straightforward recounting with dialogue of an event that couldn't have taken more than a minute and contains only the image of an elderly man speaking to a secretary or receptionist on the phone. But no matter what devices were used, they were employed to lead up to such punchy last lines that it's easy to see why these anecdotes beat out thousands of competitors.

You may not have worked in an English bakery or as a cub reporter, but you have had other experiences rich with anecdotal material. Learn to package them well and editors will come to depend on you for your stories.

CHAPTER FOUR

SECRET FORMULAS

Is there an easier way? Nothing is so perfect that it can't be improved upon . . .

Heloise

riters are busy people. To carve maximum writing time out of each twenty-four hours, you and I have learned to get everyday chores and projects out of the way fast. In the process, we have become shortcut specialists.

But many of us haven't learned to become successful tipsters—to capitalize on our timesaving strategies by typing them up and sending them off to magazines that buy hints and tips.

These guides to everyday efficiency are the easiest filler material to put together. Most of them take only minutes to write. The ideas are right in our kitchens, offices, workshops, and gardens. They sometimes require a bit of experimentation, but as far as research is concerned, that's all.

Granted, pay for solutions to the little problems of everyday life won't solve the big problems of paying for the kids' orthodontia or the month's groceries. But the $5, $20, and $50 checks that come regularly to writers who have mastered the tricks of tip writing will buy a lot of extra treats.

TIPS ON TOPICS

When you have a spare half hour or so, walk through your home, shop, or office. Spend some time in each room, thinking about what you do there, how you have saved time on some jobs and what you might do to streamline others.

Look around my kitchen with me, and you'll see how the process works.

On my kitchen desk is a pile of checkout receipts from the supermarket and other stores. When I have collected fifteen or twenty of them, I turn them to their blank sides, staple them at the top and have a handy, no-cost tablet on which to write grocery lists. That tip has a good chance of selling.

In my freezer are cubes of frozen lemon juice, each just the right size for making a glass of lemonade. Though they're convenient, the idea doesn't seem innovative enough for a tip. But there's also homemade soup in the freezer. I freeze meal-sized portions in a kettle and then store the frozen soup rounds in plastic bags. When I want to serve the soup, I simply slip the frozen rounds into the same kettle and heat. That tip could sell.

I keep kitchen wipes in a drawer but rarely use them in the kitchen. Instead, I take them traveling. They become lap cloths for hotel-room snacks, washcloths in countries where those niceties aren't provided, or turban-style shower caps. The basic idea here is a good one, but the concept needs more work—and more specifics—before it will be ready to submit.

Our breakfast place mats are recycled—an old set made new by pasting postcard collages on top of the mats and then coating them in plastic. That idea might sell, especially if you suggest pictures of grandchildren for grandparents' place mats or of storybook characters for kiddies.

We've examined only part of my kitchen and have come up with several ideas that are workable. Your surroundings also contain innovations that you take for granted but that, when put into the appropriate formats, will be salable.

Another idea generator involves making lists. Use such headings as Children, Garden, Cost-Cutting, Cleaning, Entertaining, Sewing, and Car. Under each heading jot down any jobs you have made easier, ways you have saved money, problems you've coped with successfully. Include problems you haven't solved and experiment with solutions.

You'll find the time spent is doubly worthwhile. Not only will you have made your own life easier, but you'll also be paid for your efforts when you sell your tips.

Your list headed Children might look something like this. Fill in your own solutions and use them as the bases for your own hints.

CHILDREN

Problem	Solution
Keeping clothing (mittens, socks) from getting lost	?
Helping the kids keep their rooms neat	?
Keeping them occupied on car trips or when they're sick in bed	?
Helping them adjust to new neighborhoods, new communities, new schools	?

Teaching them to share	?
Helping them learn to spend money wisely	?

Another list might be headed Disposables. Skyhook a little and write down all the uses you can think of for each one—no matter how far out.

Take plastic margarine tubs, for instance—or plastic gift ribbon spools or cardboard paper towel cylinders. What about the egg-shaped panty hose containers? If you can think up original, practical uses for any of them you're on your way to a sale. Coming up with ideas will become a sort of game that you'll play automatically as you get into the swing of writing hints and tips.

The best tips I've come up with have been a result of conversations with friends. Once, at a dinner party, the hostess brought out a scrapbook of her latest trip. Each page of the scrapbook had mementos of each day's events. I combined that idea with another (putting each day's trip mementos into a different manila envelope while traveling) and sold the item to *Family Circle* for $25.

When you discover a new way of doing something, don't dismiss it by thinking, "That's so elementary, anyone could figure it out." I say this from sad experience. I've had many ideas I thought were too ordinary to submit, only to see them in print six months later with someone else's by-line.

But how can you be sure that your tips don't duplicate those that have already been printed? You can never tell for sure. You will, however, know that your idea has a chance if (1) you originated it or (2) you got it from another source but have refined the idea or piggy-backed it on another.

TIPS ON SELLING HINTS
Once you become hooked on hinting, you'll be on the alert not only for ideas to sell but also for where to send them. To find out which publications use hints and tips, go through the listings in *Writer's Market*. I mark each one "H&T" in the book's margin. Check the newspaper in your area, too. Still another market most freelancers don't consider are products' manufacturers. If you have found an unusual use for cleanser or plastic bags, for example, write the manufacturers to ask if they pay for tips on uses for their products. If their replies are affirmative, send them your submissions.

Editors of magazines that use hints and tips (and of some magazines that don't) receive dozens of submissions each month and can use only a small fraction of them. High-visibility publications such as *Woman's Day* and *Family Circle* get thousands. (According to department editor Erika Douglas, the figure is from 3,000 to 4,000 per month at *Family Circle*.)

Though the odds are horrendous, don't let them keep you from submitting. Douglas says that the reason most ideas don't make it at her magazine is that too many of them are duplications—they're not new. She advises contributors to try to be as original as possible.

SHAPING UP YOUR IDEAS

You will increase your handy helps' chances of being among the "select" group by putting them into the form your intended publication uses. That way, the editor won't have to do anything to your copy but pass it on to the typesetter.

In analyzing hints and tips, you'll notice that those in paragraph form usually begin in one of five ways:

1. With an imperative verb: "Keep some extra flour in a shaker jar." "Place a marshmallow in the point of your child's ice-cream cone."
2. With an adverbial phrase: "When transferring the pattern to the wood . . ." "While preparing for my annual garage sale . . ."
3. With an infinitive phrase: "To help your children keep the yard clean . . ."
4. With a statement defining the problem or setting forth the tip, followed by explanatory sentences that develop the idea in detail: "Teething is the pits for parents as well as children."
5. With a conditional clause: "If you use steel-wool scouring pads for cleaning pots and pans . . ."

Though most hints and tips departments use material written with all five types of beginnings, some publications such as the *Globe's* "$$-Savers" lean heavily toward the imperative verb lead.

Warm a bottle of furniture polish in a tub of hot water—it'll penetrate wood more easily.

Sprinkle ground cinnamon on top of your range to create a pleasant spicy aroma in your home.

Waterproof leather shoe soles by soaking them overnight in a pie tin with heated linseed oil.

Spruce up stained coat collars with a solution of ammonia, water, and salt. Apply the mixture with a cloth or soft brush.

Add a little bluing to dishwasher to make cut glass sparkle.

A few publications present their tips in the problem/solution structure. The format in *Make It with Leather's* "Tips and Hints" involves a maximum of about twenty words. The following example by Tina Hecker is typical.

THE PROBLEM: Pulling lace tight on handbags

THE ANSWER: An old-fashioned button hook

"Tips, Tools and Techniques" in *Better Homes and Gardens* uses material that is somewhat longer. Seventy to eighty words seems to be the average length, and a "Problem" with its "Solution" is the format used.

LOOKING BEYOND FORM TO SUBSTANCE

More important than the proper format is the material itself. Tips that are appropriate for some magazines just won't do for others.

The hints in *Weight Watchers'* "Around the House" include household hints of the same kinds that appear in other magazines as well as tips for dieters. The blurb at the beginning of the *Better Homes and Gardens* tips department describes it as "a wide-ranging collection of shop hints, installation tips, and repair shortcuts."

Model Airplane News uses only tips about making model airplanes in its "Hints and Kinks." *The Family Handyman* prints hints on a variety of subjects—from cleaning small parts to extending ladder legs to removing wall-covering adhesive—but all of them focus on jobs around the house and workshop.

Friendly Exchange's "Helpful Hints" are the same kind bought by *Woman's Day* and *Family Circle*—suggesting clever ways of doing tasks usually considered women's jobs. "Around the House" in *Good Housekeeping* offers housekeeping tips and ways to solve problems and save time.

You can't always tell what kinds of material to submit merely by reading the departments' names and blurbs. Though the tips in "Parent's Exchange" in *Parents' Magazine* all have to do with children, "Household Hints" in *True Confessions* also includes advice on solving kiddies' problems, as does "Household How-Tos" in *Modern Romances*.

HINTS ON BOOSTING YOUR SALES APPEAL

In many publications, each tip has a title, usually two to four words: "Stocking Stuffers," "A Patch in Time," "Hints for Joggers," and the like. If your target magazine uses titles, include them with your submissions. They may take more effort to craft than the hints themselves but will be worth every minute of time spent. An eye-catching, "just right" title will distinguish your piece from the hundreds of others.

Pay close attention to the length of previously published tips. The hints in *Woman's World*'s "Tips & Tricks" usually consist of no more than 30 words. They're written in two, or at the most three, sentences:

> Save the plastic trays from packages of meat and poultry to use as disposable pet dishes. You won't have to wash them afterward; just toss them out.

"Successful Swaps" in *The Mother Earth News* features tips of up to 300 words on bartering:

> With extra money being virtually nonexistent in our household, my friend and I hadn't been able to indulge in one of our favorite pastimes: traveling. But then our sightseeing urge was fulfilled in a way that we hadn't ever imagined!

> A buddy of ours had quit his factory job to make a career as a cross-country tractor-trailer jockey . . . and whenever he was in our area, the wandering trucker would stop by and fill our evening hours with tales of places he had been. Finally we realized that *he* was our ticket to adventure!

> Our long-haul friend, you see, needed helping hands to load, unload, and secure the freight in his rig . . . and we wanted to see some new sights. So (and what could be more fitting?) we simply traded our labor for a free ride *and* a guided tour of the country!

No matter what the length, hints and tips waste no words. After you've written yours, go over each of them, asking yourself which material is absolutely essential and deleting the rest.

KEEPING IN CIRCULATION

A time-efficient procedure for keeping track of your submissions is to list each of them on a separate file card by title (or using key words) along with as many potential markets as you can think of.

Along with each submission, be sure to include a self-addressed, stamped envelope. Though some magazines inform contributors on their hints pages that no material will be returned, it will usually be sent back when rejected if an SASE has accompanied it.

The biggest obstacle to keeping material circulating is that editors will hold items they like for a *very long* time. Maureen Kenney, editor of the "Neighbors" department in *Woman's Day,* says she has used items five to seven years after they were received. If you haven't heard anything on the status of your tip six months after you've submitted it, write to the editor, especially if you have alternate markets in mind.

You'll give your seasonal hints a better chance of seeing publication if you submit them six to eight months ahead of the appropriate season. According to Kenney, people send her Saint Patrick's Day ideas when the March issue is already on its way to the newsstands.

If you have a choice of markets, start with the best-paying publications and work your way down. The highest rates I've seen are paid by *Woman's Day and Family Circle. Parents* and *Better Homes and Gardens* pay well, too, considering the small amount of time and energy you'll have to expend. Your chances will be best, however, with publications where the competition isn't so intense.

THE RECIPE FILE
While you're waiting for the checks for your hints and tips, stir up some excitement with your culinary efforts. Even if you don't consider yourself a writer, you can submit a favorite recipe without having to acquire special skills.

Recipe Markets
Recipes generally bring more money than hints and tips, but there aren't as many potential markets for them.

The *Woman's Day* "Silver Spoon Award" is the best-paying of the recipe markets. Each month the person who submits the winning entry receives a Tiffany sterling silver spoon in addition to payment at the magazine's regular rates, which are very good. The contributor must "list all ingredients by their usual names and give level measurements, complete mixing and cooking instructions and any necessary pan sizes." A menu and brief description of the occasion for which you serve the food must be included along with information on where you got the recipe.

Among the recipes recently printed have been Lamb-Pistachio Pie, Chicken Avocado and Rice, Pork Roast with Tangy Sauce, Greek Honey-Spice Cookies, and the following one for Cheese Crescents (including the introduction written by the editor from information provided by the contributor):

When Marilyn Mayo and her husband entertain informally at their Brooklyn home, Marilyn's Cheese Crescents, served with fruit, make up the light, pleasing fare. Prepared with farmer cheese or with a combination of farmer and feta cheese, the crescents are rich pastries in the Sephardic-Jewish tradition. Marilyn uses the cheese two ways—to enrich the dough, then to fill the crescent before it's rolled. (We've also worked out a version using cottage cheese for those who can't find farmer cheese.) She bakes several dozen crescents at a time, serves some fresh and freezes the rest.

Cheese Crescents

1 cup flour
$1/2$ cup margarine
1 cup (8 ounces) farmer cheese, divided (see Note)
$1/4$ teaspoon salt, divided
1 egg

In medium bowl with hands or wooden spoon, mix flour, margarine, $1/2$ cup cheese and $1/8$ teaspoon salt until well blended and soft dough forms. Divide in thirds; wrap individually in waxed paper. Chill several hours or until firm enough to roll. (Dough can be refrigerated several days.) On lightly floured pastry cloth with stockinette-covered rolling pin, roll each third into a 10-inch circle about $1/8$ inch thick. Cut in 8 wedges. Mix well remaining $1/2$ cup cheese, egg and remaining $1/8$ teaspoon salt. Spoon $1/2$ teaspoon cheese mixture on wide end of each wedge. Starting from wide end, roll up each wedge. Place on greased baking sheet; gently bend in crescent shape. Bake on top rack of preheated 400° oven 18 to 20 minutes or until golden. Remove to racks to cool. Serve at room temperature. Makes 24. *Per crescent: 65 cal, 2 g pro, 4 g car, 4 g fat, 11 mg chol, 99 mg sod.* NOTE: Well-drained cottage cheese may be substituted for farmer cheese, or use a mixture of half farmer cheese and half feta cheese in pastry and filling. [The magazine staff provides the nutritional analysis.]

Contributors competing for the Silver Spoon Award should remember that no matter how delicious a dish may be, the recipe alone won't make the grade. Be sure to choose a recipe that has an interesting story to go with it. Perhaps you found it while going through Great-Aunt Sally's trunk, or your mother brought it with her from Scotland, or you've served the dish at all of your eight children's first communion receptions.

Two other markets that require a short bit of prose along with the recipe are the "Home Cooking" department in *Ladycom* and "My Turn to Cook" in *Better Homes and Gardens. Ladycom's* invitation to submit recipes says, "We're looking for interesting original recipes (no entries from cookbooks or other magazines, please) that might appeal to other *Ladycom* readers. And we want to know all about you, too: how you learned to cook, how you developed the recipe you have submitted to *Ladycom*, what your family likes to eat, how you entertain. The more you can tell us about yourself and your cooking, the better!" Since *Ladycom* is a magazine for service wives, all contributors must have a service tie-in: e.g., retired military, a son or daughter in the armed forces.

Each month, "My Turn to Cook" features a recipe submitted by a man.

Two brother publications, *Farm & Ranch Living* and *Country People*, regularly feature farmers and ranchers who love to cook in a series called "Men Who Run the Range." Details of the chef's culinary skills as well as recipes are required.

Better Homes and Gardens also has a recipe department for the ladies. Two Cooks-of-the-Month receive $50 each; four runners-up and ten honor roll winners receive smaller amounts. Each month the focus is on two different kinds of recipes: for example, "meatless soups and stews" and "tarts and turnovers"; "jams and jellies" and "barbequed main dishes"; "holiday meats" and "festive candies."

Each issue of *Lady's Circle* contains a "Cut-Out Cookbook" of recipes from readers. As many as twenty-five recipes are printed in an issue. After the list of ingredients (in order of use), the method is presented in paragraph form. Directions for most of the recipes are from 30 to 120 words long. Each sentence begins with an imperative verb:

PEANUT BUTTER CUPCAKES
by Peggy Revels

1/2 C shortening
1 1/2 C brown sugar
1/2 C peanut butter

2 eggs
2 C flour
1/2 tsp salt
2 tsp baking powder
3/4 C milk
1 tsp vanilla

Cream shortening and 1 C brown sugar together; add peanut butter and mix well. Add eggs beaten with remaining 1/2 C brown sugar. Sift flour, salt, and baking powder together and add alternately with milk and vanilla to peanut butter mixture. Fill 24 greased muffin tins half full. Bake at 350° for 25 minutes.

Note that in this recipe, abbreviations were used for measurements. When you submit your recipes, keep that busy editor in mind and type your submissions in the *exact* form as those previously published. If the editor is torn between two recipe choices, the one that won't need any rewriting will almost always be the one that's selected.

Be sure, too, that you have listed your ingredients and steps in proper order. A "Whoops, you should have mixed together the flour and milk before you added the beaten egg whites," even if it should slip past the editors, will bring batter-smudged letters from irate cooks.

While introductions to many recipes are prepared by the editor from information provided by the contributor, you will sometimes need to write the opening text yourself, "spicing" the instructions with personal hints for success. The following recipe for Extravagant Granola, which appeared in *The Mother Earth News*, is a good example of the genre:

I don't mean to brag, but I've converted a family of devoted sugar-frosted-cereal eaters into devout granola lovers with my own home-made version of "a good way to start the day." I must admit, though, that I spent quite a bit of time throwing together mediocre batches of the breakfast food before I finally hit on what I believe to be a *great* combination of ingredients (including unrefined peanut oil for an especially nutty flavor . . . molasses *and* honey for added body . . . and a goodly dose of energy-giving nuts, seeds, and dried fruit).

One of the basic secrets of mixing tasty granola is mixing the ingredients well, so—when you set out to try this recipe—conduct the operation in a very *large* bowl or pan . . . or, lacking that, in your (clean and wiped!) kitchen sink. Also, it's best to combine the wet and dry ingredients separately before stirring them together thoroughly.

First, blend 6 cups of old-fashioned (*not* quick-cooking) oat flakes, 2 cups of roasted soy splits, 2 cups of raw sunflower seeds (use 4 cups of the seeds if soy splits aren't available), 2 cups of wheat germ, 1 cup of bran, 1 1/2 cups of milk powder, 2 teaspoons of sea salt, and 3 tablespoons of cinnamon.

Then, in a separate bowl, blend 3/4 cup of molasses, 1/2 cup of honey, 1 cup of unrefined peanut oil, and 3 tablespoons of vanilla extract.

Now, combine the two mixtures well . . . spread the granola on large, flat pans . . . and bake it in a 250°F oven (a higher temperature will scorch the *outside* of the cereal before its inside is done), stirring occasionally until it turns just barely brown. At that point, dump the toasted treat out onto your clean-paper-covered kitchen table and add 2 cups each of coconut, raw cashew pieces, and raisins or diced dates. While the healthful fare is still warm, put it into tightly sealed containers, where it'll keep for ages (though the food is much too delicious to hang around your house for *very* long). You'll find this comestible a great morning cereal . . . a perfect snack . . . and an excellent topping for fruit salad, ice cream or apple crisp!

Note how the writer establishes rapport with her audience through phrases like, "I spent quite a bit of time throwing together mediocre batches of the breakfast food before . . ." The chatty tone of the piece makes the instructions sound like they're advice from a good friend.

Concocting the Perfect Submission Mix

In deciding what recipes to submit, it's important to read recipes in back issues of the magazine. Just as a master chef selects the correct seasonings for his creations, the master recipe contributor chooses recipes that suit each publication. A magazine may favor budget dishes, gourmet fare, ethnic foods, or recipes incorporating certain ingredients.

Desserts and entrées are the dishes most frequently printed in *Lady's Circle*, but recipes for relishes, salads, soups, and breads are purchased, too. *Farm Wife News* buys recipes that focus on different foods, such as squash, each month.

As you can see from the emphasis I've placed on marketing your recipes, sending them to magazines where they will please the editorial palates is paramount. To get ideas after you have decided what kinds of recipes are appropriate for your intended publication, pore over the various categories in your cookbooks. Don't forget the recipes you've clipped from magazines and newspapers or those you have collected from family and friends.

When you're reading the recipes, consider substitutions for the ingredients—crabmeat for chicken, alfalfa sprouts for chopped celery; curry powder for paprika. Although most magazines will buy recipes that are "old family favorites," they don't want a recipe you copied out of a competing publication three years ago unless it has been substantially changed.

Flavor any recipe you submit with a dash of originality. But don't be too original. Editors know that few readers will try cookies that combine onion soup mix, cheddar cheese, and chocolate. Unless the changes you've made in a recipe have been minor ones, it's a good idea to kitchen-test your submissions. Often, it's possible to experiment with four or five variations of a single recipe, adding different flavorings to a batch of basic cookie dough or dividing a casserole into quarters and using a different sauce with each. While you're kitchen-testing, be on the lookout for ways of simplifying preparations and enchancing the appearance of the dish. When your finished product brings raves at the dinner table, type up the recipe and send it off.

There's more to the selection process than the type of recipe or its principal ingredient. If your recipe calls for truffles and imported baby eel, it won't make it beyond the editor's wastebasket at most magazines. Those expensive and sometimes difficult-to-obtain ingredients aren't what most cooks have in mind when they're thinking of gourmet dinners cooked at home. On the other hand, a basic recipe for Sloppy Joes isn't what editors yearn for when they're putting together a group of economy recipes. Fancy can't be *too* fancy, but plain must be a bit out of the ordinary.

When you've selected your recipes, take care in naming them. Editors' preferences vary. Sometimes "Rice Pudding" will do nicely; other times "Ritzy Rice Royale" will be more appropriate. Also, watch for blurbs: "My mother made this easy, delicious pie for many years" or "This dish is delightfully flavored and nutritious. It's slimming too." A few well-chosen words, tailored to the publication, can clinch your sale.

Each editor has his or her perfect recipe for submission. Editor Adele Malott of *Friendly Exchange* describes hers as "one that fits our specified subject for the month. We'd like the recipe to appear to be easy to make and economical. We'd also like the recipe to have some special extra touch such as being good for a large group, be submitted along with some bit of family nostalgia, be good for using up leftovers or making use of a bumper crop of some item from the garden." William A. Coop, editor of *Road King*, notes that "editors of *Road King* believe that it is very important to hang on to the magazine's women readers. It's not because there are so many women truckers on the highway. Matter of fact, only about 3.9 percent are women. But truckers have wives, and the wives of the independent truckers (owner/operators, gypsies) usually keep the books. Influencing these women is very important to those advertisers who sell trucks, parts, tires, fuel, etc."

Coop uses both household hints and recipes in a column called "Wives are Winners." Each selected recipe is sent to dozens of families that have been enlisted to help in the selection process. According to Coop, "The wife makes the dish and serves it to her family. The questionnaire (accompanying the recipe) asks how each member of the family liked the dish, asks how much it cost to make, asks how difficult it was to make and if the cook followed the directions exactly as provided. The questionnaire also asks if the cook would make it again and what, if any, improvements she might suggest."

Coop also says, "We shoot for hearty dishes that even steak-and-potatoes eaters will at least try. What we don't like and won't test are recipes that specify, Jell-O or Crisco or some other brand name. Usually the inclusion of brand names means the recipe came off a box somewhere. We also discard immediately all recipes where the instructions are not absolutely exact. For instance, 'some ginger' is not an accurate instruction . . . although 'salt to taste' is acceptable."

Writing tips, hints, and recipes (unless you're another Heloise or Craig Claiborne) won't pave your path to the life of the writing rich, but it will have its rewards. Not only will the mailman drop a check in your mailbox now and then, but you'll dream up recipes that become your family's favorites and devise shortcuts for handling everyday chores. And the quicker you can get routine jobs done, the more time you'll have to write.

CHAPTER FIVE

HAVE YOU GOT A PROBLEM?

The message from the moon . . . is that no problem need any longer be considered insoluble.
                                        Norman Cousins

f your problem is deciding what kind of shorts you should warm up your typewriter on, why not begin with how-tos? Writing problem-solving pieces may solve the problem of your writing future.

The market has never been larger for instructional pieces. We're living in the do-it-yourself era, and almost every publication that uses short material—from *National Enquirer* to *Gardens for All*—prints how-tos on every conceivable subject, from raising one's consciousness to tearing down chicken coops. The ideas won't run out as long as people want to expand their skills, embellish their homes, improve their relationships, and otherwise enhance their lives.

A number of fringe benefits come the problem solver's way. The discipline required to write tightly and precisely—a must for short how-tos—sharpens any writer's skills. These kinds of articles can also lead to publishing plums. Research could show you that your subject is big enough for a book. You need only stop by the nearest bookstore to find out how problem-solution books are selling. They're the hottest items on the bookstore shelves and promise to remain so for a long time to come.

How-tos fall into four basic types: *project, procedure, personal enhancement/problem solution,* and *community/organization problem solution.* Some magazines use all four types; others, only one or two.

Project and procedure pieces are the easiest to write. No fancy prose is needed, just straightforward information about how to accomplish results. Most of these pieces are essentially expanded versions of the single hint or tip—a group of hints and tips with a common theme. If you've ever left a note for your child (or spouse or employee) explaining how to perform a task, you've already written this kind of how-to.

Although most publications use how-tos, that doesn't mean that they are interchangeable—that any how-to will sell to any magazine. A study of the market reveals that while both general interest and specialized magazines like to give readers the lowdown on projects and procedures, the focus varies with a publication's emphasis.

PROJECTING A PROJECT

Go through your how-to files (which you've set up as recommended in Chapter 1), looking for articles whose subjects are similar to yours. Your idea for a piece on making a backpack from a discarded nylon jacket, for instance, will be the sort of material used by *The Mother Earth News*, which has printed such recycling ideas as making a baby carrier out of a pair of blue jeans and remodeling an abandoned privy.

When you don't have any ideas in your file, you can conjure up dozens of them in a hurry. Walk through your home, workshop, or office, noting all the items you have made from scratch. Note kit items, too, and whether you can improve on them by starting with raw materials and your own design.

After you've finished your list, go over each idea and mark those you originated with an asterisk. Include those ideas that aren't completely original but incorporated your own improvisations. Then turn your attention to the remaining ideas, and, wherever possible, give them twists that will add the originality necessary to make them salable.

I find that flyers and brochures announcing craft fairs are another good source of ideas when they list the demonstrations that will be presented. For example, one brochure in my files lists eight demonstrations: napkin folding, flower arranging, kitchen magic, cake decorating, china painting, weaving, calligraphy, and oil painting.

Don't overlook your hobbies. Consider, too, expertise you've gained from employment or formal education.

But don't stop with the things you can learn or know how to do already. You can broaden your list of how-to possibilities by tapping hobbies and interests of friends and relatives. By looking over your list of potentials, you can come up with a number of salable ideas in minutes. Each of these will trigger others by the process of association. For instance, my mother is a porcelain painter and has crafted hand-painted soap dishes, light-switch plates, and other items for our home. With her help, I might write "Customize Your Home with China Painting" or "How to China Paint Your Light-Switch Plates" (or soap dishes, coffee mugs, kitchen tiles and scads of other items).

Sometimes the connections between the subjects and your ideas are less direct. The word *calligraphy* reminded me that my daughter-in-law used calligraphy to write "Remember When" at the top of sheets of colored paper to create a memory book for a favorite aunt. Why not, I asked myself, do a piece on "How to Make a Memory Book for Someone You Love"?

But your mother doesn't china paint, you say, and you don't have a daughter-in-law. Well, maybe your neighbor makes cornhusk dolls or seashell suncatchers. Perhaps your uncle Charlie builds decorative items out of scrap lumber. Let your mind buzz without restraints and you'll come up with ideas.

Any action that can be duplicated by following a step-by-step set of directions is material for a how-to: how to make macramé hammocks, construct picture frames, fashion biscuit-can jewelry, craft pocket sundials, or sew sleeping bag canopies.

Project Marketability

To test a project idea's marketability with a specific publication, I ask the following questions:

1. Are the materials used in the project similar to those used in previously published how-tos? Magazines that focus exclusively on needlepoint and crewel creations aren't going to want those that use jute or macramé cord. *Make It with Leather* selects one project for each issue's "Crafty Critters" department. Obviously, a successful submission requires a project using leather as one of the materials.

2. Can the steps necessary in creating the item be sufficiently explained within the limitations imposed by the publication's length requirements?

3. Are the skill levels required comparable to those called for in previously published pieces? For example, if techniques required for projects printed in back issues have been those any beginner could duplicate with ease, don't include complicated instructions in your submissions.

4. Does the project compete with products advertised in the magazine? In large-circulation magazines this consideration isn't as important as in the smaller ones.

Though project how-tos occasionally run 1,000 and more words in length, 300 to 600 words is the average. The format is frequently one or two paragraphs of prose, followed by directions in list form, numbered or bulleted. Even if numbers or bullets aren't used, each step should still be given in sequential order.

The following project how-to, "Potpourri—The Scents of Gardening," from *Crafts 'n Things*, illustrates the numbered or bulleted steps format:

The word, "potpourri," is French and is pronounced "po poo ree." Potpourris are a mixture of several kinds of fragrant flowers, herbs and spices that have been dried and still retain their lovely scent.

Give a Potpourri Bubble to a bride, to an invalid who can't get out to smell the flowers, to anyone who loves gardening . . . and to yourself!

MATERIALS

8-inch or 10-inch bubble bowl. Drinking glass, about 2 inches taller than the bowl. Floral clay. Votive candle. Potpourri mixture sufficient to surround the drinking glass and to come up the sides of the bubble bowl about halfway. OPTIONAL: Rose oil or other preferred volatile oil such as lavender or a combination. OPTIONAL: A few flowers that you might have pressed or preserved can be used to decorate the bubble bowl, from the inside, before you add the glass drinking tumbler or potpourri mixture. (For Sources of Supplies, see page 66.)

INSTRUCTIONS

Step 1. Using a glass cleaner, clean and thoroughly dry the bubble bowl and glass tumbler.

Step 2. If you wish to decorate the bubble bowl with pressed ferns and flowers, this is the time to do it. Using a white craft glue that will dry clear, place a small dot or two on the petals of the flower you wish to attach to the inside of the glass bowl. Gently press the flower in place. The larger flowers should be at the bottom of the bowl and the smaller flowers nearer the middle of the bowl.

Step 3. Make a small ball of floral clay and press it to the bottom of the drinking glass. Do not flatten it.

Step 4. Now place the glass in the center of the bubble bowl. As you press down on the glass, the clay ball will flatten and cause a tight bond.

Step 5. Add a tablespoon of water to the glass tumbler and then center a votive candle in it. The water will keep the heat generated from the candle from cracking the glass as the candle burns down.

Step 6. Use a packaged potpourri mixture from the craft store, or use the recipe in this article to make your own. Slowly add this fragrant concoction to the inside of the bubble bowl. Use a funnel to direct the potpourri against the outside of the drinking glass and away from the flowers you have glued to the bubble bowl.

Step 7. When you have added as much potpourri mixture as you desire, you may wish to place a few choice dried rosebuds, delphinium florets or other flowers on top of the potpourri, toward the outer edge of the glass bowl, for a finishing touch.

When lighting the votive candle, use a long fireplace match or a soda straw. When replacing the candle, avoid disturbing your arrangement by lifting the candle out with tongs or an ice pick.

To store this arrangement when not in use, place it in your linen closet (with a piece of plastic food wrap covering the opening). Any scent that escapes will be quickly captured by the towels and bed linens!

The recipe for potpourri mix that follows the article is written in the same format.

Another how-to pattern, as used in "A Sleeping Bag Canopy," by Norma Gaffron, from *Field & Stream*, shows how instructions can be incorporated into the text. An easy-to-understand sketch accompanies the piece.

Camping is more fun if the bugs don't disturb your sleep. You can convert your sleeping bag into a refuge from unwelcome visitors with a canopy designed for use under the stars or in a tent. A mosquito netting "box" is sewn onto a muslin base, the sleeping bag slips inside, and a zipper keeps the canopy closed. It's lightweight and can be rolled to take up a minimum of space. Twill tape at the four corners ties the enclosure to stout sticks stuck in the ground or to sticks tied to the corners of a cot.

Here's how to make the canopy:

Cut a 16-inch square out of each corner of a length of netting that measures 104 inches by 62 inches. That leaves 30 inches across for the "roof"—the approximate width of a sleeping bag (the 16 inches gives adequate clearance for turning over, but if wider netting is available,

18 inches would be even better). Across the 30-inch roof piece, sew two pieces of twill tape, each 52 inches long, at the point where the drop will be, one at each end. The tape reinforces the points of stress and then extends outward 11 inches on either side for tying.

Cut a second 11-inch piece of tape for each corner to make tying a knot possible. Sew these on securely.

Next, attach a zipper down one side seam to join the netting top to the muslin base. This should be done before the other side seam is sewn, for easy handling on a sewing machine. Once the zipper is in place, the other side seam is sewn. Stitch all seams twice.

Now, being careful not to catch the ties in the seams, sew the corners of the netting "box" together, stitching a piece of twill tape to the seam for added strength. Sew the head end to the muslin base, and then to the foot, and the canopy is complete. It can be turned right side out through the zipper opening.

Materials needed for the canopy:

- Muslin—2 yards of 30-inch fabric.
- Mosquito netting—3 yards, 62 inches or wider. Available at stores that carry camping equipment (do not use cheesecloth).
- Zipper—one approximately 72 inches long, or two 36-inch zippers opening from the center out to the ends.
- Twill tape—about 212 inches.

The cost of our canopy was $5.98, which included the netting at $1.60 a yard and twill tape at 3 yards for 59 cents. We had muslin and thread on hand, and our zippers were salvaged from discarded slipcovers.

Although some articles written in this format include material quantities needed in the instructions, you will notice that those necessary for this project were listed at the article's end—a rather unusual procedure.

A third project how-to pattern—the step-by-step photo piece— uses even fewer words. A photograph of each procedure is presented in sequential order, accompanied by a sentence or two explaining the step it illustrates. Photos must be uncluttered and show clearly what the person making the item is doing (usually only hands appear in the pictures). You may want to enlist the aid of a freelance photographer (with whom you've come to an agreement on how to split the article proceeds) to take the necessary shots if your camera skills aren't up to the publication's standards. The way to determine which of the three project how-to formats is appropriate is by studying back issues to see what format your target publication has used in the past.

Checking Specifications

When I've finished the rough draft of a project how-to, I consult my checklist to see that I've followed the magazine's format to the letter and have included all the necessary information. This is what the checklist looks like:

1. Terminology. Does the editor prefer that you say "directions" or "instructions"? "Materials" or "supplies"? Where is information on necessary equipment and material listed—at the beginning, at the end, or scattered throughout?

2. Are all the ingredients, materials, supplies, and tools listed, and are they in proper order?

3. Are all the steps included?

4. Are the steps in sequence? Writing down the steps necessary to complete a project you've done many times can be more difficult than one that is a first attempt, simply because you may take the simpler steps for granted and may therefore omit them. To be sure that you include all the information, jot down the steps while you're making the item or write the directions and then follow them exactly to see if they work. An alternate testing method is to write out the directions and then ask a friend or family member to make the item while you look on.

Spell out every detail. Don't say, "Take a handful of X ingredient." Who knows whether the hand will be that of a reader 4 feet, 10 inches tall or one 6 feet, 10 inches?

5. Can any process be simplified or shortened without changing the result?

6. Would the process be easier to understand if more instructions were added?

7. Is each word precise or might any of them be misinterpreted?

8. Are there any sketches, line drawings, or illustrations that should be included? The magazine's art department usually takes care of finals on these, so your sketches need only be clear, with scale indicated.

PROCEEDING TO PROCEDURES

Instructions for procedures differ from those for projects in that they explain how to go about doing something rather than making a specific item. They may teach readers how to lighten their hair or lightning-proof a tree; how to train their children to make simple skiing turns or wean them away from a diet of peanut-butter-and-jelly sandwiches. Think of your own shortcuts for accomplishing daily tasks—say, getting the children clothed for school or breaking in a new employee—shared by millions of Americans. Concentrate on time- and money-saving procedures; you'll find they are the most popular in the majority of today's markets. What's selling should dictate which ideas you choose to develop. Again, read back issues. They'll tell you the kinds of agencies you'll need to contact for statistics, the kinds of experts and authorities (and how many of them) from whom you'll need to obtain quotes, and so on.

Like the project how-to, the procedure is tightly written. These pieces rarely include anecdotes or figures of speech. Quotes, when they appear, are short and to the point. Statistics are often used.

This article from *EveryWoman*, "Protect Your Property from Burglars," by Robert Grayson and Diana Drew, gives readers a procedure they can follow. Notice that like the project how-to, it employs an abundance of imperative verbs. Like most procedural how-tos, it is written in the second person.

Do you know what property you own? Come on, really know it? Do you know it well enough to describe it in detail to the police if it were stolen? Take a minute and give yourself this quiz. Let's say that you come home and discover that your television has been stolen. Or maybe your stereo. Do you know:

- What color it is?
- How big it is?
- Who the manufacturer was?
- What model it is?
- Where you bought it?
- How much it cost?
- How long you've owned it?
- If it has any unusual identifying characteristics?
- What the serial number is?

That quiz probably wasn't as easy as you first thought. But if you don't know all the answers, you're not alone. Most people don't.

That is what makes theft of personal property so appealing to criminals. For example, a robber can actually carry your TV on the street with no fear of being apprehended because the serial number is unknown, or the manufacturer.

In 1980 (the last year for final statistics), a burglary was committed in the United States every eight seconds. And burglaries cost victims more than 3.3 billion dollars. The majority of victims had only their memories to rely on when trying to give the police a rundown of stolen items.

If you think it's hard to remember some simple facts about your property now, think how difficult it must be when you're still shaken by a burglary.

There is a simple and inexpensive method that helps—a personal property inventory. All you need to get started is a pen, spiral notebook and some property. Your inventory should include not only entertainment units, but all household appliances, antiques, paintings, jewelry, and anything else you value.

Start by making a chart. List eight columns with the following headings: item, serial number, make/model, color, size, purchase price, place of purchase, additional information. If an item is missing a key aid, like a serial number, photograph it. Such items as jewelry, works of art and collectibles are much easier to identify from a snapshot than a verbal description.

Remember to update your list as you acquire new property. And store the list and photos in a safe, out-of-the way place.

Today, there are inventory services available. For a fee, someone will make up a list of your valuables, or even film them. Unless your art collection rivals Peggy Guggenheim's, this seems to us to be an extravagance. However, there is a program we recommend. *Operation Identification* is a crime prevention effort sponsored by local police departments in a growing number of communities. Police supply residents with a special engraving tool needed to mark property. Every item of value in your home is thus registered with the police with its own special code number. Operation Identification often supplies residents with a warning sticker as well to place on windows or doors. It works like a charm to scare away burglars.

Call your police department to see if this program is available in your area. If not, see what you can do about starting one.

We hope that you're never burglarized, but we certainly don't want to have you lose something forever in the event theft occurs. Make up that inventory list right now and be prepared.

The next excerpt, from "Tips on Buying Real Bargains at Yard Sales, Flea Markets and Auctions," which appeared in the *Star*, illustrates the procedure format in which the first word or phrase of each point is emphasized by capital letters rather than numbers or bullets. It also exemplifies the pattern most popular with tabloids for both procedure and personal enhancement how-tos. The first sentence summarizes the theme of the article; the next paragraph or two cites authorities; and the remainder of the article consists of point-by-point advice.

Garage sales, auctions and flea markets are full of great buys—if you know what to look for.

Two experts, Sylvia F. Griffin, an extension home economist in Monmouth County, New Jersey, and Bunny Shore, who operates a flea market in Langhorne, Pennsylvania, offer some advice.

Mrs. Griffin has these suggestions for buying bargains at garage sales and flea markets:

KNOW YOUR measurements (or measurements of anyone else you are shopping for), as you may not be able to try items on, and bring a tape measure along so you can measure clothes that appeal to you.

EXAMINE clothing carefully for quality and signs of wear.

Has the color faded? Are the seams straight and strong? Do zippers work easily? Are the collars, cuffs, elbows or hems frayed?

Check closely for spots. If there is a grease stain, chances are someone else has already tried unsuccessfully to remove it.

HOW MUCH work will be needed to get the clothing up to your standards? Will it be worth the time, skill or money you will have to put into it?

GO EARLY for better choices; go late for better prices.

As you can see from the foregoing examples, ideas for successful procedure pieces have broad reader appeal. All of us are interested in protecting our possessions from theft, and an increasing number of people have become swept up in the flea market/garage sale phenomenon.

Use the same idea-producing process for procedure how-tos as you do for devising project ideas. After you have your idea, write down all your top-of-the-head information on the subject before you do any research. Determine by reading parallel articles in back issues how many experts or authorities you will have to consult.

HOW TO WIN FRIENDS, K.O. MUGGERS, AVOID KIDNEY STONES, ET AL.

Personal enhancement/problem-solution articles tell readers how to put more zest in their lives, how to have more satisfactory relationships, how to do *anything* that will enrich their lives in any way.

The adaptation/focus-changing method of idea generation lends itself especially well to these pieces. Let's take titles of two actual pieces—"How to Accept Favors Without Feeling Guilty" and "How I Fight Insomnia"—and see how it works.

First, delete the key words and substitute blanks: it's okay to delete words, too.

a. How to _____ _____ Without Feeling _____
b. How I Fight _____

Then make new titles by filling in the blanks. Here are some examples to get you started.

a. How to Accept Criticism Without Hurting Inside
How to Say No Without Feeling Guilty
How to Diet Without Feeling Hungry
How to Do Hateful Jobs Without Feeling Like a Martyr
b. How I Fight Boredom
How I Fight Jet Lag
How I Fight the Blues
How I Fight Stress
How I Fight the Compulsion to Work 16 Hours a Day
How I Fight Laziness

Problem Solving Formulas

Typically, short personal enhancement/problem solution pieces fall into either the point-by-point advice pattern or the summary/examples/summary format. "How to Change Your Life to Make It More Interesting" by Phyllis Guth from *Winning* is an example of the latter pattern—the tell-and-show in which the piece begins with one or two "this is what I'm going to tell you" paragraphs, goes on with several examples to illustrate its points, and ends with a "this is what I told you" paragraph.

At one time or another most everyone reaches a point in life where he or she realizes some changes have to be made. The symptoms might manifest themselves as boredom, a general dissatisfaction with life or just a low-level irritation with things that normally wouldn't bother you. It could take place at retirement, when you move to another town or state or when your youngest child marches off to school or leaves home. But happen it does and recognizing the problem is the first step in effecting a changing that will ultimately serve to correct the situation.

Take Margaret, for instance. When she and her husband moved to a new community where they didn't know anybody, she wanted to find a way to meet new people and keep up with her own interests. Because she had always enjoyed good literature, she decided to take a course in writing at the local YWCA. There, she not only made several new friends, including the instructor who introduced her to a group of area writers who met regularly to discuss their manuscripts, but also started down the road to selling the articles she was by now turning out with regularity.

Arthur is another case in point. A retired psychology professor, he was bored and missed getting out and being among people. So he approached a local college about teaching a course on growing old gracefully. Now back in the classroom on a part-time basis, he is happy to be active once again.

When Betty retired early as a gym teacher in a nearby high school, she was content to be home with her busy and active family . . . for a while. When she mentioned her growing discontent to a friend, the friend suggested she organize a course in Dancercize for residents of the community. The lessons proved to be so popular she had to add an extra evening to her schedule, and the following year, when all those who had signed up for the course couldn't be accommodated in two evenings, a third class was added.

Nancy, on the other hand, had been a stay-at-home mother for many years while raising her three daughters. Then, she found as her girls were growing up and needing her less, there was a void in her life. A part-time job as a teacher's aide helped to fill it. But she really found her niche when her daughter made the high school cheerleading squad and Nancy volunteered her services as unpaid assistant to the overworked coach. When the coach resigned, the school principal appointed Nancy to the part-time paying position. Now her life is one busy round of practices and football and basketball games and she has a new crop of girls each year to make her feel needed.

While Nancy went to work at the school, Bernie went back to school when her three daughters left home. All her life, she had been interested in a nursing career, but somehow with raising a family she had never found the time to get the necessary training. When her last daughter left home, she attended the local community college in pursuit of a career as a licensed practical nurse. Now in her early 50s, Bernie is happily working in the field of her choice for the first time.

Jean's interests in life were different from Bernie's but they led her, nonetheless, to a new and exciting line of part-time work. Jean had many old pieces in her country home, handed down by past generations of family members. There was a history connected to each one and Jean delighted in telling visitors the story behind each antique.

Soon people who knew of Jean's interest in antiques began asking her to speak at banquets and other special programs. When fulfilling these engagements, Jean dressed up in her grandmother's 18th century clothing and took a selection of antiques with her in old-fashioned wicker baskets. Before long, Jean developed a reputation in the area for being a lively yet knowledgeable speaker, and people in outlying communities began requesting her services also.

The story doesn't end there, though. Because she liked working with people and because of her special rapport with children, she sold a mall promotion director on the idea of conducting a story hour at the mall on a weekly basis. For these, Jean dressed up in styles from the past century and billed herself as Aunt Lillie. Like her talks on antiques, this, too, expanded and soon she was appearing at several shopping malls. As you might expect, Jean seldom has time to be bored with life; she's too busy having fun and getting paid for doing something she enjoys.

As you can see from these examples, almost anyone, regardless of age, can make constructive changes, go on to do different things, achieve new goals and generally improve the quality of his or her life. If you feel that something is lacking in your life, making a fresh start in another direction could be the answer for you. You'll be a more interesting person for it and have more fun as well. And boredom will probably disappear from your life—that will really make you a winner.

Needless to say, the idea and any top-of-the-head information you might have on the subject won't be enough to sell a piece. You will have to research your topic—in most cases by interviewing people who are active both in treating and coping with the problem you're writing about. You will also want to read articles on your subject that have been published in the past. But this doesn't mean that you have to be a seasoned article writer to tackle the personal enhancement/problem-solution piece. Simply use similar articles in your intended publication as models, learning from them the kinds of people you will need to interview and the sort of facts you will have to gather.

The problems these pieces address needn't be those you have personally faced and solved. If that were the case, those of us with relatively uncomplicated lives would run out of ideas in a hurry. As a writer of problem-solution pieces, you'll want to watch out for new theories of dealing with psychological and emotional problems (if you have a psychiatrist friend, ask him or her to keep you posted), as well as agencies in your community that have been established to deal with such problems. Cocktail-party discussions with professional people are great opportunities to gather ideas for pieces.

CHAPTER SIX

GIVING PEOPLE A PIECE OF YOUR MIND

The feeble tremble before opinion, the foolish defy it, the wise judge it, the skillful direct it.
Mme. Jeanne Roland

f there's such a thing as the Great American Pastime, it has to be giving people a piece of our mind. We tell people what we think about everything from shoppers who crowd ahead of us in the checkout line to the current administration's position on embargoes. We like to share our experiences, too. Who among us can resist relating what happened when we were snowbound with the governor of New York or went diving for doubloons off the Florida coast?

We not only like to tell our own stories; we enjoy hearing about what's happened to others and how they think. Eavesdrop a bit. In the barbershop, the deli, or at the health club—almost anywhere people gather—you'll find most of the conversations you overhear will be of the opinion/experience kind.

As a writer, you can take advantage of human nature and profit from it by putting your opinions and experiences on paper, without hours of grinding away at the typewriter.

Most personal opinion/experience articles are short. Few of them require much research; many of them, none at all. Idea gathering is a cinch, since the topics for these pieces are right inside our heads. We only need to do a little remembering and evaluating to make them rise to the surface.

Personal opinion/experience pieces fall into three general categories: personal opinion, personal experience, and personal experience/opinion.

PERSONAL OPINIONS

These articles express the author's view of a topical subject. Though the pieces may refer to experiences the writers (and others) have had that support their opinions, their primary purpose is to set forth the writer's point of view.

Where Do You Stand?

To come up with ideas, think about current controversies, where you stand on them, and why. What are your views on truth (or the lack of it) in advertising, the cost of medical care, natural fur coats, nuclear disarmament, food stamps, exotic pets such as pythons and lions, bilingual signs, the minimum wage, rights for the retarded, television's sex symbols, or mail-order merchandise that arrives with parts missing? Once you put your idea machine in motion, the list will flow on and on.

After you've come up with a dozen or so possibilities, you'll want to evaluate each of them. Ask yourself if the idea has been over-worked, if it's the kind of idea the editor to whom you are submitting has gone for in the past, whether your approach is fresh. Consider the number and kinds of words you will need to write. Do you have enough to say on the subject? Can you find the authorities and statistics necessary to support your case? Will you be able to get quotes from experts? Will you be able to make your point in a style compatible with the magazine you've chosen?

One of the best markets for opinions are the op ed (editorial pages devoted to letters from readers) departments of newspapers. Although most of us immediately think of the *New York Times,* other dailies, such as the *Baltimore News American, Newsday,* and the *San Diego Union,* as well as smaller papers throughout the country, use this kind of material. *Newsday* calls for "opinion on current events, trends, issues—whether national or local government or lifestyle. Must be timely, pertinent, articulate and opinionated." These guidelines are typical of what editors are looking for. Whatever subject you choose, the article must be a commentary. Your point may be reinforced by quotes and information from authorities, but the viewpoint must be your own.

Your subject needn't be profound in order to sell to most newspapers. Witness this piece, "This Age Bit Really Gets Old," by Caroline Clark, which appeared in the "Bite" department of the *Kansas City Star:*

I live in a retirement home where my age—79—just about strikes the happy medium. And I have a gripe.

The food is terrible, right? Wrong. The food is good. The people are dull, tedious, fussy? Absolutely not! The people here are nice and we get along fine. Then it must be the over-the-hill mentality that drives me up the wall? Not really. That sort of thing goes with the territory, and each of us has his own way of dealing with it.

My complaint is with the people "out there," the ones I sometimes encounter when I socialize or shop. Much is being written these days about what to do with older people, and a lot of good things are being done. But I'd like to put in a word, if you don't mind.

To begin with, a lot of you do mind. Away from our natural habitat we tend to become invisible. Nothing is more infuriating than to be excluded from a discussion. How often I have sat between two younger people who toss the conversational ball back and forth in front of me! The Polish situation? What would a person my age know about that? Now if the subject were crochet patterns . . . Baloney! I haven't crocheted since I made bootees for my eldest daughter.

Not long ago I sold my house through a real estate agent. I didn't know the man, having selected him solely on his professional reputation. The first time my daughter and I talked with him, he directed most of his remarks to her, as if a business transaction was beyond my feeble comprehension. The second time he did it again. Finally, he said to me, "This must be pretty boring to you, my dear." Boring wasn't quite the word I'd have used. I wanted to tell him to jump in the lake that conveniently adjoined the property, but being a nice old lady I said nothing.

If we aren't ignored we may be embarrassed by excessive kindness. Some of you out there when dealing with older people instantly succumb to the help-old-ladies-across-the-street syndrome. Would I like a more comfortable chair? A drink of water? Am I sure I'm warm enough? They fuss with the thermostat, the window shade, the cushions. Hovering makes me feel uncomfortably conspicuous.

I'm still fuming about a recent encounter with a saleswoman in a dress shop. She looked at me kindly, a patronizing little smile touching her lips, and said, "I don't believe we have anything you'd be interested in." They did. I'd seen it in the window. But I summoned what shred of dignity I had left and got the heck out of there.

I know you're not deliberately rude. You're just thoughtless. So I patiently endure being talked across and I hang on to my dignity as best I can. Until this moment I haven't "popped off."

But I'm popping off now and you'd better listen. And *don't* say, "Isn't she cute?"

Note, too, how Clark's sense of humor gets her point across without preaching. The light (or at least non-preachy) tone is important.

Most editors will reject pieces that sound like sermonettes.

The author leads readers from sentence to sentence in the first two paragraphs by enumerating the disadvantages associated with retirement homes and refuting them one by one. The reader can't help but be hooked. "If those aren't the lady's gripes," he asks himself, "what can they be?" When Clark sets forth her complaint, she expresses it in generalizations and then follows up with three specific examples. After she has written what she feels needs to be said, she closes with a short, snappily appropriate statement.

This pattern—the one-to-three paragraph introduction followed by several examples illustrating the point of the piece and a paragraph or two of summary—is the one you'll most often find in op ed pieces. But before you submit your opinions, read back issues to be sure you've followed the pattern typical of the publication to which you're submittng.

Other Viewpoints, Other Markets

More limited but generally better-paying markets for personal opinion pieces can be found among the magazines. *American Way*, American Airlines' in-flight publication, pays $200 for opinion pieces on any subject except politics, religion, or sex that are published in its "Seems to Me" column. Manuscripts, which should not exceed 800 words, have a better chance if they're light in tone.

Even better pay for personal opinion pieces is offered by *Glamour*, which runs a "Viewpoint" department featuring one article per issue. The quality of writing is high and subject matter focuses on causes and trends. By reading "Viewpoint" pieces that have appeared in back issues, you can easily zero in on what the editor likes. Here are examples to give you an idea of the sort of subjects she goes for:

"Space," "needs," "conflict," "intimacy"—the language of feelings has turned sterile and meaningless.

I am not a brainless twit, obsessed with household cleanliness. I am not superwoman, going from board meeting to nightclub. I am TV's missing woman.

I'm a full-time homemaker with three children, and I'm spending a year out of my life campaigning for equal rights. Here's why.

Crime does pay—if you write a book about it. It's time we stopped hyping—and buying—these books.

How I, a former workaholic, learned to play hookey and love it.

The *Globe* has a weekly "Have Your Say" department that uses short letters (from 50 to 100 words). The pay is modest, but about nine letters are used in each issue. Topics range from pet peeves to pats on the tabloid's editorial back.

Among the other opinion piece outlets are guest editorials or opinion pages in *Trailer Life, The Lutheran, Proceedings,* and a variety of general interest and specialized publications. Each of their editors has definite opinions on the sort of commentary he likes or the subjects she favors, so your surest route to a sale lies in studying back issues.

Here's the TV's "missing woman" piece by Mary Alice Kellogg, from *Glamour.* It is an excellent example of making one's point with style (a style that is obviously in sync with the editor's).

Once upon a time, I enjoyed watching television after a grueling day at the office. Why? Because all the women in the commercials were incredibly boring. Madison Avenue had created droves of stereotyped women who broke out in hives when their floors were dingy, suffered quietly while husbands complained about coffee and—in a modern-day version of Jacob weeping at the well—wailed when their detergent failed them.

Hardly any woman is like that in real life, of course. Yet I loved those fictional portrayals because they made me feel so superior. I knew I'd never be one of those silly ninnies who fretted about window streaks for I had more important things to worry about—running a business, reading the classics, being involved in The World Out There. But I enjoyed giving these doomed women advice on their never-ending parade of household horrors. Does your little boy complain that your chocolate cream pie is not as fluffy as Mrs. Smith's down the street? Fine—don't feed him for a week. Your husband snivels that his shirts don't smell as fresh as they did last week? Great—teach him do the laundry. Your snoopy neighbor feels it's necessary to remark that your counter tops don't shine? Terrific—tell her to freeload coffee and cake elsewhere.

Yes, those were the days and now they're gone. Today, when I come home from the office and turn on the television, I no longer feel holier-than-they. Madison Avenue has replaced its army of brainless twits with Women Who Do Everything. In the new commercials, women go directly from a corporate meeting to a nightclub, where they sing and dance all night long—then drive off in a sleek sports car to watch the sun rise over the ocean. By comparison, their jobs—airline pilot, judge, television anchor woman, fashion magnate, head of the Federal Reserve—make mine chopped liver.

I have noticed that this new breed lacks intimate contact with other people. At least the terrified wax build-up hausfrau was connected to her family, neighbors, bridge groups and children. She was never quite alone; she was always preparing for somebody to come home soon. Today's commercial woman, on the other hand, seems to view other people in her life as scenery—easily dismantled and discarded. In one current commercial, a sophisticated boutique owner, after giving firm orders to her subordinates, relishes the chance to finally be at her desk alone to call her bank and pay the bills. This, I gather, is the high point of her day.

Both stereotypes are ridiculous, of course. I don't feel that I must choose either to be armed with powerful cleaning aids or with a bulging stock portfolio. When will those wonderful folks who brought us ring around the collar and female university presidents who also climb the Alps discover the obvious, which is that most of us live somewhere in between? We are not obsessed with spots on the rug nor with looking like Bo Derek right after work. We try to get through as best we can and commercials should reflect that.

Swapping one stereotype for another is not progress. Progress will come when women are portrayed as people, with all the complexity that implies. If the ad game would give viewers—both homebound and deskbound—their due credit, we might get somewhere after all.

I'll bet you a cookie that whether you're male or female, you identified with that piece. This reader identification is extremely important to op ed pieces. If the topic is one that can't arouse more than a ho-hum from most people, it's going to bomb with editors. They know that ho-hums lead to sagging circulation. The readers don't have to agree with your point of view, but the subject must matter enough to them to elicit some sort of reaction.

MORE PEOPLE, MORE PROBLEMS

Problems on a larger scale need solving, too. Though community/organization problem-solution pieces may range from 300 to 900 words, all of them have elements in common. The focus must be on a problem that most any organization or community might face. The problem must have been addressed by a group that found a workable solution that other groups can emulate. In order to be successful, these articles must include sufficient information about these solutions that they may be adapted; if this information is not included in the piece, sources that will supply the necessary information should be listed.

The following article from Gemco's *Courier*, "Helping Keep Neighborhoods Safe," by Anita Hunter, illustrates the most common format. The first paragraph sets forth the problem and emphasizes its severity. Statistics, if they're compelling enough to shock the reader, are effective in these leads. Another popular lead device is an anecdote dramatizing the problem.

After spelling out the problem, a program to counteract it is described or a set of solutions is given. The bulk of the article is devoted to supplying information readers can adapt for use in their own organizations or communities.

Over forty million crimes are committed in the United States each year, and the number is still growing, according to the Department of Justice. Since there cannot be a law enforcement officer on every street corner, concerned citizens are working together to fight crime. A number of programs are proving to be highly effective deterrents. They include Neighborhood Watch, Home Alert, Save Our Streets, Neighbors Against Crime, and Block Watchers. When a criminal sees signs for these groups posted in a neighborhood, he is likely to decide, "This is the wrong place to be."

All it takes is a group of people who want to protect themselves and their possessions from harm. Anyone who is interested and willing can participate—whether you live in the city, the country, or the suburbs, in an apartment, a mobile home, or a house, whether you're a senior citizen, a young family, a couple, or a single.

Already more than 20,000 groups have been formed in the United States, groups of people learning to pay attention to what goes on in their communities, and learning to cooperate with each other and the police to prevent crime.

A good way to start organizing a group is to contact your local law enforcement agency. Many police and sheriff's departments have a crime prevention specialist who will gladly come to your first meeting. This expert will know about specific problems that face your particular neighborhood and can make suggestions for future programs.

Next, canvass your neighborhood to determine who's interested.

Then set a convenient meeting date, time, and place, perhaps in someone's home. It's not necessary to have 100 percent attendance by residents in your neighborhood, but the more people who participate, the better.

The first meeting is often a discussion, led by the law enforcement representative, on how to report a crime; what to look for; how to describe a person, vehicle, or activity; the importance of giving the correct location. Members are urged *not* to take personal risks in order to prevent crime. It's the job of the law enforcement agency to apprehend criminals. The job of neighborhood watchers is simply to *report* crime. Often the person reporting can remain anonymous.

GATHERING AND SHARING INFORMATION

While discussions at meetings are varied, they emphasize being alert to suspicious or unusual activities in the neighborhood. Members are encouraged to exchange home and work telephone numbers, and to know the identities and ages of people living nearby. They should also be aware of school hours, number and types of automobiles owned by neighbors, and who owns dogs.

In Grandmother's day, people sat on the front porch and observed what was going on. While being nosy is frowned upon, it is still a good idea to let your neighbors know when deliveries or repairs are scheduled, and when you will be on vacation so that they can take in your newspapers and mail.

POSSIBLE AREAS OF CRIME

In some neighborhoods, residents have developed a Block Parent system. Selected houses have signs in their windows, identifying them as places where children can find refuge if they feel threatened or if a parent is not at home.

Another area of concern is home security. A law enforcement agency can help your group by suggesting effective use of door and window locks, adequate lighting, and alarms. You should also ask about Operation Identification, a program in which residents engrave their driver's license numbers onto personal property. Check to see whether your police or sheriff's department will lend an electric engraving tool for this purpose.

There are many ways to enhance the safety of your neighborhood.

An active group in one city worked to have street lighting improved. In an apartment complex, residents use a "buddy system" to check on older residents and to assist them with shopping and other errands. Where street crime is a problem, citizen patrols equipped with two-way radios have been formed to patrol at night. One group of senior citizens in a retirement community calls itself "The Eyes and Ears Patrol." Safety for women is a subject frequently discussed at watch meetings.

HOW EFFECTIVE ARE THE PROGRAMS?

Once a program is organized, awareness and cooperation replace fear that may pervade a crime-ridden neighborhood. In most areas, criminal activity has dropped significantly where groups like Neighborhood Watch are functioning. One city reported a 25 percent reduction in burglaries in the first year. Elsewhere keen observation and reporting by local citizens broke up an auto theft ring.

The key lies in reporting suspicious activity or crimes as soon as possible, so that the police can act quickly and effectively. Even a five-minute delay reduces the chance of catching the criminal by two-thirds.

Follow-up is also essential. Many communities have special programs to help victims and witnesses with transportation, daycare services, filing claims, and scheduling their cases.

The soaring value of household goods gives thieves added incentive, but a cooperative community spirit is on the rise too. The message is loud and clear: "We don't want our block knocked off!" Neighbors are working together to find the answer to rising crime statistics.

Almost always, these articles end on a positive note: you *can* do something about child abuse; your community's efforts to halt environment-damaging projects will *not* be in vain; neighbors are working together to find the answer to rising crime statistics.

The most receptive markets for community problem how-tos are Sunday supplements, regional and city periodicals, women's magazines, and general interest publications. *McCall's* "Survival in the Suburbs" department uses four or five community/organization problem-solution pieces in almost every issue. In a study I made of these pieces from February 1980, through January 1982, I found that the 113 articles could be divided into ten categories:

Children/family related	25
Recreation/entertainment	15
Educational	14
Business	11
Protection	8
Health-related	7
Free help, advice	7
Community enhancement	6
Recycling/energy-saving	4
Miscellaneous	16

Each of the articles tells how a group of people in a community have made that community better through solving problems or initiating programs that improve the quality of life.

The majority of the pieces were between 100 and 125 words long. Fifty-three of them had titles consisting of two words; 34, three words; 23, four words, and 4, five words. The writing is extremely tight, synopsizing the improvement schemes without going into detail.

Closely related to the community problem pieces are those that tell how some individual or group solved a problem common to an organization—increasing attendance at fraternal functions, heightening children's interest in church school, gaining wider acceptance for women in a male-dominated area, and the like.

Articles about projects, procedures, and personal, community, or organizational problems can all be targeted to the right market with mini-studies like the one I did of "Survival in the Suburbs." If you take some of the advice you read in the course of those studies, you may solve some financial problems as well.

There may be times when your reason for writing stems from a desire to be heard rather than to make money. That's when your goal will be publication in the letters-to-the-editor column. Wherever you want to send your sound-off, you'll find that the following tips will help you combat the competition.

1. Avoid emotionalism. Let your concern show, but set forth your case clearly, without displaying agitation.
2. Don't ramble. State your point of view as succinctly as possible, without digressions or information that is not basic to the point.
3. Beware of unsupported claims and hearsay. Check your facts.
4. Don't make potentially libelous statements. Editors quake at the

thought of lawsuits (which wouldn't be much fun for you, either), so avoid saying anything that could be construed as damaging. See *Law and the Writer*, by Kirk Polking and Leonard Meranus (Writer's Digest Books, 1980), for more information on libel.

5. Take care not to write an "I, I, I" piece. Use first person when necessary, but note that most opinion pieces are written primarily in the third person and *imply* a point of view.

6. Don't become so involved with your message that you neglect style. Read opinion pieces in back issues to determine whether they're flip, clever, or strictly earnest and straightforward. Craft your statement in the appropriate image.

Three additional points apply specifically to letters to editors:

1. Letters to magazine editors must pertain to articles that have appeared in recent issues of the publication. Newspaper letters must focus on subjects of current concern.

2. Keep the letter brief. These departments serve as public forums, and their editors want to feature as many points of view as possible in limited space. Check word lengths of previously published letters to make sure yours aren't too long.

3. Sign your letter. If you wish the editor to withhold your name, say so and your request will be honored. Magazines and newspapers will not print anonymous letters.

SHARING YOUR EXPERIENCES

Personal experience articles simply recount incidents in the lives of their authors, without philosophizing on the effects of these experiences or drawing parallels between them and other aspects of life.

Departments of various magazines and tabloids that use personal experiences are bonanzas for writers who read their editors' mind by reading back issues. Since these articles are published regularly, it's possible to find abundant examples of what the people controlling the publications are loosening their purse strings to pay for.

Each month *True Story* prints "A True Story Miracle of Faith" that recounts a reader's experience. The magazine also pays for material used in its "Visits from the Beyond" department, such as the following piece:

March, 1976, found me lonely and depressed over a recent engagement breakup. I loved Nancy, my fiancee, very much. We spent all of our free time making plans for our future life together. But her mother disliked me and was determined that the marriage would not take place. She was right.

In February, Nancy had phoned me and told me she had fallen in love with Dan—a man her mother had introduced her to and approved of as a suitable husband for her daughter.

I was shattered beyond belief. I had lost my father to cancer in 1974, and I was just starting to get over that. Now Nancy had left me, too.

I started going to bars and knew I was drinking too much. I would have done anything to ease the pain I was feeling.

One night, I was especially lonely and depressed and I stayed home to talk to my mom about my problems. When I started to tell her how lost I was feeling, she said she was in a hurry and did not have time to talk. She was going to spend the night with my sister, who lived in a nearby town.

After my mother left, I was feeling more lonely and depressed than ever. I couldn't live with the misery any longer, so I took Mom's sleeping pills from the medicine chest. I had decided to end my life.

I locked the front and back doors to the trailer and then locked myself in my bedroom. I took the whole bottle of pills and lay down on the bed, hoping the end would come soon.

As I started feeling drowsy, I heard the door to my bedroom open. I stared in disbelief as I looked up to see my father, who had died two years before, standing in the doorway! I was scared and wanted to get up and run, but I couldn't move.

I passed out then and awoke to flashing lights all around me. I felt myself being lifted onto a stretcher, but then passed out again. I came to the next morning in a hospital. A police officer and a doctor were standing next to the bed. I couldn't believe I was still alive, so I asked them how they had found me.

The police officer explained that an anonymous phone call from an older man had alerted them and asked for an ambulance. I asked him how they had gotten into the trailer and into my bedroom, since I knew I had locked all the doors. To my surprise, the officer said that the front door was ajar and my bedroom door hadn't been locked either.

To this day, I am certain my father's spirit returned to save my life, and I am so thankful he did. I now have a lovely wife and two beautiful daughters. I'm sure that my father still keeps a watchful eye over all of us.

Grit's "Narrow Escape" department solicits true, unpublished narrow-escape stories of 300 words or less, such as this one, entitled "My Thirst Saved Me from an Accident," by Homer Walker.

One afternoon when I was about 10 years old I started to the bottom pasture, a little over a mile, to round up the cows.

That afternoon Uncle Dempse and Aunt Logan caught up with me in their Studebaker roadster, pulling a sulky plow behind the car. They were on their way to a farm they owned across the creek. Stopping, Uncle Dempse said, "Hop on that plow seat and have a ride."

I climbed on the plow and away we went down the hill, probably about 10 miles an hour. I really thought it was fun. The only thing wrong was the dust blowing in my face.

By the time we came to the well beside the road I was quite thirsty. I motioned to Uncle Dempse to slow down and I jumped off to get a drink. They went on down the road.

They were only about a quarter of a mile away when that old plow went end over end, narrowly missing the back of the car.

There had been a pecan tree in the middle of the road and that spring the road crew had cut it and graded the road up over the stump. The road had worn down enough with passing traffic that the stump stuck up a few inches—just enough for the plow point to hit it, causing it to flip.

If I hadn't been so thirsty and jumped off the plow, I would have been on that seat.

The following short account by Virginia Banghart was published in the "Tell Us About Your Worst Moment and Win $25" in *Star:*

On a trip out west, a car crashed into the back of ours and I suffered a severe injury.

A large gray hearse drove up and they lifted me into it. When I lay in the back and saw all the brass and curtains, I thought I must be dead or dying.

I did not realize the hearse was also used as an ambulance.

The foregoing examples show how important it is to submit a piece that fits the publication—not only in length, but also in style.

Coming up with ideas isn't a problem after you've read several personal experiences in a publication. The sophisticated articles in *Glamour* and the down-home pieces in *Grit* and *Star*, despite their differences in approach and length, center on ideas that can be developed without research. All you need do is ponder similar experiences in your own life.

Don't concentrate on gathering ideas, however, until you've studied the markets and know what editors are buying. Then determine the kinds of experiences (supernatural, frightening, inspiring) that are in demand. After that, spend some couch time letting your mind work over things that have happened to you. Sort them out into the various categories you've listed and evaluate their dramatic or inspirational potential.

Whereas you may upon occasion invent or radically rearrange the facts to write an anecdote, don't fabricate personal experiences. The truth, although not certain to catch up with you, could be mighty embarrassing if it did. You needn't, however, be limited to your own experiences. You can draw on those of others if they're properly attributed and not passed off as your own. Write of your own experiences in first person and of those that have happened to other people in third person.

Some personal experience writing falls into the therapy category. If something unpleasant or traumatic has happened in your life and you think it would make a great article, write about it, by all means, if the writing will act as a catharsis. But be aware that the delayed flight that caused you to miss connections or your spouse who ran off with the high school baton twirler isn't the stuff editors' dreams are made of unless your treatment of the material is fresh. Your personal experiences—or your reactions to them—must be sufficiently out of the ordinary to set them apart. Lois Duncan's *How to Write and Sell Your Personal Experiences* (Writer's Digest Books, 1979) will tell you more about this form of writing.

There are also personal experiences that should be recorded for the local historical society or your family's memoirs. In order to be salable, these accounts must include information or drama that transcends that mere recital of day-to-day life.

You can avoid wasting postage by asking yourself if your writing is as dramatic, inspiring, or informative as the pieces previously printed in your intended publication.

ADDING TO YOUR EXPERIENCES
The best-sellers in the experience/opinion category are those that combine the writer's experiences with a message—the *personal experience/opinion* pieces.

The biggest generic market for them is made up of religious/inspirational publications. These magazines and newspapers, due to the number of articles printed in each issue and the frequency of publication, are by far your most promising outlets if you have a knack of recounting experiences that teach a lesson with a message.

Titles of articles from a variety of religious/inspirational publications show the kinds of topics that prompt their editors to buy: "To Grow in Faith," "Let Me Be Aware," "I Was Once a Nun," "He Answered All My Questions," "Dealing with Things That Won't Change," "Why Resort to Retort?" and "A Stranger in My Church."

The key to selling to these magazines lies not only in appropriate subject matter but also in analyzing the publications' personalities, doctrines, and philosophies. It is essential to study back issues to determine just how heavily conservative or fundamentalist or ecumenical a magazine's view may be.

Your own religious philosophy usually is not important; a Roman Catholic friend of mine wrote for both Catholic and Protestant publications at the same time she was a stringer for a weekly Jewish newspaper. But it is vital to know how much religion an editor wants mixed in with the text and whether it must be slanted toward a particular denomination.

Writers' guidelines will tell you much of what you need to know. For example, Assemblies of God informs those who write for its publications that "a strong spiritual emphasis must be an integral part of [the] material." The *Parish Family Digest* wants "articles of timely interest to the young and growing Catholic family, particularly in its relationship and service to the Catholic parish." *Purpose* is interested in articles and stories that guide readers in their beliefs and decision making, showing what it means to follow Christ in today's world. A typical *Guideposts* story is a first-person narrative written in simple, dramatic, anecdotal style with a spiritual point that the reader can "take away" and apply to his or her own life. *The Lutheran's* guidelines do a good job of describing the kind of personal experience material most religious magazines and newspapers are looking for: "articles in which the writer describes real-life encounters with adversity, family problems, the frustrations and opportunities of everyday living."

This excerpt from *Faith and Inspiration's* guidelines for writers also applies to most religious/inspirational submissions:

Articles are basically positive and supportive in character, stressing the human and divine resources that can make life meaningful and joyful. Although this sometimes means dealing with negative elements, the total effect of the article should provide help to the reader.

Faith and Inspiration publishes "unforgettable experiences that may be specifically religious in content or of general inspirational nature." Other magazines may want a much stronger religious emphasis, but few of them buy articles that preach. Most of their editors are of the "show, don't tell" school. Take this gentle story by Mary Louise Kitsen, "The Blue Door," from *Seek:*

I live on an old street. It is a street where the houses are older than anyone who lives in them. The house I live in was built by a grandfather of generations back. It is a large structure, and a veranda wraps itself around the place like a loving guardian angel. It is shaded from the hot sun by grandfather trees who seem to believe they really own the place.

Today the old houses on my street have been given various types of face-lifts. Most have new siding of various colors, and they proudly boast shutters and other trims in harmonizing hues. Like all good citizens, the families living here have insulated and have returned old fireplaces to usefulness. Everywhere I look, I see color.

But color is reasonably new to this street. Even when I was a little girl, the street was a puritan-like place of large white houses with very little trimming. Graham's house had black shutters, and that was about it for color. Most of the families then were descendants of the first residents of the town. They pretty much went to the same church, banked at the same bank, and shopped at the same market. They liked their life-style, and they had no welcome ready for any newcomers.

I was about eight when the first old house on the old street was sold to a new family. And what a family they were! Eleven children arrived, laughing and playing with their pet dog, who barked with great vigor. I watched with a wide grin. They seemed so happy. So full of fun! My friends and I had fun, of course. Yet, there was something different about this new family.

Up went bright-colored curtains. (Our curtains were all white.) The children roamed about the street looking for friends. Carrie May and I were in the same age bracket, and we were immediately "best friends." The old families peeked out of windows at the new family.

Most felt the street had started to go downhill.

"When people come to know our new neighbors, they will be more charitable in their opinions," my mother told my brother and me. "This is a country where all peoples are welcome."

Papa said nothing. He was a quiet man who spoke mostly when it seemed vital to do so. But he was a man of action. When he felt a situation called for action, he was the one to take it. Mama always said, "Still waters run deep," when she talked about Papa.

Weeks went by. I didn't see some of the neighbors becoming charitable. There were a few who, like my Mama, made calls with hot food to show a welcome. But most simply complained about "those dreadful people." Mama would attempt in her gentle, soft-spoken way, to open their hearts. Papa would watch, but he said not a word.

Then came the Saturday morning when our new neighbor started painting his front door. It was the brightest blue I ever saw in my life. Somehow, that blue door was the final straw for one of our neighbors who charged into our kitchen to ask my mother how she could "close her eyes" to such ugly degradation of a once-fine home.

I slipped out the kitchen door. Carrie May saw me and came running over. We started playing hopscotch in my backyard and soon I had forgotten about the blue door.

Suddenly, Carrie May said, "Look at the people in front of your house." She was right. Several neighbors stood on the sidewalk, staring at the front of my house.

"Let's see what's happening," I said. Carrie May and I rushed around the side of the house and peered around the corner. Our eyes popped! There was my Papa, painting our front door—the same bright blue as our new neighbors' door!

"Look at the people," I whispered to Carrie May.

"Some of them had their heads down, looking more at the sidewalk than Papa. Little by little they moved quietly away. My quiet Papa had made his point. The street started accepting the new family. Little by little it happened.

I'm still here on my old street. Most of the families are first generation to these old homes. You can find my house with ease. It's the huge white one with the wraparound veranda and the blue door. The door is a sky blue now. But it will always be blue. It's my reminder from Papa that "God is no respecter of persons" (Acts 10:34).

Many times, the personal experience/opinion pieces in religious magazines are those you might find in secular publications. *Virtue*, a religiously oriented women's magazine, uses pieces like "Apologies of a Mother Without a Television," for example.

There are dozens of women's and other specialized magazines that occasionally use the personal experience. Just as pieces in women's magazines focus on situations with which females can identify, the subjects for personal experiences in other specialized publications must tie in with the magazine's reason for being. You'll find ecologically slanted pieces in *Sierra*, personalized accounts of trailer travel in *Trailer Life*, personal flying adventures in *The AOPA Pilot*, personal do-it-yourself experiences in *Your Home*, and articles about horse-show experiences in *Horse & Horseman*.

Two magic ingredients that will help sell any personal opinion, experience, or experience-opinion article are a dash of "everyman" and a dollop of humor.

The everyman element addresses subjects that matter to a broad segment of the publication's readership. Though we think of ourselves as individuals, in many respects most of us are very much alike. The writer who can express opinions or relate experiences that have to do with the common denominators in our lives—the need for love, food, shelter, acceptance; fears for ourselves, our families, and the world; the joys, worries, and little triumphs familiar to us all—is the writer whose readers are with him every word of the way.

The reason for adding humor is that readers (and editors) like to chuckle. Moreover, editors bemoan the fact that magazine article humor is in short supply. If your topic lends itself to a humorous touch, you'll catapult your submission ahead of the competition. You don't have to produce material that will make them roll in the aisles, but if you can give readers reason to smile a little, most editors will find it difficult to give your well-written personal experience/opinion a frown.

CHAPTER SEVEN

MINI-INFORMATIONALS

I find that a great part of the information I have was acquired by looking up something and finding something else on the way.

Franklin P. Adams

 eading patterns have changed with the advent of TV. Our attention spans are getting shorter. Savvy editors, aware of this trend, are placing increased emphasis on the mini-informational article. Readers benefit from mini-informationals, too, as they can become "instant experts" on everything from miniature horses to the sidewalk cafes of Paris by reading pieces that are only 300 to 900 words long.

The unintimidating length of the mini and the limitless subject matter of the informational make this combination a natural for beginning writers. Chances of acceptance are greater than for full-length features, and pay can be quite impressive (about $75 to $1,000 at the higher-paying publications). Even the $50 to $100 checks from the mid-paying magazines make the hours spent/money earned ratio attractive.

Established professionals who combine writing the mini-informational with full-length articles and books find that ideas for the articles often evolve from their longer works and that in some instances no additional research is required. Then, too, a longer, unsalable article can sometimes be split into two shorter ones that will sell.

The short article serves a variety of functions in magazine layout. Some publications devote a complete page or two, with several photos, to one mini-informational. Other magazines contain special sections composed of short pieces. In still others, editors use these pieces to fill the occasional empty half or three-quarters of a page.

In the latter two cases, photos may not be necessary. But when they are, your ability to obtain them is vital. Whereas editors often assign photographers or illustrators to provide art for full-length features, their budgets usually don't allow for such luxuries in the case of short articles.

If your picture-taking skills need developing, you might want to take a course or read some good books on the subject, such as the Eastman Kodak Company's *Encyclopedia of Practical Photography* (American Photographic Book Publishing Company, 1978). I didn't know an f-stop from a shutter speed when I enrolled in a five-week photography course at the local university some years ago. During those weeks, I averaged eight hours a day in the darkroom, and I emerged from the sessions doing work of professional quality.

SHORT-FORM SPECIFICS

Not all stories can be told in a few paragraphs, so before you start writing, let's talk about the requirements of the mini-informational.

First of all, the focus must be narrow. A short piece about the general subject of tennis—its stars, the history of the game, courts, equipment, rules—can't give the reader much information that he doesn't already know. By focusing on equipment or stars or first-rate tennis courts, the writer would still have a difficult time squeezing sufficient information into the prescribed length. But by talking about racquets, shoes, a specific court, a certain star—aha!—you can give your topic the kind of in-depth treatment editors like.

One of the most efficient ways to come up with mini-informational ideas is to study back issues of the publications for which you want to write. *Find a need in the market first. Then fill it.* Perhaps your target publication has printed pieces on the flowers of Grenada, the architecture of St. Lucia, and the palm trees of Puerto Rico. You can devise a host of ideas by making one list of Caribbean islands popular with tourists and another of attractions, such as birds, handicrafts, fishing grounds, native dances, superstitions, festivals, luxury resorts, golf courses, traditions, forts, and museums. Then play mix-and-match with the two lists. How about "Birds of Barbados," "Celebrations in St. Thomas," or "Dances of the Dominican Republic"?

You can follow this procedure to generate article ideas for almost any magazine. It's also possible to go back over full-length articles you have written to see if facets of those pieces can be split off or expanded upon to make mini-articles.

Decide on your focus and stick to it. A short article's success depends on the development of a single theme. You don't have enough space to expound on corollary subjects and experiences.

Then evaluate the idea itself. Is it "big," (i.e., important) enough to support a full-length feature? If it is, pursue that course first. You can always write shorter pieces on the subject, or certain aspects of it, later.

You can evaluate the idea's importance by considering a number of factors. Does the subject have depth—will you run out of things to say about it after you've written 500 words—or can it support a 1,500-word piece? Is it timely—not so avant-garde that people will have difficulty relating to it, but not so much in the mainstream that it's been overdone? Does the subject have broad appeal, human interest? Is it one that you have special qualifications to write about? (Your best friend has just invented the first robot capable of mixing twenty-five different bar drinks; you have contacts among U.S. Olympic Team coaches that most writers don't have.)

Think about style. Would your subject be showcased best in a piece filled with adjectives, anecdotes, and long quotes—all devices that use a lot of words—or can the story be told simply?

One of the best mini-informationals I've read is this one by Karen Ray, which appeared in *Family Weekly*. Notice how much information the writer has packed into only 659 words. Note, too, that the piece is sharply focused. It tells about one breed of horse. The theme is developed without inclusion of extraneous material. Sentences are predominantly declarative, and short, concise quotes contribute a good deal of information on the subject.

FAIRY-TALE HORSES

Rare and delicate, these animals are less than three feet tall and can do just about anything—except carry a rider.

Silver Dollar is a very special horse. When she was born, three doctors and five nurses were in attendance. Now, three years later, at 26 inches high, she is the smallest registered full-grown horse in the world.

Silver Dollar is one of ten miniature horses owned by Rayford Ely of Oakland, Calif. "Interest in the miniatures has been growing in recent years," says Ely. "The demand for them has risen tremendously."

The tiny animals are extremely rare, however. There are only 200 registered miniature horses of show quality in the world today.

The animals are desirable because they require little space and are gentle, intelligent and, of course, small. To qualify for the International Miniature Horse Registry, a horse must be no taller than 32 inches at the shoulder. (A half-inch difference in height can make a $1,000 difference in its value.) Ely, current president of the International Miniature Horse Association, scoffs at animals that large. All of his horses are under 30 inches.

A former Texan who was always interested in horses, Ely became fascinated by miniatures ten years ago when he saw one for the first time. He soon purchased a filly, then bought it a companion, and, before long, wanted a stallion. Arabian King (28 inches), a former South American champion, filled the bill. He was named the national champion here in 1975 and is Silver Dollar's father.

Celebrity names often pop up when discussing the horses. Recently Arabian King was mated with a mare belonging to Dean Martin. Aristotle Onassis owned three miniatures when he died. The Kennedys own several, and there are always a few in England's Royal Stables.

Perhaps part of the reason for celebrity interest in the horses is their value. Ely estimates he would have no problem selling Arabian King for $25,000, but don't bother to make an offer. Ely considers his horses members of the family. Generally, though, any horse under 30 inches is worth at least $5,000.

"Miniatures are not a new breed," says Ely. "They were bred down in the 16th and 17th centuries from Arabian stock and were the pets of royalty and the aristocracy. But then around 1900 their popularity died out and only now seems to be coming back."

Ely, who owns a foreign-car dealership, keeps the horses in his backyard. Four of them will fit nicely in a stable normally used for one standard horse.

While not exactly housebroken, the horses are often allowed inside the Ely home. "He has good manners," Ely said assuredly when asked if it was safe to bring the stallion onto the thick white carpet.

The animals are intelligent, too. Ely has trained them to "shake hoofs" when a human extends his hand. And, without training, one of his mares discovered how to escape the complicated system of gates in the Ely Horse Hotel. On several occasions she led the herd to freedom. Now the gates are double-locked. The only thing the horses can't do is give rides. They are simply too small to be ridden, even by very young children.

The horses don't require any special attention, and Ely estimates they will live as long—up to 25 years—as a standard horse that received exceptional care. Because the horses are so small, however, they often are too weak to kick themselves out of the mother at birth the way a normal foal does. Hence, when a mare approaches delivery, she is watched round the clock. And Ely's miniature horses are born at the veterinary school at the University of California at Davis, where a professor has taken a special interest in the breed.

At birth a miniature horse may be only 15 inches high, weigh 12 pounds and have all the appeal of any baby animal. The Ely household is exuberant because one of their mares recently gave birth to a 17-inch 11-pound foal, which means the miniature horse population is now 201.

Another reason this piece is a winner is the unusualness and universal appeal of its subject. Some topics are too exotic and removed from common experience for average readers to identify with them. But everyone can relate to these extraordinary little animals, because people already know something about standard-size horses. When gathering ideas, remember that superlatives—the world's *smallest* horse, the *biggest* hotel in the U.S., South America's *wealthiest* city—are perennial interest grabbers.

HOT TYPES

Although you can find mini-informationals on every conceivable topic, from wing collars to antique gas pumps to television satellites, the most popular categories of pieces focus on travel, sports, health, and business.

Travels with Profit

The short travel articles that sell best center on a single place or event. Topics run the gamut—from an Indian village in Oklahoma to a mountain range in Northeastern Nevada; from renaissance fairs and seaplane races to crab-crawling contests.

Illustrative of the structure you'll often find in the place/event genre is this piece, "A Special Island," which appeared in *Small World*. Notice that the author, Dorothy Becker, gets into her subject quickly and then weaves in historical background by describing sights that can be seen today. Her final paragraph, only 48 words, is most effective.

New Castle, a one-square mile island on the northeastern tip of New Hampshire's 18-mile-long seacoast, is home for photographer Walt Becker, who prides himself on being one of the few remaining true natives (born on the island). His photographic book *A Native*

Looks at New Castle, N.H. is proof of his love for the town.

New Castle, settled in 1623 and incorporated in 1693, has changed from a settlement of fishermen and wharves, fish houses and winding dirt footpaths, where taxes could be paid in fish and lobster was deemed fit only for bait. Shaded colonials, Cape Cods, and contemporary-styled homes dominate the area now, enhanced by velvet lawns that carpet miniature front and back yards, and flowers that spill from window boxes and iron pots into rainbow waterfalls. Deeds of a few houses have been traced back to the late 1600's and approximately 90 houses show evidence (cross beams, wide boards, old bricks, hidden fireplaces) of construction dating back 100 years and more.

The island population is inching toward 900 and "That is enough," say the residents, who consist of the retired, some young couples with children, and a few professional people. Several new houses are under construction, but few building lots remain in town.

Formerly called Great Island, New Castle is bounded by the swift-moving Piscataqua River separating Maine and New Hampshire, and the Atlantic Ocean. Wentworth Bridge on the seaward side reaches into Rye, N.H. Two bridges and a breakwater lead into the city of Portsmouth on the river side. Older residents remember when the latter were toll bridges—three cents for pedestrians, 15 cents for carriages and cars (with an occasional cold drink served on a hot day). The town's respected Judge Oliver Marvin wrote, "In 1926 when the bridges were freed and opened to the public, New Castle was discovered."

However, it was a second discovery for the rocky isle. During Colonial days, New Castle was chosen government seat of the province. Here the governor resided, and customs duties were collected. In 1774 the Sons of Liberty, a local assemblage, stormed the island's English-held Fort Constitution, overcame Captain Cockran and his five men, removed 100 barrels of gunpowder, some of which later appeared at Bunker Hill, and thereby achieved a few paragraphs in history for this first overt act of the Revolution.

In addition to Fort Constitution, formerly Fort William and Mary, there is Fort Stark. Another military installation, Camp Langdon, was sold to the town and is now a favorite recreation area known as Great Island Common.

Beams from two lighthouses sweep the rocky shores—Portsmouth Harbor Light, and Whalesback, just off Sandy Beach. Plying the river and out into the ocean, tankers, barges, fishing and pleasure boats, the cruise boat *Viking Queen*, tugs, and a submarine now and then, provide a never-ending fascination for the islanders.

Several structures, resulting from an 1800's construction boom, are still in use, including Great Island store, New Castle Library on Windmill Hill in the former Free Will Baptist Church, and the 1895 Town Hall, which recently was voted a reprieve (voters turned down demolition in favor of modest renovation).

Centered in the town and in the hearts of parishioners is the village's only church, New Castle Congregational (1835). Elongated arched windows, lofty mahogany pulpit, boxed pews with latched doors, and an altar fragrant with New Castle garden flowers in season adorn this historic house of worship.

New Castle oozes charm. It is a place that prompts tourists to stop and enthuse, "Aren't you lucky to live in such a beautiful spot?" and "Do you want to sell your little cottage?" To which the native is apt to respond with a "Yup," then a "Nope."

This piece wouldn't be nearly so effective without the visual phrases: "winding dirt footpaths," "flowers that spill from window boxes and iron pots into rainbow waterfalls." Writers of all good place and event pieces share this ability to paint pictures with their words, a you-are-there technique that transports readers to the featured place or event.

The next best sellers in short travel focus on coping with specific travel problems, such as those women might encounter when traveling alone in a motor home, or knowing how credit cards work abroad and when to use them. Most often they combine information and the sort of advice found in procedural how-tos.

The third "best bet" for writers of short travel articles is the broadbrush. Though most of these pieces exceed the word limit we're covering in this book, there are a few publications, such as some motor club magazines, tabloids, and airline in-flights, that use them regularly. The broadbrush differs from the place piece in that it covers a larger territory, rarely goes into detail, and includes only general information.

Whereas a 750-word event piece about Holland Happening in Oak Harbor, Washington, would be sufficient to tell all about that celebration, a 750-word article on annual festivals throughout the state would have to be a broadbrush affair. The writer could afford to devote just two or three sentences to a celebration, hitting only the highlights.

A fourth category of short travel pieces—travel trade-publication newsbreaks—will be discussed in Chapter 9.

In addition to taking less time to write than full-blown articles, short pieces are virtually the only way a newcomer can break into the prestigious travel publications. Editor-in-Chief Pamela Fiori says, "The best place for writers to try out for *Travel & Leisure* is in our seven regional editions—Western, Midwestern, Eastern, Southern, California, Chicago and New York. The articles appear in those editions only and should be geared to those areas. Think of the ideas you might submit to a regional or city magazine. They might work well for our regional sections."

Among the best markets for short travel pieces are *Vista USA*, *Odyssey*, *Small World*, and many of the airline in-flights. Each of them has a distinct personality, and though their short travel pieces may all seem alike to the casual reader, there are differences—sometimes subtle ones, but differences nonetheless—in style, tone, and subject matter.

The only way you will be able to zero in on your target publication's personality is by familiarizing yourself with its content. As with all kinds of writing, effective marketing will make the differences between a sale and a "sorry, but your material does not fit our editorial needs."

Scoring On Sports

The top-selling sports minis focus on equipment or events. Equipment articles generally combine information on what is available with how-to advice, as in "Sharpening Your Skate-Buying Skills," by Emily Greenspan, which appeared in *Common Cents*.

Good equipment can make a difference in any sport, but in figure skating the equipment is crucial. It can mean gliding gracefully across the ice, rather than sitting in the locker room, rubbing tender ankles and cursing the day you ever got the notion to skate.

Contrary to popular opinion, weak ankles are a myth. Instead, there are skates without proper fit or adequate support. Before you buy your boots and blades, here are some points to keep in mind.

The single most important part of a skate is the leather around the ankles. This is called the "counter." Because your ankle will be supporting the weight of your entire body, it must be firmly gripped by the skate. This means that the leather must be stiff. Rental or low-quality skates will not have stiff counters.

Buy skates at the skate shop, at a local skating rink, or at a store that specializes in skates, where a professional can fit you properly. The skate should fit snugly in three places: in the heel and arch, beside the toes, and around the ankle. Check that there is room up front for you to wiggle your toes, but not so much that you can do a dance inside the skates. Usually skate sizes run a half size smaller than your shoe size.

Although many skates come with the blade attached, it's better to buy skates without blades. Then you can select and align the blade to the boot, according to your own center of balance. Stainless steel blades are preferable to aluminum because they have sharper edges and will hold a sharpening longer. Blades are ground with an inner edge, an outer edge, and a flat in between. To check for dull blades, run a finger along either edge. If your finger can roll from the flat to the edge with little resistance, then it's time for a sharpening. Take them to an expert at a skating rink to be sharpened, rather than to the local hardware store.

Laces are available in cotton and nylon in various lengths. Cotton laces are a wiser choice, because nylon has a tendency to slip. Ninety- or one hundred-inch lengths should be about right for most figure skates.

Be sure that your skates are laced tightly over the instep; other than that, lacing is largely a matter of personal preference. Most people will prefer the top part a little looser for greater flexibility, although some like the skates tightly laced from top to bottom for support.

Good skates start at approximately $35, and can run into hundreds of dollars. Blades range from $15-$120. Although these prices may seem steep, compare them to the price of shoes these days and then consider the greater workmanship required for skates.

You should also buy blade protectors, called "guards" or "scabbards," and a flannel rag or chamois cloth for wiping the skates after use. To keep your skates looking as clean as the day you bought them, special polish is available. As for decorative accessories, pom-poms and other adornments are frowned on by serious skaters.

If you do purchase a pair of good skates with stiff counters, you may want to break them in before your first go-round on the ice.

The event piece either centers on a specific sporting event, such as the Reno Rodeo, or is what I call the generic article, telling about rodeos, bodysurfing competitions, frisbee tournaments, or any other group of happenings in a single sport.

To Your (Writing) Health

Health-related subjects lend themselves amazingly well to short formats, and given the current preoccupation with all things beneficial to the body, pieces on health-related themes may well prove to be the biggest little informationals of the decade.

Titles of these pieces range from "To Your Health: Nightmares" in *Seventeen* to "Cataract Surgery Once and For All" in *Health* to "Are Pets Good for Your Health?" in *Ms*. In all of them, the focus is on a tiny sliver of the topical pie.

The most popular kinds of health-related pieces tell of medical breakthroughs (especially new methods of treating or diagnosing disease), fitness, and nutrition. These articles often require quotes from authorities in the health field to give them credibility, as in the nightmares piece from *Seventeen*. The author is Shirley Kesselman.

Nightmares, a common occurrence in childhood, tend to become less and less frequent as we grow older. Still, they are not unusual among teens or adults.

"Everyone has occasional nightmares," says Dr. Anthony Kales, the director of the Sleep Research and Treatment Center at Pennsylvania State University College of Medicine, in Hershey. "They represent a failure by the psyche to resolve stresses, conflicts, or fears."

Sometimes, you will recognize characters in your nightmares; other times, not. Time may be confused, and past events may be mixed with those of the present. Hideous demons may appear. Often when the sleeper awakes, she vividly recalls her bad dream.

"Night terror is different from a nightmare," Dr. Kales says. Persons experiencing night terror thrash around in their beds and scream or moan. Once awake, they are confused and only remember such feelings as choking, suffocating, or falling. These experiences are usually outgrown by adolescence but can reoccur when one is feverish.

Nightmares can usually be traced to something that is bothering you. For instance, many teens report having bad dreams during exam week. In a common nightmare, the teen can't find the room where the test is being given.

Scary movies can also cause nightmares. Liquor or tranquilizers or other drugs can bring on nightmares, too. "These drugs disturb normal sleep patterns. Disruption of these patterns often causes nightmares," Dr. Kales explains.

Persons who suffer from several nightmares a week are going

through a particularly stressful time. If you have frequent bad dreams, try to determine their cause. Perhaps you are anxious about a planned move to a new town or a problem with a friend. Nightmares that are caused by current problems will subside when the situations causing the tension are resolved. Meanwhile, anything you can do to relax before bedtime, such as listening to music or taking a hot bath, should reduce the likelihood of having a nightmare.

Make It Your Business

Business topics encompass everything from creative home financing to the Oregon businessman who saves money by using horse-drawn vehicles in his sanitation service. The most salable kinds of business mini-articles are those focusing on trends and techniques—any way of doing business that is gaining popularity or enabling business people to accomplish their goals.

You'll find trends-and-techniques business articles in business publications and general-interest magazines. Your best markets, however, will be trade publications and not-so-well-known magazines such as *Americas*, which, as a matter of fact, has a department called "Trends." The following is an example of the kind of short business pieces it uses. It's called "Chilean Methane Gas."

Nine Chilean municipalities have agreed on a joint scheme to capture methane gas emanating from a sanitary landfill. With the Santiago Gas Consumers Company paying for the construction, a plant will be built to exploit the biogas created by the municipalities' dump, La Feria. The gas will be purified and shipped to local consumers. The Chilean Government believes the plant is the first of its kind.

Municipalities will be paid according to the volume they deliver to the dump. The income derived from the methane sales will probably pay for only a quarter of the region's garbage disposal costs. But finding sanitary and seemly ways of dumping waste is a growing world problem. Futhermore, the La Feria operation will carry off disagreeable odors as well as providing an energy source.

The landfill method consists of covering refuse with a layer of soil. The resulting anaerobic decomposition of organic matter generates the gas flow.

The Chilean project is a frank experiment. Estimates of how long gas production may continue range from ten to one hundred years, and the company and the municipalities must take a chance that the environmental project will pay for itself.

Still another popular type of mini-informational focuses on natural science subjects—especially plants and animals.

MASTERING THE MARKETS

There is virtually no well-written mini-informational that can't be sold *somewhere*. But finding that somewhere can be a time-consuming task if you've already written the piece. It is better to identify potential publications and then come up with appropriate ideas.

For example, in scanning magazines, you'll find that *Parade* has a department called "Significa." The department's "Invitation to Our Readers" says, "Do you know an unusual fact for Significa? If so, please send it to us with the exact source of your information. If we don't already have it and if we print it, we will send you $50." Among the contributions the weekly supplement has used is this one called "Baboon Who Ran a Railroad."

> A century ago, a baboon helped his handicapped master run a railroad switching station.
>
> In 1877, railroad man James Wide had both legs severed in an accident near Port Elizabeth, South Africa. He was reassigned as switchman at the Uitenhage Tower, where he settled into a rundown cabin and befriended a baboon named Jack. Wide had found his man Friday.
>
> Jack was extremely intelligent. He learned to pump water from a well, clean house and tend Wide's garden. Every morning, he pushed his master to work in a handcart that Wide had built to run on rails. Wide trained his hairy helpmate to perform minor chores at the signal tower, and Jack soon was manning the station. He operated the levers that set signals for approaching trains and managed the tower controls that opened or closed switches on a siding.
>
> When Jack died in 1890, he left behind a spotless record with the railroad. In the nine years he served as Wide's assistant, he never made one mistake that resulted in the loss of life or property.

Though unusual facts pop up before a writer's eyes on rare occasion, they usually take conscious effort to unearth. Short items in newspapers are one of the best sources and can often be followed up for more information by contacting a newspaper or chamber of commerce in the city given in the article's dateline. *The Queer, the Quaint, and the Quizzical* and similar volumes of amazing facts in library reference sections are other potential idea sources.

"It's All in a Woman's Day" in *Woman's Day* pays $50 for reader contributions to that department. Subject matter ranges from "Hotline on Bug Killers" to "Bargains for Brides." The "Ideas for New Businesses & Diversification" department of *Venture* uses pieces such as "Turning a Computor into a Patient Tutor."

The best way to test ideas for editor appeal is by analyzing what he or she has shown a fancy for in the past. My two-year study of the "Right Now" department in *McCall's* resulted in this chart:

Publication: McCall's

General Subject	Number of Articles
Business/Jobs	29
Education	23
Energy/Conservation	6
Family Members	22
Health & Safety Related	77
Housing	10
Money	13
Political/Social Concerns	6
Vacations	9
Women	9
Miscellaneous	34

Of the 238 articles, 30 percent are related to health and safety. That's important marketing information, telling you that your best submission bet by far is an article on a topic in that area.

To zero in more closely on slant, I listed the article titles categorically. The titles under Business/Jobs illustrate the amount of information you can get from articles' names:

Business/Jobs
Work-at-Home Warning
Help Wanted for Older Woman Workers
Motherhood and Work
Where to Find Summer Work
Job Hunting Guide
Career Planning—Getting an Early Start
Fields with a Future
How to Get Through an Interview . . . and More
What Teenage Workers Need to Know
How Resourceful Kids Earn Summer Money

Immediate Openings—Apply Today
Help from Uncle Sam
Help Wanted—Secretaries
Taking Your Talents Abroad
Working for the Public Good
Where to Learn a Trade
When Women Go Back to Work
Workshops for Laid-Off Workers
When Two Jobs are Better Than One
Fighting the Blue Collar Blues
New Jobs for Men
Temporary Work: A Timely Option
Business Women in Training
Your Own Business: The Franchise Alternative
Teenage Tycoons
Cash for Co-Ops
Home Is Where the Business Is
Making Dough
How Small Shops Renew a City

You can use the same technique to study any mini-informational market. You'll find back copies of many magazines in your library stacks. Have friends who subscribe to others save them for you. Even if you can find only five or six back issues of a publication, you will be able to get a good idea of what the editor wants.

RESEARCH MINUTE-SAVERS

Spending three full days finding facts for a $25 piece doesn't make sense when you don't need 90 percent of the information you've gathered. The "tip of the iceberg" theory—that what you write about a subject should be a small fraction of your total knowledge about it—is all well and good if you've the luxury of scads of time and money. But you'll save hours of research (and consequently have more time for writing articles) by reading similar articles in back issues of your intended publications. That way you can determine the sorts of questions you will want to answer in your piece.

It's not my intention here to tell you everything there is to know about research. Good books like *Writer's Resource Guide* (Writer's Digest Books, 1983) and *The New York Times Guide to Reference Materials* (Popular Library, 1971) will help you acquire the necessary skills. But since effective research is vital to the short-article/filler writer's economic survival, the following tips will help you get the most value out of the time you spend.

The answers you seek will in most cases be found through interviews (personal, telephone, and via letters), on-the-scene research, library research, or a combination of these methods.

You'll need to do some detective work to locate authorities when your piece calls for quotes, statistics, and opinions from experts. My starting point is usually the library's reference section. There I can find books containing lists of individuals in a given profession (lawyers or psychiatrists, for instance) and organizations such as the National Association of Manufacturers or the Future Farmers of America. These directories give addresses and phone numbers that will help you track down your experts. Don't neglect to consult *Books in Print* for the names of authors of books on your subject (contact them by writing in care of their publishers).

Suppose, for example, that you need views from three authorities on the relationship of soil selenium levels to the incidence of certain diseases. Your first step would be to look at *Subject Guide to Books in Print* under *vitamins* and *minerals*. Next, you would seek out any directories of organizations dealing with nutrition. You would either call or write to those organizations that sound most promising to ask for names and addresses of experts in the field of selenium research. A half-hour of well-spent research time should in most cases yield a bumper crop of experts' names.

You will also often find experts named in articles that have been written on your subject (tracing them can be difficult, however, unless the articles mention their affiliations with organizations, universities, or the like). Other expert-locating aid is available at colleges and universities. Simply phone the department related to your subject and ask for names of the kinds of authorities you need.

Before any interview, write down the questions you plan to ask. Make them specific and sharply focused on your subject. General, vague questions produce general, vague answers.

Don't let your interview paraphernalia slow you down. If you plan to use a tape recorder, know how to operate it and be sure the batteries are fresh. Have your prepared questions where you can find them immediately. If you plan to take notes, be sure that you have two or three functioning ball-points or pencils.

To avoid confusion, at the outset of the interview tell the interviewee what the article will be about—even if you have given the same information over the phone when you made the appointment. You might add a phrase like, "Since it will be a rather short piece, I'm hoping to keep questions and answers as sharply focused as possible." That will alert your subject not to ramble.

A young friend of mine was the victim of a runaway interview. The interviewee was an octogenarian who loved to remember the old days. Since my friend is a well-brought-up young lady who respects her elders, she was loath to interrupt. As a result, she got sixty minutes of taped reminiscences and not one of her questions was answered—wonderful for an historical society, but totally useless for the article she had in mind.

If, despite your comments about sharply focused answers at the beginning of the interview, your subject meanders, digresses, and tells you everything you don't want to know, persist. Break in as politely as possible with, "That's very interesting and maybe we can talk about it another time, but what I need to know now is . . ."

When nothing works, call a halt to the interview with a "Thank you so much" and try to get your information from other sources or abandon the project altogether.

When a face-to-face interview with an expert isn't possible, make an appointment for a telephone interview or send a letter. Keep your questions brief and specific, asking only what you need to know. Too many questions will cause your telephone interviewee to fabricate a long-distance call on another line or your correspondent to put off answering your letter (sometimes indefinitely).

If your piece involves library research, it's easier to keep the time you spend under control. Through the years, I've developed a great working relationship with the reference librarians at our local library. I suggest that you get to know yours, too. Tell them about your current projects and they will often direct you to research sources you didn't know about or have overlooked.

When the regular librarians are busy—or when the only people on duty are new or part-timers who don't know as much about research as you do—reference librarians advise that you search through the volumes to which they turn.

Reference Books for Small and Medium-Sized Libraries contains more than 750 annotated listings of reference sources. The second half of *The New York Times Guide to Reference Materials* lists reference books in such fields as art, current events, education, government, history, literature, and science. *Finding Facts Fast: How to Find Out What You*

Want and Need to Know contains a wealth of information on library resources as well as other methods of obtaining information. *Readers' Guide* and other periodical directories will lead you to articles that have been written about your subject.

Other resource gold mines include *Reference Books: A Brief Guide*, *Writer's Resource Guide*, *1001 Free Sources of Travel Information* and *The Information Report* (government pamphlets and other forms of information).

The yellow pages of telephone directories can also prove invaluable as reference sources, as do *Access* and *Popular Periodicals*. Suppose you're writing a short travel piece on Nashville for a recreational vehicle magazine and need information on campgrounds in the area. Get their names and addresses as well as telephone numbers from the Nashville phone book (available at the phone company or the library). Perhaps you need facts on import stores in New York or substance-abuse clinics in San Francisco. Though you might use other kinds of directories to obtain the information you need, the yellow pages are often the fastest method of getting results.

Don't forget business and industry as information suppliers. (Contact their public relations departments.) Many of them put out printed material, not only about their specific products, but also about their businesses in general. Then, too, one source of information will often lead to another. The first person you contact may not be able to supply the facts you need, but you will be referred to someone who can. You must cast aside any reluctance you might have about asking questions. After all, as a researcher/interviewer, that's your job.

Time-saving on-the-scene research also involves pre-preparation. Before attending an event or visiting a point of interest about which I plan to write, I read everything I can on the subject. Then I make a list of the features I especially want to investigate and another list of picture possibilities if the piece will require photos.

STRUCTURING SHORTCUTS

The mini-article is written in brief paragraphs with strong active verbs and nouns. To be effective, writing has to be clear, crisp, and concise. Adjectives and adverbs are used sparingly.

Summary leads and endings are most often used in mini-informationals, for the simple reason that they get to the point fast and exit quickly. In short travel pieces especially, the descriptive lead is also a favorite.

When you begin writing, you'll save yourself rewriting grief if you abide by these rules:

1. Stick to the article's focus. With each sentence, ask yourself, "Does this relate directly to my subject? Would the purpose of the piece suffer if I left it out?"

2. Present your points in logical order. An article that goes directly from facet A to B to C requires fewer transitions.

3. Don't waste words tells6ing readers what they already know. Avoid phrases like "Have you ever wondered . . .?" and "You know, of course, that . . ."

4. Delete unnecessary examples and anecdotes. One fact or little story (or two at most) will illustrate a point sufficiently.

5. Look for word wasters. Instead of writing "at the present time" say "now." "If" conveys the same meaning as "in the event of." *Elements of Style* by Strunk and White will help you pare your prose.

6. Cut the negative from any positive/negative portions of the piece. For example, "The solution is not in watering your plants every day. It lies in watering them when the soil feels dry" uses twenty words. "Water your plants when the soil feels dry" says the same thing with eight.

I've found, too, that fitting my material into the prescribed length is much easier if I make a rough outline after I've completed my research but before I begin writing. I read my research notes and put asterisks in the margins opposite the material I would like to include (three asterisks for the most important, two for that next in importance and one for "if there's room" material). Then I write my "lead" or "intro,' followed by the number of points I would like to make if length permits and then the word "closing."

Next, I scan my notes for good lead material and write the appropriate number of words I'll need to use opposite "lead." I try to use material I've marked with three asterisks in that lead, killing two space-takers with one stroke of the pen. Important information used in the lead won't have to go in the body of the piece, thus freeing more words for that part of the article.

After "closing" I almost always write "100 words." It's the maximum number one can use to wind up a short piece. The writing job becomes easier if you can hone your closing shot to 50 words.

With a 100-word lead and 100-word closing, 550 words are left for the body of a 750-word article. I've learned from experience that at least 100 words are usually needed to make a specific point, so I look at my asterisked notes to find the four or five most important facets of the subject. I begin writing when my outline looks something like this:

Lead: 100 words—statistics on pet abuse

Point 1 and example: 150 words—outright mistreatment

Point 2 and example: 150 words—negligence

Point 3 and example: 100 words—thoughtlessness

Point 4 and example: 150 words—what's being done to correct situation

Closing: 100 words—sources of information on getting help for abused pets

If, after writing according to this advice, your piece is still too long (one of the most common problems for novices, by the way), cutting it down need not be a teeth-gritting task. If your piece is more than 50 words too long, try to delete whole paragraphs. If the excess is less than 50, you'll probably be able to meet the limit by eliminating superfluous words and phrases rather than resorting to major cuts.

If you've gathered more facts than you need, you haven't wasted your time. Look at that information as input you've acquired for your personal knowledge bank—or use it to write another mini-informational.

CHAPTER EIGHT

PEOPLE PIECES

What is the dividing line between gossip mongering and good personal journalism? I think it is this: gossipists are figures outside the window peeking in. When a journalist knocks and is admitted, the situation changes. You are in a close consultation which you cannot abuse. You're involved. You have a relationship, hence a responsibility not to betray.
Shana Alexander, McCall's, February 1970

 hough it takes years to get to know a person well, it is possible to give readers more than a passing acquaintance with people in only a few hundred words, as masters of the short personality piece prove issue after issue. Although they're still not as prevalent as longer personality pieces, the 300-900 word articles showcasing interesting people are appearing in an increasing number of magazines.

These cameos are among the most interesting and lucrative minis to write. Interviews are as exciting as those for longer personality pieces but less demanding, since they don't require as much time or as many questions. And if you ask the right questions, you can get twice the information you'll ever need from a half-hour interview. (We'll get to that later in the chapter.) As for other research, there often isn't any material at the library on your subject, so you can eliminate that step.

Then too, you can use the leftovers from interviews for full-length profiles to write shorter personality pieces about the same people for different publications. Los Angeles-based Jill Williams, best known for her articles about celebrities and their pets, deliberately asks a few "extra" questions at each interview. The responses provide material that she can use for other pieces.

Best of all, the central figures in abbreviated personality pieces don't have to be headline entertainers or Nobel Prize winners. They don't even have to be as "slightly famous" as the winner of Nathan's annual hotdog-eating competition.

The only requirement for most mini-personalities is a subject who does or has done something just a bit out of the ordinary. Counterparts of Thelma Williams, the 70-year-old peewee baseball league coordinator and coach whose profile appeared in *Modern Maturity*, and wildlife warden Jeremiah Johnson, featured in one of *The Mother Earth News* profiles, can be found in cities and hamlets all over the world.

What this means to you, the writer, is that you can craft mini-personalities about people who are readily accessible. It is often difficult to obtain interviews with celebrities (Martin Agronsky, the story goes, persevered four years before getting a television interview with Justice Hugo L. Black of the U.S. Supreme Court.) Most non-celebrities, on the other hand, are flattered by the idea that someone thinks they're interesting enough to write about. In time, as your skills expand and credits pile up, you may find yourself interviewing the world's famous. But for starters, you've a better chance interviewing the not-so-well-knowns.

REJECTION-PROOFING YOUR PERSONALITY

Just as each potential subject has his or her individual characteristics, so do the magazines to which you must match them. Some tie-ins are obvious: people 50 years and older for *50 Plus;* practicing Christians (often of a certain denomination) for Christian publications; professional truck drivers for *American Trucker.* Others are less apparent. But everything you need to know about targeting your profile material can be learned by reading a few issues of the publications you think might accept your ideas.

Personality pieces in *Channels* center on people in business. One issue, for example, contained articles about owners of a furniture mart, a boot shop, and a steak house in Nebraska; a health food store proprietor in Pierre, South Dakota; a grocery store owner and a barber pole manufacturer in St. Paul; a public accountant in Bismarck, North Dakota; Des Moines hearing aid company and employment agency owners; and the owner of an Omaha jewelry store. Contributors who submit pieces about theatrical agency owners in New York or citrus growers in Florida, however interesting the subjects and their businesses may be, won't have a chance with this publication, since it uses material about businesses in the midsection of the United States only. The pieces give insights into their owners' business philosophies and tell about their companies as well. This piece, "Kay Brown's Health Food," is typical:

"Business is going exceptionally well," says Kay Brown, who calls herself owner, clerk, stock person, bookkeeper, local philosopher and cleaning woman of Brown's Nutrition Market in Pierre.

Kay started the store in July, 1977, with "a little help from my friends" and a loan from the Small Business Administration. She did it because she couldn't find a food store to satisfy her personal health food needs after she had quit smoking two and a half packs of cigarettes a day, and had changed her eating habits.

Kay, a former English teacher, believes, "People should try the things they dream of being. A lot of people see what they should be but don't do anything about it. If this doesn't work, at least I've tried."

The market is stocked with natural foods such as freshly stone ground wheat, freshly ground peanut butter, puffed millet, charcoal tablets, dried banana chips, tiger's milk and sea water.

Kay likes to think of her store as a place people can buy fresh natural foods without preservatives, and a place where people can come to talk, too. "I like a place where you know your customers by their first names and where you care about them."

Her customers range from the kids who run in after school for licorice to older folks who stock up on grains or fig newtons just like they used to at the old general store.

Kay also has books on nutrition, a line of natural cosmetics and some fresh dairy products. She hopes to add fresh produce organically grown by local farmers to involve the community more in the store.

Kay Brown matches display of a bulletin board in her store with a weekly radio program featuring discussion of the items posted. She ties in tips on diet and nutrition. While she lauds the program as her best promotion, Kay Brown has used other techniques as well—newspaper and shopper ads, a combined birthday and grand opening open house and a display table featuring new and sale merchandise.

Pieces in *Odyssey's* "People in Travel" department, as you might assume from its name, focus on interesting personalities who do a lot of traveling, though not necessarily by car (*Odyssey* is Gulf Oil's Motor Club Magazine). The following article about a person who does get around by auto shows how the travel theme is woven into the piece. It's called "Don Kir Van Collects Barns" and was written by Joel Schwarz.

Some people collect stamps, coins, antiques or dolls. Not Don Kir Van. He collects old barns.

For the past 25 years the Woodinville, Washington, landscape contractor and nurseryman has scoured the back roads of the west looking for abandoned and run-down barns to buy.

Unlike other hobbyists, Kir Van doesn't display his collection. Rather he buys and dismantles his finds, salvaging the usable boards to sell to architects and designers for use in homes, restaurants, hotels, department stores—even at San Diego's Sea World.

Kir Van estimates he's driven more than one million miles throughout the West hunting for barns. That distance is only a guess; he's put five odometers and 10 engines into his truck.

Kir Van got into the barn board business in the 1960s when an architect friend mentioned he was looking for weathered timbers to use in a restaurant with an old sailing ship motif.

"I told him it would be easy to find a barn," he recalls, "but it didn't turn out that way."

Months and Miles

Several months and thousands of miles later, after discovering that most of the old barns in Western Washington and Oregon were termite-infested, Kir Van brought back his first barn.

Since then, his business has grown considerably. However, his barn collecting is still on a custom basis. He keeps no inventory because "it's difficult to store the boards without an air-controlled environment. If you stack them they lose their beauty."

When he does get an order, Kir Van hops into his truck and heads out for his favorite hunting grounds in Idaho, Montana or eastern Oregon.

"It can take quite a while to find a good barn," he says. "A lot depends on the size and other details of the order."

He may hire a local person to find a suitable barn, or he may check out a barn that is offered for sale. But most of the time, Kir Van just drives down back roads looking for abandoned structures. At times, finding a barn is easier than locating its owner. "It's almost like detective work because the owner may live halfway across the country," he says.

Just any old barn won't do, especially if a customer wants a particular wood, or boards sprinkled with a specific color of lichen.

"You also have to look at the texture of the wood, its age, and whether the barn has been used by animals," he cautions.

Kir Van pays between $300 and $800 for a barn, depending on its size and condition and the amount of cleanup work he has to do once he dismantles it.

Most of the time he takes down the barn piece by piece, with a hammer, although he occasionally uses a stick of dynamite in the rafters to "pop the boards loose." Approximately half of the boards in a barn are usually salvageable. The rest are too insect-riddled for use.

What Kir Van stacks in his truck are weathered boards in sizes impossible to find today—boards an inch thick, two feet wide and 20 feet long. He also has discovered other rare items: brass beds, branding irons from the 1880s, old mining and farming implements, cans of salmon with 8¢ price tags, and even an old still with 24 bottles of moonshine under one barn.

But even though good barns are scarce and the work hard, as long as people continue to appreciate the beauty of weathered siding, Kir Van will continue to jump into his truck and hunt for old barns to add to his collection. He sees a lot of country that way, too.

Both the nutrition storekeeper and barn collector pieces were tailor-made for their publications. The articles' topics—small businesses and reliance on transportation—fit perfectly into their magazines' themes. But either of the pieces, with minor changes in style or emphasis, might have been sold to other publications. Grocery and health food trade magazines would be the most promising alternate markets for the first piece. Possibilities for the second encompass a wider variety of publications, since an offbeat hobby has a broader readership appeal than running a nutrition store. Church, fraternal, and retirement magazines (depending on the subject's age and affiliations), general interest and regional publications, tabloids and lumber trade newsletters are all potential markets.

PSA Magazine has a "VIP" (very interesting people) department that features people who live in or near the airline's route cities. These profiles are anywhere from 300 to 500 words long; and though the first sale won't make you rich, the editors pay more for subsequent pieces.

Small World, the Volkswagen publication, uses two or more miniprofiles in each of its quarterly issues. Though subjects have ranged from a Cleveland TV weatherman to a Connecticut couple who design hot-air balloons to a Chicago fencing coach, they have one thing in common: all of them drive Volkswagens. Each of these people-focused featurettes is accompanied by two photos: one of the subject going about his business or hobby; the other showing him in or near his automobile.

People and *Us* print more cameos than other magazines. Unfortunately, they're usually either staff-written or assigned to a group of regulars. The only non-staffer I know personally who has done a *People* piece isn't a writer by trade and didn't seek the assignment. She was traveling on a Barbara Cartland tour and was asked by one of the magazine's editors to write down everything that happened during the tour group's meeting with the author.

But both *People* and *Us* do use freelance material to some extent. According to Brendan Elliott, staff assistant at *Us*, 15 percent of the magazine's editorial material comes from stringers and about 30 percent is written by freelancers. "But," Elliott says, "80 percent of those who query don't know the magazine. We are what you call a personality book; most of our stories are about celebrities, with a few of them about ordinary persons doing extraordinary things. To sell to us, an article must be hot, on, timely. Assignments go to those who really understand the book, and writers have to establish themselves as being able to write in our 'up, contemporary' style of journalism."

Personality departments in several magazines are linked to nostalgia, among them "Where Are They Today?" in *Sports Parade*, which features athletic greats of yesteryear. Other publications in the Meridian group, including *Inflight* and *People on Parade*, use the same logo and "Where Are They Today?" title but center on former show business celebrities.

"Whatever happened to . . ." in *Woman's World* focuses on celebrities who have faded from the limelight such as Noel Neil (Lois Lane in the original *Superman* movie serial) and Mark Spitz, the swimmer who won seven gold medals at the 1972 Summer Olympics (he owns a Los Angeles real estate and development firm).

Occasionally, you'll find a short article that contains micro-profiles of several people based on a single theme, as in "When I Grow Up," which appeared in *Mature Living*, by G. Ward Walker.

It's a "monkey see, monkey do" world, I know. I learned that from my dad.

I'm young now, but I'm getting older. I've been watching several senior adults to learn what to do when I grow up. Look with me.

The short article then goes on to tell about several people and how they have enriched their lives through Christian involvement.

Whereas longer personality pieces fall into five basic categories (profiles, question-and-answer interviews, a day in the life of . . ., roundup, and group), most mini-personalities are single-facet profiles. Simply stated, these are pieces that tell about one dimension of the featured subject's life—how he entertains the disabled; how she climbed to the top as a time-management expert; her involvement with migrant workers.

Your choice of the featured personality, as well as the aspect of his or her life that will be emphasized, is largely determined by the focus of the publication in which you hope to publish.

LEADING INTO YOUR SUBJECT

Summary leads are great when you have to get into your subject fast, as is the case with the mini-profile. Take this one from *PSA Magazine*, "What's in a Namesake?" by Chris Barnett:

> It's tough to have a famous name. Just ask Max Schmeling, night bartender at the popular Buena Vista Cafe in San Francisco. He's no kin to the German heavyweight who knocked out Joe Louis, though his grandfather claims that they were both from the same hometown outside Munich. When Max calls up to book a hotel room, wags invariably say, "Yeah, we'll give you a suite right next to Jack Dempsey." Getting a restaurant reservation isn't any easier.
>
> But Max Schmeling is an honest-to-gosh champ.

Here is an even shorter summary lead from a piece in the "Profiles" department of *The Mother Earth News:*

> When Jay Brown first decided to take up his current hobby—building stagecoaches—he was disappointed to discover that there was little information to be found on the subject. So Brown decided to get some hands-on experience.

You can see from this lead and others in *Mother Earth* that the pieces are not so much about the personalities as some back-to-nature/old-times activity they're involved in.

Here is a still shorter summary lead from "Where Are They Today? Lana Turner" from *Inflight:*

> Lana Turner, unquestionably one of Hollywood's remaining superstars, still attracts the attention of moviegoers the world over.

Quote Leads

The **quote lead,** using an appropriate statement, by either the featured person or one of his or her associates, also is a favorite curtain raiser for the mini-profile. This one appeared in a *Modern Maturity* piece called "The Magic of Josef Muench":

"His work is incredible and his eye gets better every year."

So speaks a magazine editor, praising the echanting landscape photography of Josef Muench, whose eye, by the way, is 78 years old.

Whether or not they begin with quotes, most mini-profiles contain a large proportion of direct quotations. People telling about their work or hobbies or adventures *in their own words* give readers not only information but also insight into their personalities.

In an article about a woman puppeteer in *New Woman,* for instance, 180 of the 526 words in the piece were directly quoted.

Not all mini-profiles contain so many quotes. But it's a rare personality piece that doesn't call for at least two or three. This can present real problems when your subject is a mumbler or answers in monosyllables—people who do interesting things aren't necessarily interesting to talk to. When you've failed to coax scintillating sayings from your subject's lips despite your best efforts (read John Brady's *The Craft of Interviewing* [Writer's Digest Books, 1976] and *The Journalistic Interview,* by Hugh C. Sherwood [Harper & Row, 1969], for interviewing tips), don't despair. Talk to his friends, her business associates, the family priest, and quote *their* comments.

Descriptive Leads

Although the **descriptive** is the least often used of the three most popular mini-profile leads, it can be extremely effective in giving readers a feel for the subject's personality or his surroundings. This one is from "Woodcarver" by Monte Hansen in *Small World:*

It was a cool day, but inside the tiny shop a glowing wood-burning stove radiated a friendly warmth. In the corner of the shop a small man huddled over his work and noted that Minnesota's weather seemed to be growing increasingly harsh with the passing of each year.

As he spoke, Edward Dietmaier made use of the last bit of afternoon sun to carve an intricate pattern on a small wood statue. Working with a pick-like tool, he meticulously shaped each piece of fruit in a sackload of grapes which was slung over the shoulder of a carved figure of a farmer:

"Ah, if you don't have patience you go crazy," he said.

The refined wooden figurines scattered throughout Dietmaier's shop are testaments that this German-born craftsman possesses the all-important patience required of a true woodcarver.

Anecdote Leads

A fourth lead, the **anecdote,** while used for longer personality pieces, is difficult to incorporate into the shorter piece, since most anecdotes require a disproportionately large number of words to work well.

Which Lead Should Lead?

To determine which of these leads to use, consider the editor's past preferences. Some editors favor summary leads; others consistently buy pieces that begin with quotes. Try to fashion your lead after those *your* editor prefers. But keep your material in mind, too. The information gleaned from some interviews simply doesn't lend itself to certain kinds of leads. If you have to interview your subject in a bare and blah-looking room or if he answers your questions soberly and directly without smiling or exhibiting any distinguishing mannerisms, you won't have much material to write a descriptive lead. On the other hand, your subject may greet you in her pink satin boudoir, wearing an orange antebellum gown and fifteen pieces of jewelry, surrounded by her pet chimp and three talking birds.

GIVING LIFE TO THE BODY

However you lead into your article, you must from the beginning do everything you can to let readers know what makes your archeologist or dogsled maker or Supreme Court justice tick. Is he short or tall? Does she speak like a nuclear physicist or with down-home simplicity? How does he feel about traditional family life? What are her views on keeping pets in apartments? A peek at a personality, however fleeting, must reveal a three-dimensional, flesh-and-blood character.

As you read mini-profiles, be aware of why you do or do not enjoy reading them. Chances are, those that don't interest you are just characteristics on paper instead of human beings to whom you can relate. This piece, "Home Is Where the Chili Is," by Marjorie Menzies from *Odyssey's* "People in Travel," graphically demonstrates techniques that make the personality come alive: quotes, personal trivia related to the topic, background information about family and career, likes and dislikes.

Home for singer Kelly Garrett is somewhere between New York and California. "On a plane," suggests the brown-eyed performer with the infectious smile.

And in her luggage—chili and tortillas.

Kelly's career takes her throughout the world, and she often has to fly from 300,000 to a half-million miles a year. But her heart is in her hometown of Santa Fe, New Mexico. And Kelly, born Ellen Boulton, the daughter of an English father and Spanish-American mother, never stops extolling her native state, whether she's on the *Tonight Show* or playing a state fair.

Kelly was the second daughter in a family of 10 children. Everyone in the family sang—it was as much a part of life as learning to cook New Mexican-style in her mother's kitchen. But Kelly wanted a career as a singer.

Accepted at a Cincinnati conservatory on the basis of her operatic tapes, she got a job at a nearby hospital to pay her way. When school officials found she couldn't read music, didn't speak any foreign languages except Spanish and had no formal training, they were horrified.

"I had memorized everything from old Deanna Durbin and Mario Lanza records," she explains, laughing at the memory.

Hard Work

Working full time, trying to catch up on the background basics and carrying the regular program proved too much. With her family unable to help financially, Kelly had to give up.

"I was never so depressed in my life," she admits.

But when local boys asked her to audition with their rock group in Santa Fe, she pulled herself together to help them out. It was the start of her career in popular music, a career that has gone up and up—Broadway shows, nightclub acts, television, supper theaters and recordings.

The flood of jobs means Kelly is on the go most of the time.

"Stewardesses who see me fly to Los Angeles one day are always startled to see me heading back to New York the next," Kelly says with a laugh. "They say, 'Didn't I see you yesterday?' "

Winging West

"I like jobs in Denver or Texas—then I can sneak home to Santa Fe for a few days to see my family," she says with her big happy smile.

"Winter is the worst time to fly," she continues. "Airports get closed by snow in the East and fog in the West, and I always worry whether I'm going to get to my concert on time. And the luggage!" Kelly moans in dismay.

"If time is tight, I have to hand-carry my gown—and roll up my music and carry it with me. All that and the usual bags and maybe a winter coat and boots!" Not to mention the frozen green chili, the tortillas and the dried red chili she likes to carry along as gifts for friends or as a touch of home for herself.

But when vacation time comes, does Kelly relax at home?

"Now don't laugh—but I usually find myself on a plane going somewhere!" she exclaims, laughing at herself. "When I had a week free last year, I headed for Calgary to visit a friend. After I got on the plane, I suddenly said to myself, 'What are you doing here on a plane? Are you crazy?' But I had a marvelous time."

Next winter, she's planning a trip to Greece to "visit the little places and relax."

But, Kelly adds ruefully, "I'll probably go crazy with nothing to do. And no green chili or tortillas."

Without interviewing Kelly Garrett, I have a good idea of the questions author Marjorie Menzies asked. Of course, there were the standard queries: "Where were you born?" "How many brothers and sisters do you have?" "Where did you receive your training?" But there also must have been some "What do you do for fun?" and "What's your favorite food?" questions, too.

As an exercise, reread the piece and make a list of the questions that would elicit the article's information. To get you started, here are the questions that were probably asked to obtain the first hundred words:

Where do you live?
What do you pack in your luggage?
How many miles do you fly in a year?
Is Kelly Garrett your real name?
Where have you performed?
Where were you born?
What nationality are you?

BOWING OUT

The quote ending, as used in the piece above, is the one you'll most often find wrapping up the mini-personality. While they're interviewing their subjects, the pros look for appropriate end quotes and note those that are possibilities.

Ending the mini-personality is not a difficult task if you keep the purpose of your piece in mind. Whatever facet of your subject the article focuses on should be reiterated or reinforced in those final sentences. If the piece points up your subject's sunny nature in the face of adversity, close with a quote from one of his friends about the man's marvelous sense of humor. When your article focuses on a person's athletic prowess, you might want to close with a summary (the second most popular mini-personality ending) about her past accomplishments or goals for the future.

INSIGHTS FOR INTERVIEWERS

The interviewing tips for mini-informationals (see Chapter 7, "Research Minute-Savers") apply to mini-personalities as well. Sharp interviewers have other tricks to make every minute of the short interview count. Celia Scully, who has interviewed such authorities as Frederick LeBoyer, the French obstetrician who pioneered non-violent childbirth; and Lester A. Kirkendall, grandfather of family life education in the United States, says, "When I've only got a few minutes with a V.I.P., I'm forced to reverse my usual procedure of building up to the tough questions. I've found that if I wait, the interviewee may signal 'time's up' before I've gotten to the answers I want most."

Jill Williams advises, "Don't be intimidated. You have to be the director, never letting your subject take charge of the interview. Be resourceful in planning your questions, and be sure you've done all the research you can about the person in advance."

Good interviewers agree that it's a plus if you can interview your subject in his or her natural habitat—home, office, or place of business. Try to arrive a bit early so that you can concentrate on the atmosphere and make notes on the surroundings.

You'll often be called upon to provide photos of your personality. Sometimes the interviewee will be able to supply them (show business people, especially, seem to have stacks of black-and-white glossies), but most of the time the job will be up to you. If you don't feel that your photographic ability measures up to the magazine's standards, make a deal with a freelance photographer. When the magazine pays separately for photos, you can afford to pay that amount to the photographer. If payment is made for the text/photo package, arrange to pay her a percentage of the total amount. Even if photos aren't required by the editor, snap a few, if you can, to refer to while you're writing the piece. It's amazing how many details you will recall simply by looking at the pictures.

PICKING PEOPLE

I hope that while you've been reading the examples in this chapter, you have been reminded of interesting people you might feature in mini-personalities of your own. They are everywhere—appearing in town on the lecture circuit or sitting on the front porch two houses down. Look for people in unlikely professions or with unusual hobbies. People who have conquered adversity are naturals for the tabloids and women's magazines. The subject of the following article, which appeared in *National Enquirer,* was also featured in a longer *Family Circle* article. The article is entitled "Miracle Mom Gives Handicapped Kids Her Special Brand of Love." Chris Benton wrote it.

Life dealt Grace Sandness a terrible blow . . . but she has returned only kindness and love.

Paralyzed from the neck down, Grace has lived her past 31 years in a wheelchair. Yet the courageous woman has taken into her heart and home 12 children, many with handicaps of their own.

"God doesn't give us disabilities we can't handle," said the 50-year-old miracle worker.

"He wants to see what we do with our own set of circumstances."

Grace has been a United Nations of love. Her family of twelve foster and adopted children include four Americans, four Koreans, three Ethiopians and one Vietnamese.

"I want to reach out and touch my children even though I can't move my arms."

"But because I'm handicapped too, I can reach out to them with understanding and love," said Grace, who was felled by polio at age 19.

When schoolmates tease her children, she said, "It breaks my heart, and I can't dry their tears. But I can make them understand that they aren't as handicapped as the children who make fun of them."

Grace can't move her arms or legs, and she operates her wheelchair by blowing through a tube that controls the motor. A respirator that fits across her chest keeps her breathing.

Grace's heartwarming courage in the face of her handicap inspires her children to make the most of their lives.

"Aesoon, 27, had heart surgery," said Grace. "Now she works as a nurse on a heart surgery team in Korea."

"And before Kim, 25, became a nurse's aide, she had severe emotional problems. Cindy, 23, has cerebral palsy and attends the University of Minnesota. Jennifer, also 23, had polio. Now she's an office manager at an insurance company."

Three others have handicaps too, said Grace. "They listen to me because we have our handicaps in common and I am able to help them in ways that a normal mother couldn't."

For instance, 19-year-old Dezirae, who suffered a spinal cord injury, sometimes becomes discouraged about having to be in a wheelchair.

"When she's so tired of sitting in that chair, she talks to me and I listen to her frustrations and try to help her by making her understand that I know what it is she's going through," said the gutsy Edina, Minn., woman.

Grace has also written two books, typing out the words with a plastic stick clenched between her teeth.

"I put my faith in God," she says.

"I do the best I can with what I have. Giving up is not part of life."

Despite Grace's handicap, she and her husband, Dave, have also founded an adoption agency. And since 1976, she's placed hundreds of homeless children from around the word with loving families.

"She doesn't sit around pitying herself," said Dave. "And her faith in the Lord has helped her do the things she's had to do."

Grace doesn't question the physical disabilities of her family.

"It's never even crossed my mind that the Lord was cruel for handicapping me or the children," she said, adding that raising her family has been one of the greatest blessings of her life.

And, she says, she's determined to continue her good works.

"God wants to see if we turn to Him—or if we lie down and give up. I've just tried to do the best I can and look to the Lord for help when I need it."

I chose this particular piece because it typifies the *Enquirer's* profiles, to be sure. But I also selected it to emphasize a most important point. The best subjects for personality pieces are often too close for us to see them. I should have written that piece. As a child, I walked to school with Grace. We went to the same Sunday school. Though my family moved from the town where both Gracie and I grew up, I knew about her tragedy and subsequent triumphs.

Every one of you has courageous, interesting, daring, inventive, inspiring, famous, exciting people in your life. Don't pass them by.

CHAPTER NINE

THE NEWS IN BRIEF

A people without reliable news is, sooner or later, a people without the basis of freedom.

Harold J. Laski

he newsbreak is considered the bread-and-butter piece by many freelancers. It is relatively easy to write and, for writers who can keep up production, a steady source of income.

Most newsbreaks fall into the 200-500 word range. Whereas the mini-informational has a lifespan of several months (or even years), the newsbreak has an immediacy about it, a "this is the latest" slant.

You'll find these timely news items in a host of publications, both general interest and specialized: trade publications, technological journals, and magazines about opera, boating, and cats.

The basic classifications of newsbreaks, according to my system of keeping track, are *breakthrough/innovation, event, place,* and *business briefs.* All of them are written in journalism's inverted-pyramid format, the form used for the majority of newspaper articles. The main point is presented in the lead paragraph (almost always in the first sentence), and succeeding points are given in order of importance.

Each point is generally amplified by a sentence or two of additional information (referred to as *New York Times* style by editors). Paragraphs most often consist of two or three sentences—rarely more than four. The practical reasons for this style are that readers get the most important information in a hurry and editors can cut the article to fit available space at the end of any paragraph.

Style is crisp and reportorial, seldom employing devices such as similes, metaphors, and anecdotes. This makes the newsbreak a natural for writers with newspaper experience, but it's an easy style for any writer to catch on to quickly.

NEW NEWS
The *breakthrough/innovation* category covers new developments (especially in science and medicine), new ways of doing things (big in the trade journals), and new products.

Science Digest uses a good many of these kinds of articles, and such titles as "Plastic Car Batteries," "Messages by Meteor," and "New Easter Island Data" give an idea of the variety of topics it accepts. This one, "Woodpeckers Lured by Plastic Trees," is written in typical newsbreak style:

Woodpeckers, it seems, aren't too finicky about where they hang their hats. They usually make their nests in the soft decaying wood of dead trees. But as researchers at Ohio State University have found, they will also peck at plastic trees.

When timber growers weed out deadwood in a forest, they inadvertently remove the woodpeckers' nesting sites, causing the birds to look elsewhere for a home. Without woodpeckers, which are natural insect predators, bugs that live beneath tree bark go to town feeding on the wood. In hopes of luring woodpeckers back into pest-infested forests, zoologists Thomas Grubb, Jr., and Alan Peterson are pressing plastic trees into service.

To see if the birds would be attracted to the artificial trees, the researchers "planted" 50 eight-foot-tall cylinders of soft, foamlike plastic in a woodlot. They found that within a few months, the birds pecked roosting cavities in about 85 percent of the brown-painted impostors. "But we didn't see any birds actually nesting in any of them," Peterson reports.

The zoologists speculate that the nesting cycle was not completed because the plastic trees did not resonate as real ones do when the birds drum out their love songs. Woodpeckers, they say, may rely on the familiar rat-a-tat to attract mates. So in order to refine the mimicry, the researchers are planning to cover parts of the plastic trees with a resonant material such as plywood.

"Once perfected," says Peterson, "the devices should provide easily portable nesting sites." He hopes the pseudo-trees will attract enough woodpeckers to the forests to keep pest outbreaks under control. If so, the technique may provide a natural means of insect control that works as well as insecticide sprays, which can be hazardous to human health.

Psychology Today uses newsbreaks on psychological findings in its "Newsline" department, such as this one, called "The Slump of the Secure Player."

A team of psychologists has mustered statistical evidence to show that long-term contracts take some of the hustle out of professional baseball players.

Multiyear contracts became common in 1977, two years after a federal arbitration panel ruled that players were no longer bound indefinitely to the teams that originally signed them, a decision that made it advantageous for owners to tie up their stars. Richard O'Brien and other psychologists at Hofstra University studied how the ruling affected players' performance. The researchers examined the records of 38 pitchers during the three years before and after they signed contracts for three or more years, comparing their play with that of 38 randomly chosen pitchers who signed only single-season contracts for the same period.

As long as they had to get their contracts renewed each year, the players who eventually won long-term berths improved steadily, from an average of 3.66 earned runs scored against them per game in 1974 to 2.91 in 1976. After signing their long-term agreements, however, their earned run averages (ERAs) climbed to an average of 4.04 three years later. The pitchers with one-year contracts showed no consistent pattern during the six years.

The researchers recommend that owners combine a base salary with incentive payments for achieving goals such as a specified ERA or batting average. Negotiated peformance targets, they say, "would allow equitable rewards for productive seasons for all players."

Just before the findings were published, the Baltimore Orioles' ace pitcher, Jim Palmer, provided independent support for that conclusion in a *New York Times* interview. Having a long-term contract himself, Palmer noted that "up until 1975, my next year's salary always depended on every pitch I threw. I never relaxed. I never took anything for granted. It would seem to be hard for some players to have that kind of intensity after signing a multiyear contract. Some players are making a lot more money than they should."

Note that the two examples above have several elements in common. Both contain their leads in the first sentence, which is amplified in the text that follows. They are narrowly focused, telling about a single breakthrough or set of findings. Both include statistics and quotes to support their basic premises. Moreover, in true newspaper style, both could end at the close of any of the paragraphs if space were not available to print the pieces in their entirety.

WHAT'S GOING ON
The *event* piece tells about a happening of interest to the magazine's readers, be it a church conclave, an antique show, or a bowling tournament. The event piece is either printed in advance of the

occasion, letting readers know what is about to take place, or run after the event, providing a rundown of its highlights.

You'll find event pieces in *Yacht Racing/Cruising* in the form of post-race recaps and in *Dancemagazine* as roundups of performances that have been held around the world. *Horizon* uses these newsbreaks to announce forthcoming exhibits and performances. *Cats Magazine* reports results of cat shows. This one, "The Leslie Year," appeared in *The Highlander* and is typical of postevent articles:

> Two major Clan Gatherings, various meetings and ceilidhs, plus the visit of the Clan Chief, the Earl of Rothes and the Countess to the United States were the highlights of the American Clan Leslie in 1981.
>
> Its combined National and Western Gathering was held in August during the San Diego Highland Games and in September an eastern Gathering was held at the Charleston Games. In addition Clan Leslie tents were manned by ACLS members at Ligonier and both the Rocky Mountain and Stone Mountain Games as was the Leslie booth at the Edinburgh International Gathering.
>
> Clan Chief Ian and Lady Marigold were guests of honor at the American-Scottish Foundation Ball in September and later flew to California to visit with Leslies on the west coast. A ceilidh was given in their honor by the Southern California chapter. This is the first ACLS regional chapter to be formed with Charles H. Leslie of San Diego as president.
>
> At the National Gathering the Society established the position of musicologist and elected Dr. Jane Moore Bolen of Greenwood, S.C., an expert in Scottish and Celtic music, to that position. Also established were "Inceptor" memberships to bring persons under 18 into the societies' activities and to stimulate their interest in Scottish culture and their Clan Leslie heritage.
>
> Of importance to Leslies was the re-acquisition by a Leslie of one of the Leslie Castles in Scotland. This was the one at Leslie, near Aberdeen, which was acquired by Baron David C. Leslie of Aberdeen, who will completely restore the Castle. It is successor to the very first Leslie Seat, of the 11th Century. Whatever remained of it was built anew in 1661, later passed out of the family and in this century fell into ruin.
>
> Readers wanting more information about American Clan Leslie may write to the Society at PO Box 28332, San Diego, CA 92128.

Event pieces figure heavily in trade publications, informing professionals of upcoming conferences and sales meetings and reporting on what transpired at them after they're over. An especially promising market is publications for people in the travel industry. One issue of *Travel Trade*, for example, contained these articles: "Election Jitters Jolting ASTA [American Society of Travel Agents]; Tough Race Seen," "Women's Travel Meeting Slated for Niagara Falls," "TIPS/NJ [The New Jersey Travel Industry Travel Society] Joint Meeting," and "Integrity in Tourism Keynotes 1978 USTOA [United States Tour Operators Association] Annual Meeting."

Travel trade publications also feature several newsbreaks about forthcoming tours and similar events in each issue, such as this one, "Italian Cooking Classes, Tours Set," in *TravelAge West*.

ROME—Cooking buffs who also enjoy traveling will have the best of two worlds when they join a Gourmet Adventure tour developed by the Bettoja Hotels, Lo Scaldavivande Cooking School, Guaranteed Travel and E&M Assoc.

The seven-day tour of Rome includes four morning sessions at the school. Classes are in English and Italian by Jo Bettoja or Anna Maria Cornetto.

Two afternoons are devoted to Italian Mosaic guided sightseeing in Rome. On the last day, participants drive to Barbarano in Romano for a graduation lunch at Angelo Bettoja's country villa.

Cost starts at $855, depending on departure, including air via Pan Am. Tour members stay at the Bettoja's Mediterraneo Hotel in Rome.

Departures are scheduled from Oct. 21 through May 19.

Contact E&M Assoc., 667 Madison Ave., NYC 10021. Telephone: 800-223-9832.

Note in your market study that the event piece begins by telling what event was held (or is to take place). Succeeding information includes location and time, topics to be covered, guest speakers, entertainment highlights, cost to participants, and/or where further information may be obtained.

PLACES IN THE NEWS

The place newsbreak is most often found in travel publications—primarily in the trades and travel bulletins, such as *The Travelore Report*. In travel trade publications, these pieces focus on news of vacation spots: hotels that are offering special rates, theme parks and other attractions that are opening or expanding, sporting facilities that are adding new equipment (such as ski lifts), and the like.

This article, "New Safari Lodge Introduced to Industry," illustrates the longer place newsbreaks used by travel trade publications. It was published in *Travel Trade*.

Cecil Evans, owner and manager of Musungwa Safaris Limited of Zambia, carried out a brief promotional visit to the U.S. as a guest of Zambia Airways to personally introduce Musungwa Safari Lodge to the travel industry.

The lodge, Evans said, was named for an old friend, Chief Musungwa of a neighboring Ilo tribe. It commands the banks of a lake formed by the construction of the Itezi-Itezi Dam and is just without the border of Zambia's Kafue National Park, one of the largest animal reserves in Africa.

The complex presently consists of 16 double-bedded chalets facing the lake and plans for an additional nine for the 1979 season are well underway.

Architecturally, the chalets are based on the traditional African style: thatched roofs, reed ceilings, double doors and all but wrap-around windows make air conditioning superfluous. Each chalet is attractively decorated and comfortably furnished with, of course, private facilities.

Other amenities he listed include a swimming pool, 24-hour electricity and, thanks to the talents of his wife, Connie, a hair-dressing salon.

Game Viewing

Rates are about $53 per day, per person, including accommodations, all meals, game-viewing drives twice daily and the services of safari leaders.

For maximum visibility, game-viewing drives are in open Land Rovers, each drive covering from 50 to 60 miles within the national reserve. When safari leaders believe it appropriate, passengers may leave the vehicles and track game on foot in groups of not more than six, accompanied by their leader and a guard.

Evans has found this technique to be effective and especially suitable to Kafue, as certain species can best be observed and photographed from the Land Rover; others on foot. One nocturnal game-viewing drive will normally be arranged during an average 3- to 5-day stay.

Lake fishing is also a major attraction aboard a shallow draft "sea truck." Evans's hearty and excellently prepared meals always include freshly caught fish at breakfast and lunch. The sea truck is also used for lake cruises in the late afternoon.

Safari Camp

Other scheduled diversions include nightly dancing by groups of young people from neighboring villages and a daytime visit to at least one of those villages, as unspoiled and as natural as Zambia itself.

A safari camp, built within Dafue's boundaries, is another Evans's facility. The compound, about 15 miles from the main lodge, can accomodate 30 persons in huts made of reed and thatch. These huts, Evans contends, are far cooler and more comfortable than tents and in no way detract from the life in the bush. Visitors may opt for the camp, or it may be possible to arrange at least one night at the safari camp for lodge guests.

Further information or reservations for Musungwa Safari Lodge are available from Zambia Airways, One Rockefeller Plaza, New York, N.Y. 10020; (212) 582-6637.

Notice that this type of travel newsbreak differs from the travel mini-informational only as far as style is concerned; the newsbreak is more reportorial in tone.

Travel bulletin newsbreaks are usually much shorter (one or two paragraphs) and give readers the scoop on destinations around the world, like these two from the *Travel Advisor:*

225 "SNOWPLAY" AREAS IN U.S.—MOST FREE

Many people don't know that the Forest Service, U.S. Department of Agriculture, has set aside 225 special sections in *154 national forests* for *winter recreation:* downhill and cross-country skiing, snowmobiling, snowshoeing, and winter camping. While some are operated by concessionaires who put up facilities such as ski lifts and restaurants, others are kept in a completely natural state and are *free to all comers*. Contact the district office of the *Forest Service* for details about "snowplay" areas near you. If you have trouble finding the address of this office, write to the *Travel Advisor* (15 Park Place, Bronxville, N.Y. 10708) and we'll send you a list of all the regional offices.

CUT MEAL COSTS WITH FLORIDA DINER'S CLUB

If you're planning to spend 3 weeks or more in south Florida, particularly Ft. Lauderdale, Hollywood or Pompano Beach, you can save money on restaurant bills if you join the *Carriage Dinner Club*. "As a longtime newspaperman and restaurant writer I like to check on these things, and I tried it six times without a hitch. I honestly recommend it," says Ben Schneider, owner of Four Seasons Travel. The membership fee of $15 entitles you to pay for one dinner and get the second one *free* in more than fifty restaurants in the area. For a listing of participating restaurants, write to *Carriage Dinner Club, 2573 N. Federal Hwy, Ft. Lauderdale, FL 33339*.

MINDING THEIR BUSINESS

Business briefs report on everything from mergers to the employment picture to the machinations of the prime rate. You will encounter these bits of information from the financial world not only in business magazines, but also in publications like *Ad Forum* and *Constructor*. This brief, "Philadelphia Story," appeared in *Black Enterprise*:

If you ask black contractors in Philadelphia whether the rise in defense spending means better business for them, the answer will be a resounding no.

In fiscal 1981, there were $63.4 million of contracts awarded by the Philadelphia Naval Shipyard as part of the $269 million overhaul of the carrier USS Saratoga. But according to a study by the office of Congressman William H. Gray III, only $1.1 million, or 1.8 percent of those contracts went to minority businesses.

Naval officials point out that $30 million of the $63 million had to go to original contractors: "You cannot send a high-pressure turbine to a local shop for repairs," said one. Added another, "I think we've done a good job."

Gray says that the lack of black contractors "borders on a system of economic apartheid," and has threatened legal action.

In analyzing newsbreaks, you'll see that they are composed principally of declarative sentences. Writing is straightforward and tight; there is no attempt to dazzle the reader. In the newsbreak, the only function of the words is to get the message to the reader, as succinctly and accurately as possible.

Once you have discovered a market and submitted successfully, it's not difficult to become a regular contributor, contributing editor, or stringer. Since most national magazines that use newsbreaks want information from around the country, they arrange to have stringers in various regions—writers who will send in copy on the latest developments in the magazine's area of interest and on whom they can call to cover local events.

There are a number of ways to become a stringer, even without having previously written for a magazine. One of my writer friends obtained a job by answering an ad in *The Quill*, a publication for journalists. Another responded to an advertisement in the local newspaper and earns her grocery money by writing about openings of area supermarkets for a food trade magazine. Still another method is to contact various trade publications (you'll find the names of hundreds of them in *Working Press of the Nation*), sending your resumé and qualifications to them along with a cover letter inquiring about openings for stringers.

MARKETING MOXIE

To maximize your marketing mileage, concentrate on trade publications—the periodicals aimed at people engaged in a specific occupation, business, or industry. Most writers aren't aware that many of these markets exist.

Obtain sample copies of from 50 to 100 magazines. Study them closely; then start matching up publications with ideas. Whereas marketing most other short pieces works better if you identify publications first and then come up with ideas for them, the newsbreak marketing process works the other way around because of the timeliness factor. When you come upon a newsbreak idea, you must find a place to sell it right away. Finding that place is much easier if you already have a good knowledge of the trade publications.

Your local and area newspapers will be your number-one source of newsbreak inspiration. When you read that a convention of beekeepers or loggers or hardware salespeople will be held in your area, look through your trade magazine files. If you can't find the appropriate publication there, check *Writer's Market* and scurry down to the library to search through their publication directories.

Take down all the pertinent information: name of publication, editor, address, and telephone number. If you don't have much lead time, you may want to phone editors to see if they would like coverage. When you receive assignments, contact the convention bureau or organization handling the event to obtain press credentials.

If your city hosts a number of conventions, as mine does, you'll want to check regularly with the convention bureau or chamber of commerce to see what's coming up (most conventions are scheduled at least a year in advance). With this head start, you will be able to contact editors well in advance.

The papers will also report new businesses and industries in your area or, if you live in crop and livestock land, the latest agricultural developments.

Information about new resorts and tourist attractions appears in local papers long before the rest of the world learns of their existence. The astute newspaper reader should watch for applications to construct hotels, convention centers, and the like. That gives plenty of lead time to study potential publications and query their editors.

As far as breakthroughs and innovations are concerned, there are several ways to translate them into salable newsbreaks. Read technical journals for ideas that can be submitted to less specialized magazines. Attend seminars (find out who's in charge and get a press pass if meetings aren't open to the public). Make it a habit to ask "What's new?" whenever you talk to acquaintances in the scientific, medical, and business worlds. Ask your storekeeper friends what new products are being introduced or will be in the near future. Quiz your stockbroker and banker about business trends.

Another source of scoops is government publications. The prolific newsbreak writer will also see that he or she is on all sorts of press release lists—from tourism bureaus, art foundations, and corporations. In short, cultivate every informational source you can.

Several magazines have columns that, although by-lined, use newsbreaks from contributors. Sometimes this information is spelled out in *Writer's Market* or in the magazine itself. Most of the time, however, you'll have to discover this information for yourself. Phrases like "Betty Hanna from Greensboro reports that" are good indicators that the person mentioned was paid for his or her report. If you're in doubt, write to the columnist and ask.

Since your material will be rewritten and you won't get by-lines providing items for columnists, it's more gratifying to sell your pieces to markets that promise a by-line, pay, and the pleasure of seeing your words printed relatively intact.

Bread-and-butter pieces though they may be, newsbreaks can of-

ten be a freelancer's entrée into a magazine's inner circle—the people who get assignments for the really big pieces and that, I'm sure
you'll agree, is the frosting on any writer's cake.

CHAPTER TEN

THE GREETING-CARD MESSAGE

It's nice to receive a greeting card in the mail, but a greeting card with your words on it—and a check with your name on it—is the nicest greeting of all.
Patricia Ann Emme

 hen cousin Martha has her appendix out in Louisville, what do you do? Send her a card. What about when Mike and Barbara finally take that world cruise, your neighbor's grandson has his Bar Mitzvah, the new gal in your bridge club gives birth to twins? You hurry down to the shop to find just the right card for each of them.

You've *bought* cards galore. But have you ever thought about *writing* them? Every day hundreds of thousands of greeting cards are flying through the mails, bringing wishes for happy anniversaries, happy birthdays, happy holidays—messages of sympathy and congratulations and love. The people who produce these cards are always on the lookout for new ways of expressing these thoughts, and they often pay well for ideas ($1 a word isn't uncommon). You don't have to be a seasoned writer to submit successfully. In fact, your greeting-card sales could well be the first writing sales you'll make.

My first sale to a greeting-card company was made in a roundabout way. It was the fourth piece I had ever submitted—a 120-line children's fantasy in rhymed verse. It had been rejected by all the children's book publishers I knew about in those days (four)—except one. I was getting tired of rejection. In desperation, I sent the piece to Hallmark Books.

A letter came back, not from the book division but from the writing manager (Hallmark's person in charge of greeting-card messages). The manager wanted to buy it for $100 for use in a large-size greeting card.

I had never considered the story as a greeting card because it not only wasn't the length the company customarily buys from freelancers, but didn't contain the kind of material the listings say they're looking for.

Two months later I sold another rhymed fantasy to them (Hallmark built a whole line of products—gift wrap, decorations, paper plates—around the story's central character, Barnaby Bunny, and the things that happened in the story), and a productive relationship with a series of assignments began.

Chances are that you will find it easier, and more fun, to craft certain kinds of greeting verse and product ideas. Due to the diversity of possibilities, you may have to experiment with several forms before you find your niche. The diversity makes it imperative that you study the markets thoroughly in order to make sales. Each greeting-card company differs from its competitors, both in the style of its product and the kind of material it needs. Don't depend on the sort of dumb luck I had.

MONITORING THE MARKETS

Before you send off a single line of sentiment, you should do some market research. Begin by studying the greeting-card company listings in *Writer's Market*. You might also send for *Artist's and Writer's Market List*, put out by the National Association of Greeting Card Publishers (600 Pennsylvania Avenue, Suite 300, Washington, D.C. 20003; include SASE).

Note each company that buys freelance material and send for their writers' guidelines. These guidelines list the company's current needs: birthday, anniversary, party invitations, thank you notes, and the like. They also state submission requirements, rate of pay, and taboos.

Without these guidelines, you will waste a good deal of time sending material to companies that don't want it and can't use it. For the sake of illustration, let's take the guidelines of two companies, Fran Mar Greeting Cards, Ltd., and Amberley Greeting Card Company.

Fran Mar's guidelines for contributors contain sketched examples of the kinds of material they're looking for. They want ideas for 4x6-inch novelty pads and 6x8-inch novelty stationery. Their guidelines also stipulate that invitations and thank-you-note ideas should contain the complete text on one side.

Amberley spells out its needs as follows: "Humorous cards with 'heavy punches.' Don't be subtle. That's not our market. There are four major categories that we need—birthday, friendship, get well and anniversary. We need ideas that are positive and don't 'put down' the recipient. The shorter the better. Risqué and non-risqué ideas accepted. Any new greeting card concepts or promotions."

That information is followed by an equally helpful list headed, "This is what we do not need":
1. Any seasonal cards (Christmas, Valentines, etc.)
2. Insulting cards
3. Odd category cards (Happy Birthday to my brother-in-law, etc.)
4. Poetry
5. Cards that require any type of attachment
6. Children's cards
7. Religious cards

Fran Mar's sketched illustrations provide the information you need for the form of your submissions. Amberley instructs contributors to type ideas on 3x5-inch cards with name and address on the back of each.

To submit to other companies pieces written according to the foregoing guidelines (they're all greeting card companies, aren't they?) would be tantamount to throwing your hard-crafted prose and poetry and your expensive SASEs into the garbage can.

Hallmark, for example, currently uses freelancers only for their Contemporary (studio) line of greeting cards. All their other writing needs are met by staffers. Likewise, while Amberley doesn't want seasonal cards, Red Farm Studios and lots of other companies do. They're looking for Easter, Mother's Day, Father's Day, and Valentine messages in addition to lines for most other holidays.

There are companies that buy writing only if accompanied by finished art. Others buy no messages at all—only ideas for greeting-card art or for related products such as plaques.

Greeting-card companies have a good idea of who their customers are and what they will buy. The profile of the typical Hallmark sender is that of a woman (about 90% of Hallmark's customers are female) 30 to 35 years old, upscale in income and education, and "more socially than intellectually oriented."

The cards put out by Panache-Papeterie Products are aimed at the sophisticated professional from 25 to 40. Good avant-garde poetry and haiku please the Panache-Papeterie people. Sugary, sentimental messages don't.

At different greeting-card houses certain phrases, subjects, and rhyme words are taboo. Some of these don'ts are spelled out in the guidelines. It's up to the writer to find out about the others.

My favorite taboo tale involves a Valentine's story in rhyme I submitted. It was purchased but sent back for revisions. The first two lines were:

Did you ever hear of the State of Dismay
Where people were gloomy and no one was gay?

The writing manager had circled gay and written in the margin, "We try to avoid use of this word whenever possible."

In another rhymed story I was asked to revise, a fat baker was one of the principal characters. The editor pointed out that many senders are overweight and sensitive about it, so references to obesity should be avoided.

This list, provided in Hallmark's guidelines, is typical of the dos and don'ts of many companies in the social expression industry:

1. **"Brevity is the soul of wit."** Eliminate all copy that has little or nothing to do with the greeting (the actual wish) or the gag (the humorous "twist" given to the greeting to make it funny).

2. **Pay close attention to the greeting.** Funny cards will not sell if there is no "sending situation." While there are exceptions, most successful cards must contain a wish or greeting of some kind for the recipient.

3. **Avoid slams.** Customers buy Contemporary Cards to make the recipient laugh—not to hurt his feelings. If the card does include a slam, it must be extremely funny to offset the handicap of the insult.

4. **Avoid obscene references.** We prefer to leave the vulgar and offensive card ideas to our competitors.

5. **Avoid ethnic and political references.** The purpose of greeting cards is to convey a message or wish, not to furnish editorial comment on subjects unrelated to our cards or insulting to ethnic or minority groups.

6. **Avoid archaic expressions.** Most Contemporary Cards derive their humor from current expressions, phrases, slogans, advertisements, etc. However, these expressions should be "household words" and familiar to all our customers.

7. **Be funny.** It takes a certain amount of experience to build humorous gags into sendable greeting-card situations. While many of our successful Contemporary Cards are cute or clever, most everyone likes to laugh, and, therefore, it would be best to concentrate on a humorous sending situation, for it stands the best chance of being accepted by us.

CASING THE COUNTERS

While those guidelines will serve you well when you're writing for most companies, they won't work for all of them. Take a look at the cards on the racks at liquor and adult book stores. You'll see that many of them are built around slams and obscene, ethnic, and religious references.

Which brings us to your next task if you want to become successful in the greeting-card field. Study the products.

Go to the stores that sell cards and spend time studying the various product lines. I've found that I feel much more comfortable casing the counters at card shops and drugstores than I do trying to read magazines at newsstands. After all, card department employees expect customers to browse. As long as your hands are clean and you don't mangle or mix up the cards, no one will raise an eyebrow.

You will find that your job is much easier if, after you read the writers' guidelines, you make lists, on separate sheets of paper, of what each company tells you it needs. Then you won't waste time poring over cards you have no chance of selling. Make some preliminary phone calls to determine what stores carry which brands. Granted, your market survey will take several hours. But when you begin to write, the results will reflect your knowledge of what is marketable. Every few months or so, do a bit of brush-up browsing to see if any new concepts—kinds of cards and related items—have been introduced.

Your research will show you there are three basic kinds of cards:

1. *Sentimental/conventional:* cute, formal or sentimental cards, usually verse or simple prose.
2. *Humorous:* calculated to produce snickers and guffaws. For instance, Hallmark put out a card shaped like a double-decker hamburger with all the trimmings. It says:
   (cover)
   "Wishing You a Birthday"
   (inside)
   "With Everything on it!
   Happy Birthday!"
   The card derives its humor from a cleverly stated message employing a sight gag. Other humorous cards depend for impact on funny illustrations—an ape dressed up like a judge, Miss Piggy in evening gown and furs—as well as their messages.
3. *Studio/contemporary:* snappy, upbeat gags, often irreverent (and always printed vertically on rectangular cards).

Although slams are to be avoided, clever put-downs that don't cause hurt feelings are the basis of many studio cards' humor. However, you'll rarely find a put-down in a humorous card. There are times when the same messages will work for both humorous and studio cards, but the visual treatment won't be the same. In addition to their differences as far as shape is concerned, humorous cards usually have "cutesy" illustrations: ears of corn with faces on them, dogs in detective gear, elephants walking tightropes. Studio card illustrations tend to be more sophisticated and/or zany: stick figures with big heads, unmanageable hair, and little bodies with weird expressions on their faces.

A fourth variety, the *personal expression* card, features a picture on front (sometimes with a short message) and a blank inside, leaving room for a tailor-made message from the sender.

You will also learn that there are three primary sending situations: *occasions, seasonals,* and *everydays.* The majority of cards that fall into each of these categories are of the following kinds:

Occasions

Birthday/Belated Birthday	Confirmation
Wedding Anniversary	Bar Mitzvah/Bat Mitzvah
Engagement	Congratulations to
Get Well/Convalescent	Expectant Mother
Bon Voyage	New Baby
Sympathy	Graduation
Congratulations	Retirement
First Communion	New Job

Seasonals

New Year's	Father's Day
Valentine's	Fourth of July
St. Patrick's	Halloween
Easter	Thanksgiving
Passover	Hanukkah
Mother's Day	Christmas

Everyday

Why Haven't You	Thank You
Written?	Missing You
Thinking of You	Goodbye

| Friendship | Sorry I Haven't |
| Thank You | Written |

You'll also notice that while a large number of cards are designed to be sent to people in general, there are cards for Grandpa, Grandma, Mom, Dad, Uncle, Aunt, Sister, Brother, Sister-in-Law, Brother-in-Law, Son, Daughter, Nephew, Niece, Grandson, Granddaughter, Godfather, Godson, Goddaughter, Special Friend, Secret Pal, Boss, Sweetheart, Husband, Wife, Neighbor, and others. In addition, some cards are meant to be sent by an individual, others by a couple and still others by a group of people. The possible combinations of occasions, seasonals, and everydays with their potential recipients as well as their senders yield hundreds of options for greeting-card writers.

MARKET RESEARCH TIPS

Even the more conservative companies are moving away from stereotypes and towards accommodating senders and buyers with nontraditional lifestyles, who may want an anniversary card for an unmarried couple living together or a birth announcement appropriate for a single mother to send.

As you browse, note the tones of various cards. Are they sophisticated, corny, sentimental, formal, quippy, cute? You'll realize after reading several sentiments that sincerity is an absolute necessity in all messages except those of studio and humorous cards.

Pay attention to how your targeted company handles punctuation. Hallmark is heavy on exclamation points, for example. Since the purpose of punctuation is to facilitate reading, you will want to use commas only when they're necessary and periods only to end complete thoughts unless the company you're trying to sell to does otherwise.

A Glossary of Greeting-Card Terms

The greeting-card industry has a lingo all its own, and you'd better know how to speak it. The following terms are a part of the greeting writer's basic vocabulary:

Mechanicals: cards with moving parts.

Pop-ups: cards with a form that protrudes from the inside of the card when the card is opened.

Cute: informal, gentle humor calculated to evoke a smile, not a belly laugh.

Juvenile: designed to be sent to children to the age of 10 or 12.
Sensitivity: sensitive, personal greetings.
Topical: based on a subject of current interest.
Punch-outs: with sections perforated so they can be easily removed, usually in juvenile cards.
Soft line: gentle me-to-you messages.
Visual gags: cards in which most, if not all, of the humor depends upon the illustration or illustrations.
Risque: a card that jokes about sex.
Inspirational: more poetic than conventional. Meant to inspire; can be religious or nonreligious.
Novelty: items sent on same occasions as greeting cards but not in standard card format.
Attachments: gimmicks, such as safety pins, bandaids, or miniature mirrors, attached to certain cards as part of the message.

MORE THAN JUST A PRETTY CARD
Your on-site research shouldn't stop at the greeting card displays. Almost every drugstore, five-and-dime, gift shop, card shop, department store, and discount center sells non-card products manufactured by the greeting-card companies. You'll find humorous buttons, calendars, bumper stickers, posters, coloring books, place mats, mottoes, and a host of other items whose ideas originated with freelancers.

You might have an idea for collapsible gift boxes shaped like Santas or birthday party decorations that can be dismantled to make take-home favors for the guests. Your brainstorm might involve inflatable beach pillows or book jackets with slogans on them, punch-out sticker books, decals, puzzles, or plaques.

To devise ideas and determine who will be likely to buy them, make separate lists of products sold by each company that makes greeting-related items. One list might look something like this:

balloons with short sayings
coffee mugs and cocktail napkins with quips
books of party games, entertaining tips, or things to make from used gift wrap
offbeat posters—heavy on supernatural themes
buttons with love-related messages
plastic cookie cutters
disposable bibs for birthday parties

sealing wax and unusual stamps
super-size jigsaw puzzles
kite kits
"get well" play packets for kiddies

Then take each item, devising slogans or concepts to fit in with existing product lines or using existing products as springboards for similar ideas. For instance, you might have some great ideas for outer-space cookie cutters or a travel-activity packet for children. In your craft experience, you may have originated lots of projects using empty plastic ribbon spools which could be the basis for a little book.

If you can come up with a new wrinkle, submit the idea, with examples, to each company in turn. But don't waste time approaching organizations whose only business is manufacturing cards.

TURNING ON THE IDEA MACHINE

When you have finished your research—and only then—you can start writing. But you can't start unless you have some ideas. Once you have them, don't let them get away. Write each on a 3x5-inch card.

Your idea producer should have begun perking back there at those greeting-card counters via the process of association. A message structured on baseball terms brings to mind other sport vocabularies; a verse about flowers should trigger thoughts of nature's other wonders.

Then there's the old reliable list-making device. Choose an occasion—say, Halloween—and write down all the words that come to mind: *ghosts, goblins, ghouls, apple cider, doughnuts, spooks, spirits, skeletons, haunted houses, witches, broomsticks, pointed hats, black cats, graveyards, jack-o-lanterns, pumpkins, cobwebs, Frankenstein, Dracula.* Concentrate on each of the words you have listed. Reverse stereotypes. Look at your subject from an out-of-the-ordinary perspective. Remember Caspar the Friendly Ghost? Your goblin could be a scaredy-cat. Have your witch streaking through the sky on a motorcycle (a Vrrrooooooom-stick, perhaps?). Dream up unlikely happenings: the Monster experimenting on Dr. Frankenstein; Count Dracula turning his castle into a Transylvanian real estate office specializing in the sale of haunted houses.

Attribute unusual properties to items: magic apple cider, a sad jack-o-lantern, cobwebs in the form of naked ladies. Don't worry if some of your ideas are pretty bizarre. Nothing stifles creativity like saying "dumb" to your imagination. When you have two or three good ideas, concentrate on messages to go with them.

Another method is to think about possible **plays on words.** The idea for this Buzza card is a simple one, hinging on two meanings of one word.

(cover)
We hope you're feeling better
We know you need the rest, it's true

(inside)
But all the rest of us need you!
Get well soon!

This card, put out by American, utilized the same method:

(cover)
I think of you a lot . . .

(inside)
Because I think a lot of you!

Second cousin to the play on words is **parody.** It's one of the devices greeting-card writers most often use—a play on words of a quotation, proverb, song or movie title, or well-known phrase. Take that common phrase, quotation, or whatever, and give it a new twist, as the writer of this Gibson card did:

(cover—illustration of a lion behind bars)
Caged up in the hospital?

(inside—illustration of lion with big R-R-R-R-R coming out of his mouth)
Hope you're soon well and roarin' to go!

Analogy—likening one thing to another ("You remind me of the Rock of Gibraltar"; "Friends are like flowers")—works well too. Another effective device is the *coining of words* ("supermama"; "swella-bration," for a great party; "pairents," for the mother and father of twins). However, it works only if the new words make sense.

Think of current fads, fashions, and fancies. Topical subjects are always potential hits. Two of the many cards that have emerged from the Pac-Man mania carry these messages (both are Hallmark Contemporary Cards):

(cover)
*I like two things in life—
being with you and
playing Pac-Man!*

(inside)
*Both give me
something to do
with my hands!*

(cover)
Birthdays are Like the Monsters in a Pac-Man Game!

(inside)
*They Keep Creeping Up on You!
Have a Happy Day!*

One of the most popular studio card formats is a question with appropriate illustration on the cover and a gag answer inside, such as this one produced by Gibson:

(cover)
*What Rhymes With Hex,
Starts with an S,
and is Needed Often by People
Your age . . .*

(inside)
*. . . Specs.
Happy Birthday.*

Others, like this Gibson card, have the first part of a gag on the cover and a punch line inside:

(cover)
We Were Made for Each Other . . .

(inside)
I've Got a Screw Loose And You're a Nut!

MOLDING THE MESSAGE

Greeting-card and product messages usually fall into one of three categories: one- or two-liners, rhymed verse, and prose.

One-liners have to be clever. They can't be obscure or ho-hum. It helps a great deal if you can supply ideas for art as well as copy.

The secret of short prose is knowing exactly what you want to communicate, then working over each word to be sure it's the most appropriate one you can possibly use.

Of course, in order to make sales you must have a fresh approach. Come up with new ways of saying "I love you" or "I care" and you'll be on your way to success. Remember that all cards must bear a me-to-you (or us-to-you) message: I like you, we miss you, I think you're a great mother, Your friendship really matters to me, We're glad you invited us to be your guests, I wish you joy, or the like. If you haven't got a greeting, you don't have a salable idea.

Your writing should have a conversational, easygoing tone. Messages should be simple and carry warmth and sincerity. Studio material must be snappy. Humorous and "cutesy" messages have to be funny.

Steer away from being too specific; for example, don't write messages aimed at a single occupational group. That limits the situation in which a card can be sent. Although personal pronouns also restrict sending situations, most companies produce cards to be sent by both individuals and couples, as well as a smaller number for group sending.

Rhymed verse (we will talk about foot and meter in the next chapter) must be in perfect rhythm and involve true rhyme—not rhymes like *presence/presents* or *sparkle/startle*.

Whenever you're rhyming, avoid (or use sparingly) words and phrases like *'tis, 'twas, o'er, e'er, ne'er, gladsome, true-blue, 'mid, 'neath, 'mongst, bliss, glee, natal day, wondrous, friend o'mine, mother mine,* and *wee one.* These terms are not in common use and sound affected and contrived.

Also stay away from inverted word orders. For instance, a cart-before-the-horse rhyme like this one is a no-no:

I'm plucking a wish from the wishing tree
And hoping your birthday will TREEmendous be.

If you fall into this trap, go back to the typewriter or hot tub or wher-

ever your creativity turns on and rework the verse until it doesn't
sound forced.

The rhyme pattern you will come across more than 90 percent of
the time is *a b c b* (second and fourth lines rhyming), as in this card
from Ambassador:

> (cover)
> *TWICE remembered*
> *your birthday date!*
>
> (first page)
> *Once . . . too early*
>
> (second page)
> *Once . . . too late.*
> *Hope It Was Happy!*

Less common forms are *aabb* (with first and second lines rhyming, as
do third and fourth), *abcdec* (third and sixth lines rhyming in six-line
verse), and *abcbdefe* (second and fourth lines rhyming, as do the
sixth and eighth).

As a general rule, the only time you will submit anything longer
than 16 lines (and some companies don't use messages that long) is
after you've established a firm relationship with a company. My experience in selling a 120-line piece of work as a first-time submission
was definitely a fluke.

SUBMISSION STIPULATIONS

Most greeting-card companies ask for submissions on 3x5-inch
cards. Some call for special formats for different cards, such as a
9x9^1/2-inch sheet of paper folded to the size of the traditional studio
card. Be sure to check your guidelines.

You are usually also required to type your name and address *on
each submission* (usually on the back). In most cases material should
be double-spaced.

Companies often ask that you assign a code number to each submission. I've found that my initials, followed by three numbers
(CE200, CE201, CE202, and so on) work well. Start with a different
century mark (200, 300, 400) when coding submissions to different
companies, or use different letters to start each sequence.

If no specific instructions are given, your submission cards should
look like this:

```
Name
Street Address
City, State, Zip
Phone Number


                        _____
                        _____
                        _____


```

Remember always to include an SASE accompanied by sufficient postage with every batch of submissions.

Although greeting companies ask that you send your submissions in batches, concentrate on quality rather than quantity. Send the number of items suggested (if no number is suggested, send at least five and not more than fifteen at one time), but don't include a couple of so-sos just to fulfill the numerical requirement. Don't send the envelope off until it contains only your best efforts.

You will want to keep copies of these submissions for your files, but getting the lines of type straight on one card is enough of a challenge without making carbons. Therefore, I type each message twice, once on the card and the second time on a piece of paper from 3x5-inch colored tablets. If you use different colors for different kinds of submissions—green for Christmas, pink for Valentine's, and so on—you will make your filing system more efficient. But if you're sending material to several companies, with several kinds of sentiments, you'll get snarled up in your own system unless you keep a master list of your color-code and number designations.

No matter how much you detest keeping records, some organizational scheme is necessary if you decide that writing for the greeting-card markets will be more than a sometimes thing. It's not hard to keep track of ten submissions, but hundreds of them make for confusion if they're not logically catalogued.

Your bookkeeping investment can be minor. You need only three recipe files (the dime store variety will work fine) and dividers. Try to find those with blank spaces rather than letters of the alphabet (or designations like breads, chafing dishes, and so on). If you can't, just turn the cards around and write on the side without printing (or use self-adhesive labels to cover the undesired categories).

In your first file you'll keep ideas, perhaps segregated according to various occasions and seasonal days: Congratulations, Bon Voyage, Valentine's, Easter, and so on. The second will contain your submission copies, and the third, copies of items that have sold. Note dates of sale and amounts of payment on the backs of these cards.

Considering the number of words you have to write, that pay is usually very high indeed. Hallmark pays $72 for each original Contemporary Card idea accepted. Amberley pays $40 for each idea it buys; Red Farm Studios, $3 per line for verse and $20 for verse/card illustration suggestions.

Most writers, unless they have established a big name for themselves, don't get by-lines. But the good ones do get a steady supply of checks. Besides, there's the thrill of standing at the greeting-card counter next to the lady who's reading your card—and laughing.

CHAPTER ELEVEN

DABBLING IN DOGGEREL (OR IT COULD BE VERSE)

If you want to be a poet,
You have to know the score;
It's true that meter matters,
But matter matters more.

Agnes W. Thomas,
Writer's Digest, July 1979

 am not a poet. Sonnets mystify me. I draw a blank when it comes to blank verse. My family laughed at my one attempt at haiku (and they weren't supposed to).

Life, however, has its compensations. Instead of the poet's sensitivity and soul, I got rhythm.

And as the song says, who could ask for anything more? Especially if you want to write light verse.

But why should you want to?

You won't have much chance of becoming immortalized like Keats if you write odes to salad bowls rather than Grecian urns. You will get those nifty little checks, though. Maybe ten cents a line, maybe a dollar.

Your poetically phrased thoughts on love and honor and bravery won't be memorized by eighth-grade English students. Instead, you'll have the satisfaction of knowing that somewhere, someone's day is a little brighter because you have a way with thoughts about carpools and microwaves and elevator operators. What's more, you don't have to suffer to write light verse. It's actually fun. Who knows? You might become the next Ogden Nash or Dorothy Parker.

Light verse doesn't sell like hotcakes. Although about one-third of the magazines listed in *Writer's Market* say they buy poetry, many of them aren't interested in this frivolous form. But when you do make a sale, you get paid money for it, which is more than can be said for payment in copies (the most common form of compensation for traditional poetry).

If you've followed the advice in Chapter 1 and cannibalized as many magazines as you can lay your hands on, you've probably accumulated a stack of these little verses, all marked with the magazine's name and other pertinent information. Among the better-paying markets are *Good Housekeeping* and the *Saturday Evening Post*. You will also discover bits of rhymed whimsey tucked into little spaces in magazines like *Women's Circle*, *Home Cooking*, *Capper's Weekly*, and *Grit*. Let's talk about writing them.

THE BEAT GOES ON

The cardinal rule in constructing light verse is that it must have perfect rhythm. In reality, however, editors do buy verses with imperfect rhythm. To increase your chances, whether you're submitting a couplet, a quatrain, or longer verse, you must arrange syllables and stresses with precision.

I realize some readers might prefer that I ease into the subject gently (or not at all), but rhythm is so essential to light verse that in my book (or at least in this chapter of it) the rules of construction get top billing.

Rhythm is the repetition of accented and unaccented syllables. A verse's rhythm is its **meter**. Each line of verse is made up of **feet** (beats). A line of four feet has four stressed (or accented) syllables, as illustrated by this piece from *Good Housekeeping's* "Light Housekeeping" department:

A Calculated Gain

Sometimes a slight discrepancy
Exists between the bank and me,
But the only difference that I savor
Is when it's five dollars in my favor!
—Muriel Lilker

In dashes and slashes, the poem looks like this:

— / — / — / — /
— / — / — / — /
— — / — / — / — /
— / — — / — / — /

Near-perfect rhythm comes into play here, since the last two lines aren't *exactly* on beat with the first two. What saves the rhythm is the fact that the number of stressed syllables, or feet, in each line is consistent.

There are four kinds of feet you will use in light verse: *iambic*, *trochaic*, *anapestic*, and *dactylic*. Using a / for accented syllables and — for those that are unaccented, the iambic line goes like this: — / — / — / — / (— / = one iambic foot). This first stanza from a poem by Freda Jacobs is written in iambic meter, the kind most often used in light verse. It appeared in *Capper's Weekly*.

Go Fly a Kite!

> Don't ask me, "Have you put on
>   weight?"
> (A question I most surely
>   hate!)

The trochaic foot is exactly the opposite as far as stressed syllables are concerned: / — / — / — / — (/ — = one trochaic foot). The first two lines of this piece, printed in the *Saturday Evening Post's* "Post Scripts," are trochaic; the last two, iambic.

Reflections

> Mirror, mirror, on the wall,
> You're not pleasing me at all;
> I know you cannot lie, forsooth,
> But can't you slightly bend the truth?
>   Nora B. Kathrins

An anapestic line goes — — / — — / — — / — — / (— — / = one anapestic foot; e.g., "Twas the *night* before *Christ*mas and *all* through the *house*"). Dactylic reverses the accent: / — — / — — / — — / — — (/ — — = one dactylic foot; e.g., "*One* for the *money* and *two* for the *show*").

As you've probably noticed, rhythm patterns in light verse aren't always in the classic forms. They may have more than the prescribed number of unaccented syllables. But the stressed syllables must fall on the right words to make the rhythm work.

When a line has three feet, it's called *trimeter*; four feet, *tetrameter*; five feet, *pentameter*.

The meter of verse is expressed by referring to the kind of foot and number of feet in a line. The most common forms of light verse are iambic trimeter, iambic tetrameter, and iambic pentameter—the — / foot with three, four, or five feet in a line.

There are several ways to test your rhythm. The first is to write it out in dashes and slashes. Another way is to say your rhyme aloud and see if your feet can dance a little jig to it. If you can't do a jig and are unsure whether the verse scans perfectly, have someone else read it to you.

The method that works best for me is to type the verse, using lowercase letters for the unaccented syllables and UPPERCASE for syllables that are accented, then read it aloud, stressing the uppercase syllables.

RHYME WITH REASON

Then there's the matter of rhyme—not to be confused with rhythm. Rhyme is produced by pairing up words with the same sounds and stresses on parallel syllables: *fate* and *weight*, *blizzard* and *wizard*, *vermouth* and *uncouth*. A rhyming directory is indispensible when the perfect rhyme doesn't pop into your head. (My favorite is *Whitfield's Rhyming Dictionary* [Thomas Y. Crowell Company, 1964].)

Rhyme words do not have to contain the same number of syllables, but their accented syllables must coincide. The rhyme words from this verse, which appeared in the *Saturday Evening Post*, work even though one word contains a single syllable and the other, two.

Sound of Music

Most folks don't really listen,
A trait we all condemn.
Yet people rarely interrupt
When someone's praising them.
—Evelyn Amuedo Wade

The rhyme pattern you'll most often find in light verse is *abcb*, second and fourth lines rhyming. Other common schemes are aabb (first and second lines rhyme, as do third and fourth) and *abab* (first and third, second and fourth).

Occasionally, you'll run across a rhyme scheme that departs from the standard form, such as in this poem from *Farm Wife News*:

Spring List

Grasses windswept, tulips starched √
New leaves waxed and buffed √
Orchards tie dyed √
Meadows mopped √
Fields all turned and fluffed √
Bird rehearsal, polished sky √
Clouds well aired and puffed √
—Jane Wilson

Not only is the form unusual (it's actually an *abcbdb* rhyme pattern, with what would traditionally be the third line split into lines three and four), but the author's imaginative way of looking at a common theme and the creative use of checkmarks at the end of each line make this piece special.

No discussion of rhyme would be complete without defining a few terms. *Masculine* rhyme involves rhyme words that end with stressed syllables. *Feminine* rhyme words end with unstressed syllables. Now that you've heard that, you can forget it.

Internal rhyme, on the other hand, is something you shouldn't forget. It's a great device: rhyming two or more words in the same line with each other. To remember how internal rhyme goes, think of "The rain in Spain falls mainly on the plain."

Mini-Glossary of Light Verse Terms

Masculine rhyme: rhyme words ending with stressed syllables.
Feminine rhyme: rhyme words ending with unstressed syllables.
Couplet: two successive lines rhyming with each other.
Quatrain: a stanza of four lines.
Meter: systematically arranged and measured rhythm in verse.
Foot: a metrical unit in verse.
Iambic, trochaic, anapestic, dactylic: the four basic kinds of feet.
Trimeter: a line with three feet.
Tetrameter: a line with four feet.
Pentameter: a line with five feet.
Rhyme scheme: the pattern lines of a poem follow in rhyming with each other.

When you're testing for rhythm and rhyme, be aware of differences in pronunciation. People in the South pronounce the word *suite* "suit" instead of "sweet," so rhyming suite with neat wouldn't work for them. Words like *tomato*, *aunt*, and *fragile* fall into this category. Other words vary in pronunciation according to accented syllables: *Caribbean*, *Caribbean*, for example.

The more good light verse you read, the better you'll become at crafting it. Study the rhymes of Ogden Nash, Richard Armour and Dorothy Parker. Reading well-written song lyrics will develop your sense of rhythm. The two books of lyrics I read time and again (they're in the stacks of most fairly large libraries) are those of Cole Porter and Lorenz Hart. Hart, especially, was a master of internal rhyme.

MATTER MATTERS

To get the light verse idea-machine running, prime it by making lists. Give them headings like "goof-ups," "problems," and "pet peeves"—for light verse is spun around commonplace, everyday themes to which any reader can relate. Witness the following, the first of which appeared in the *Post* and the second in *Modern Maturity:*

Taxing Malady

Of all the causes of strain and stress,
Heading the list is the IRS.
                                                —Frank Tyger

Writing Without Readers

No man can count the cost
Of all the time that has been lost
Forfeiting fruits of more
    useful deeds,
Filling out forms that nobody reads.
                                                —Frank Goodwyn

As you can see from these examples, the secret of light verse is saying something people have heard or thought about hundreds of times, but phrasing it in a clever, fresh way.

With targeted marketing, you can use this commonality to hit smaller groups of the population who read specialized magazines: golfers, organic gardeners, veterinarians, beekeepers, geologists, and so on. But when you're aiming at general interest magazines, you'll be more successful sticking to everyman experiences.

If your life is anything like mine, your lists will look something like these:

Goof-Ups

Missed appointments
Mail-order merchandise mix-ups
Errors in credit card/bank statement billings
Wrong-number phone calls
Brushing teeth with shaving cream; spraying hair with room
  freshener

Problems

Household appliance or office equipment breakdowns
Overweight/diets
Company that overstays
Neighbors' bumper crop of dandelions
Housecleaning
Running out of milk, butter, eggs

Pet Peeves

Getting into the slowest line at the market, bank, post office
Overabundance of singing commercials on radio, TV
Being put on hold by a receptionist, then cut off
Unsynchronized traffic lights
Products that don't give their money's worth

All of the troubles and grumbles I've listed are common to almost everyone, and any one of them can provide the basis for several rhymes. Take the following, which appeared in the *Saturday Evening Post*. Its author took one example (and there have to be hundreds) of the last pet peeve on the list and wove it into a six-line sale.

> *Sheer Disaster*
> I paid through the nose
> For the best pantyhose,
> In a creamy shade of honey.
> What I wanted to get
> Were the nicest legs yet;
> What I got was a run for my money.
> —Jill H. Walker

You can also compile lists of general topics: babies, children, personal appearance, nature, inanimate objects. The more common a subject is to everyone's experience, the broader its appeal will be to the editors.

After you've listed your general topics, expand on each of them with specific themes or situations around which you might fashion verses. For instance, some of your themes/situations for babies might be:

1. Always seem to wet right after you've changed their diapers.
2. Make dignified grandfathers into baby talkers.
3. Cry at the most inopportune moments.
4. Force smiles from frowning shoppers.
5. Act like little dictators.
6. Have to be the sweetest things in the world.

After you have your idea, it's time to begin putting your verse in shape. As in anecdotes, you want a punch line that will surprise the reader. Effective devices are puns, parody, or rearranged clichés.

The easiest way I've found to write light verse is the "bottoms-up" method. Get your last line first and work from there. After you've thought of the punch line, write down associated words or phrases.

For example, while at the dinner table one hot July night, the phrase "waiting for chips that never come in" streaked through my head. I got up from the macaroni salad and cold cuts and wrote the phrase down (though I do carry a notepad with me, I draw the line at bringing it to the table).

Later, while scraping plates, I started playing with the idea. Since we live in Reno, my first association was with gambling. I also came up with potato, wood, and computer chips. Next, I thought of rhyme words. *Win* was one that could be used for a gambling theme. *Chagrin* would go well with computers. Plates scraped, I tucked everything into my subconscious.

The following morning, I decided to concentrate on the computer theme, since that subject would have a more universal appeal. Markets for the gambling verse would be limited. Then I wrote down words and phrases associated with computers: *software, technology, marvel, information retrieval, malfunction, program,* and so on.

Later that day—again while I was doing a task unrelated to writing—the verse started taking form. It would be in dactylic feet, since "waiting for chips that never come in" scans that way, with a slight variation in the midsection. Content would focus on computer breakdown, and I would use *chagrin* as the rhyme word in an *abcb* pattern. After a half hour of conscious effort and a few more hours of subconscious simmering, this is what evolved. You'll notice that the meter isn't perfect—anapestic trimeter for the first three lines with imperfect anapests in the fourth—but the rhythm works.

> *Technology Gap*
> My computer is in the repair shop,
> I've waited for months with chagrin;
> It seems *their* computer's malfunctioned,
> So I'm waiting for chips that might never come in.

CHRISTENING YOUR CREATION

What you call your verse can be just as important as the lines that follow the title. "For the Birds" is a great name for this piece, sold to *Good Housekeeping:*

> My feeder is loaded with sparrows,
> And starlings in droves get the word . . .
> But if I'm going to be a bird fancier,
> I'd fancy a fancier bird!
>
> —Jeanne Westerdale

I especially like the play on words in the title of this verse, which *True Confessions* bought:

> *The Yolk's on Me*
>
> "Good," say I, "the sun is out,
> Our picnic won't be spoiled."
> Until—with a hearty crack—I find:
> The eggs I packed weren't boiled!
>
> —Jill Williams

Though the rhythm pattern in the following light verse, which appeared in *Modern Bride,* is a bit shaky in the last two lines, it's easy to see why the editor found it irresistible. The content fulfills the universal experience requirement, and the subject matter is suitable for the publication. But to my mind, it's the title that clinched the sale:

Home on the Range

Among my many hurdles
Are these: my gravy curdles,
My hollandaise has no éclat,
My cheese soufflés are pancake
  flat,
My vegetables look put upon,
My frosting seems more off than
  on,
My salad sags, my roast's
  defiled . . .
But, better than a Julia Child
Beside me, is my darling groom
Who's sizing up in the kitchen
  gloom
Takes noble charge . . . my love,
  my sweet breadwinner . . .
With "Get your coat, we're
  going OUT to dinner!"
                    —Maureen Cannon

The same devices that work for punch lines, two words that
rhyme with each other, short quotations, and names of well-known
songs, books, and movies make good title material.

FORM-FITTING YOUR VERSE
When your verse is as near to perfection as you can make it—
when you're sure it will wow the editor—type it in traditional verse
form. As for punctuation, use it sparingly: commas when you must,
semicolons or colons only when absolutely necessary, and periods
only to end a complete thought. Remember that light verse is a casual form, best if it flows easily off the eye. Unnecessary punctuation
marks are visual impediments.

Once in a while you will find light verse in prose format, like the
following pieces, published in *Sunshine:*

*Hats Are Back and Guess Who
Hasn't Got One?*

I'm gauche in a cloche and any-

thing else designed to adorn
my head. While I simply adore a fe-
dora on you, it makes me look
quite dead.

I'm not at all svelte in a felt or a
straw, whether pillbox or derby or
fez, though my hat's off to those
who care about clothes from their
toes to the tips of their heads.

As for me I'll stay free of bur-
dens on high. My brain has
enough of a load. Bare heads may
be old hat, but why should I care if
I'm not à la mode?

—Pat Myren

Horoscope Hangup

Did you ever notice Fate's peculiar ways, in that many famous
men were born on holidays?

—Ruth M. Walsh

If you wish to submit to a market that uses this form, type your
piece as traditional verse first to be sure your meter is perfect. Then
transfer it to prose with the appropriate punctuation.

After you've typed your light verse neatly, all that remains is to
pop it into an envelope with your SASE, making sure that the envelope is addressed to the right editor. Though many light verses
could fit into any number of publications, it's important to match
tone, subject, and length to the magazine.

You'll see, after reading various magazines, that while most editors go for the carefree, flip verse we've been talking about, others
define light verse as traditional rhymed poetry with a light subject.
For example, this piece, printed in *Grit*—and considered light verse
by its editors—is different in tone from that printed in *Good Housekeeping:*

Pin-up Girl

My favorite pin-up girl

Has all the others beat
She's loveliest by far
From head down to her feet.

There's dimples, oh, so deep
In cheeks of rosy hue
Ne'er hidden is the gleam
In her eyes of azure blue.

Her curls are golden strands
And you should see her clothes—
A diaper and two pins—
Oh, camera catch that pose!
—Vivian L. Hall

You'll find definite editorial preferences for subjects, too, if you read several back issues on your target publications. Retirement magazines like verse that centers on universal situations or treats growing older with a light touch. Light verse in men's magazines deal with stereotypically masculine subjects.

You are on the right track if you send a clever food-oriented submission to *Gourmet* only if it is the right length. Although most editors go for two, four, or at the most twelve lines, the editors at *Gourmet* and a few other publications like poems to be much longer. This piece illustrates both the length and the strong gastronomic tie-in a piece must have in order to make it with *Gourmet*'s editors:

A Memo to the Chef
of the United Nations
Cafeteria

The Italians eat plates of spaghetti,
And the French like their fours to be petits.
Now, the couscous is meant for the Arabs,
But the Chinese eat fried rice and sparabs.

For the Greeks, there is tasty souvlakia,
Japanese like a cup of hot sakia.
If the Russians have borscht they're not fussy,
And the Polish just want their kielbussy.

For Americans, steak is ambrosia
While a shashlik for Czechs make life rosia.
For the Spanish, whip up some paella,
Make some waffles for Belgians, I tellya.

Mamaliga for those from Romania,
And some cheese for the Swiss wouldn't strainia.
Don't forget the Hungarian goulash,
If you've no Irish stew, then you're foolash.

The Israelis, if kosher, shun bacon
(Served to Moslems, it's also mistaken).
And roast beef is saved for the British,
While the halvah is Turkish, not Yiddish.

If you keep all this straight in your head,
The ambassadors all will be fed.
They'll have food that to them isn't crummy,
And at least we'll have peace of the tummy.
                                    —Dan Carlinsky

The snippets of time you spend writing light verse can provide you with both profit and pleasure. U.S. Representative Mickey Edwards (R-Okla.) is quoted as saying, "The biggest thrill of my life was . . . not getting elected to this office . . . [but] when I had a poem published."

Reading those magic words, "Pay to the order of," on the first check for your little poems may not be the highlight of *your* life, but it's bound to be a day brightener.

CHAPTER TWELVE

BRAIN TEASERS

I've always said that you can't worry about your bills when you're worrying about 7-Down.

Margaret Farrar

People have been fascinated by puzzles for hundreds of years. Anagrams (from the Greek *ana*, backward, and *gramma*, writing) evolved as a form of entertainment in the third century A.D. The 119th psalm is written in an early acrostic form.

It wasn't until the early twentieth century that the crossword was invented. But they caught on quickly, and countless puzzle fans became addicted. During World War II, the Germans bombarded England with leaflets that included crosswords using propaganda definitions.

Even the advent of video games hasn't made a dent in the puzzle phenomenon. In fact, they seem to be more popular than ever—witness the amount of space bookstores devote to puzzle books. Newspapers wouldn't be the same without their daily crosswords. (The story is that songwriter Jerome Kern frequently phoned the *New York World* office for a crossword solution that was keeping him from his work). Hundreds of magazines have a puzzle of some kind in every issue.

All of this means that when you get tired of writing and want to flex your brain in a different dimension, there are scads of puzzle markets waiting out there.

THE FIRST PIECE OF THE PUZZLE

The solution to the puzzling problem of where to submit your brain benders lies in the pages of these hundreds of magazines. Editors are as consistent in their puzzle choices as they are regarding editorial content. The magazine chief who has run crosswords (or word finds or word jumbles) in the past twenty-four issues is pretty sure to keep buying them. An editor whose monthly puzzle page is a mixed bag of visual mind stretchers will be looking for original ideas in the same vein.

Magazines devoted strictly to games and puzzles comprise the biggest market. Most of them come out every month and contain twenty or more puzzles in each issue. You won't get a by-line in some of them, but there's the chance that your puzzles will also be used in books put out by the same companies that publish the magazines, and that means extra money.

As a group, airline in-flights use puzzles more often than any other category of magazines except those devoted exclusively to them. But don't send puzzles off to any of the in-flights until you have checked to see exactly what kinds they use.

That advice also goes for any of the other markets: both general interest magazines and specialized publications. Your choice of markets will depend largely on the kinds of puzzles you enjoy making and find easiest to construct.

FITTING IN THE OTHER PIECES

The easiest puzzle for most people to put together is the *word find* (sometimes called "find-the-words" or "word search"). As the name implies, they're squares or rectangles filled with letters, among which are hidden words, generally focusing on a single theme. Here's what you have to do to make them:

1. *Count the number of letters both across and down* in word finds the magazine has previously published (15 or 16 both across and down is most common, but you will occasionally find formats using as many as 25 each way).

2. *Count the number of words to be found in these same puzzles.* I've seen lists of anywhere from 40 to 156 of them in various publications.

3. *Decide on a theme that is compatible* with those used by the magazine in the past (e.g., railroad-related terms for *Model Railroader*).

Choosing the theme is easiest if you use the process of association. Let's take *Modern Maturity* as an example. The magazine publishes a word find in each issue. Themes run the gamut from names of inventors to terms relating to forms of water to words that date back to the days of knighthood. One puzzle centered on famous painters; another, scenic attractions in the United States and Canada.

Each of these themes offers the base from which the associative process can take off to provide scores of new ideas. The following are only a few ideas triggered by the scenic attractions puzzle:

Scenic Wonders of the Far East
Historic Spots of Europe
Nature's Attractions in South America
Seaports of the World
Capitals of the World
Namesake Cities

4. *When you have settled on a theme, start listing related terms, names and the like*, using reference books as your sources: basic chemistry, biology, and other texts; an atlas; guidebooks. It's frequently possible to get all the words than you need from a book's index. Write down at least ten more words you will need to use. You can determine the mix of common and obscure words by studying previously published puzzles in your targeted magazine.

5. *Using graph paper (four or five squares to the inch are easy to work with)*, draw lines enclosing the appropriate number of squares (each square will represent one letter).

6. *With pencil, lightly write in the words you have chosen*, forward, backward, up, down and diagonally. This part of the project may require some juggling, but since it is possible to use common letters in words that intersect each other, you shouldn't have too much trouble fitting them all in. Your extra words will come in handy here, since they can be substituted for those that don't fit.

7. *Encircle all the words with lines* in the same manner as on the answer pages of the publication. Copy the puzzle neatly on another sheet of graph paper and label it "Answers to [title of puzzle] Word Find."

8. *On your original puzzle, fill in the blank squares* with any letters you choose. Again, study previously published puzzles to see if you've made yours difficult enough. The letters you fill in (making unrelated words with letters similar to those on the list, or using the same letters that are used in the words), add difficulty. Then copy it neatly and below it list the words that are to be found.

SOLVING THE CROSSWORD PUZZLE PUZZLE

Although crosswords are a bit more difficult to create, they're the most popular puzzle, and therefore you may find it worth your time to master the skill. As with other fillers, the easiest markets to sell are low-profile, specialized magazines that don't receive a large number of submissions.

The tools of your crossword-making trade will be graph paper (four squares to the inch), a crossword dictionary, a regular dictionary, a book that lists words in easy-to-find order (such as *Instant Word Finder*), and a selection of crossword puzzle magazines. Use the puzzles in these magazines to build your own grids. It's perfectly permissible to copy these grids, but be sure you choose only those patterns with symmetrical designs. A symmetrical design is one in which the juxtaposition of white and black squares results in one of the following: the left and right halves of the grid are the same as (or mirror) each other; the bottom is the same as (or the exact reverse of) the top; one-half of the diagram, cut diagonally, mirrors the other.

Also be sure that the pattern you choose contains the same number of squares as the crosswords in your intended publication. Although 15 by 15 and 16 by 16 are the most common sizes for both magazine and newspaper puzzles, you'll find others as well. Books and Sunday supplements may use a larger format. The world's largest published crossword, by the way, was constructed by Robert M. Stilgenbauer of Los Angeles over an eleven-year period and contained 3,185 clues across and 3,149 clues down.

Basic crossword construction rules stipulate that no more than one-sixth of the squares should be black and that there should be an overall interlock of words with no cutoff segments or unkeyed letters. There should be no isolated white boxes (except in children's puzzles; see Chapter 17).

According to William J. Sunners, who is considered one of the two foremost crossword makers in America (the other is Margaret Farrar), the accepted ratios of white to black squares (called *outs*) are the following:

Size of Puzzle	Outs	Size of Puzzle	Outs
11 x 11 squares	20	19 x 19	60
13 x 13	28	21 x 21	74
15 x 15	36	23 x 23	88
17 x 17	49	25 x 25	104

Most editors, for some reason, prefer an odd number of squares. The majority of them won't buy puzzles that contain more than four two-letter words (some markets won't buy crosswords containing any).

After you have copied your design onto graph paper, legibly number the white squares in their upper left-hand corners to correspond with those of your pattern. Remember that only those squares containing the first letter of a word are numbered. Sunner's book, *How to Make and Sell Original Crosswords and Other Puzzles* (Sterling Publishing Co., Inc., 1981) is a marvelous reference for numbering as well as other procedures involved in puzzle making.

Although you will find general interest crosswords in a number of magazines, many crosswords are keyed to a specialized audience, like the one from *Cruise Travel* on page 165.

Your first job, therefore, will usually be to think of a theme that is appropriate to the readers of your target publication. The best place to start looking for themes is in the library's reference section. Seek out trivia and terminology in baseball, movies, science, business, mythology, Egyptian art, radio programs of the 1930s, plants, and animals. You'll find ideas falling off the shelves.

Next, compile a list of words keyed to your theme. Try to think of at least a hundred, though you may not use them all. For example, if your theme is French cooking, you'll use words like *brie*, *ragout*, *truffles*, *pâte*, *cassoulet*, *bouillabaisse*, *genoise*, *crème*, and lots of others you can find quickly in the index to a French cookbook. You'll also want a crossword dictionary for reference.

Experts advise that you begin by filling in the answers and then make up the questions. Starting with questions first will leave you with a jumble of impossible-to-complete constructions. Will Weng, the former crossword puzzle editor of the *New York Times*, advises "Do the longer *across* words first," and all master puzzle makers agree that you should start from the middle and work out.

The ten letters used most often in the English language are (from most to least) E, T, A, O, I, N, S, H, R and D. If you use words containing these letters, your work will go more smoothly. Those ten also serve well as beginning letters of words. Avoid words that contain more than two vowels or three consonants in a row.

After you've filled in all your answers and numbered the squares consecutively, going from left to right on each line, it's time to compose the *across* and *down* questions, keying them to the numbered

Cruise Crossword

by Jack Luzzatto

Nearly every word has to do with cruise ships, ports-of-call and the bargains they bring, plus the whole wide geographic world of travel. Try your hand—we think you'll find these crosswords a unique fun way to increase your travel knowledge.

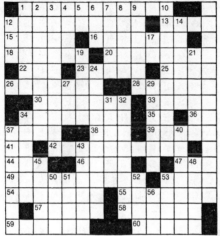

Across

1. Eastern cruise liner to Nassau
12. Island named by Columbus in 1493
13. Israeli circle dance
15. Scottish isle
16. Cheese to enjoy in Britain
18. Anglers
20. Least hazy
22. Camera memento (slang)
23. Theater guide
25. Charles Lamb's pen name
26. Italians call it Livorno
28. Sandwich meat
30. Coral-colored beach (2 wds.)
33. Refasten
34. Famous old guidebook
35. State prosecutor (abbr.)
36. While
37. Game fish
38. Little _____, girl in "Uncle Tom"
39. Great occasion on board
41. Carson sidekick (init.)
42. Moonlighting benefit (2 wds.)
44. Capitals of Texas, Idaho and Indiana (1st letters)
46. Verdi opera
47. Outgoing tide
49. Shared room
53. Unlucky son of Adam
54. Road hazard needing repair
55. A ships' cost (2 wds.)
57. More mature and sweeter
58. Blue color
59. Machined
60. Earl or baron

Down

1. Overseas Continent
2. Former Empress of Canada, Carnival Line's ship
3. Tasty export from Holland (2 wds.)
4. Glass designer Monsieur Lalique
5. Capitals are Montgomery and Baton Rouge (1st letters)
6. _____ Angeles
7. Hollanders
8. Pier's supporting timber
9. Snake-like fish catchers
10. Time for fun off the ship (2 wds.)
11. Where the VIP cruise guests eat (2 wds.)
12. Spear-nosed fish
14. Once around the deck or track (2 wds.)
17. Capitals of Florida and Maryland (1st letters)
19. Hospital member
21. Monkey
24. Idaho's great waterway (2 wds.)
27. Peculiar
29. Warmly romantic
31. State that shares Lake Tahoe
32. Vivid
34. Chinas' former "curtain"!
37. Boston cooking utensil
40. Look over closely
43. Followed car ahead
45. Introduction, for short
48. Actress Davis
50. Yankee broadcaster Rizzuto
51. Sheet, on a sailboat
52. English school
53. Saudi native
56. Capitals of Illinois, North Dakota and Washington (1st letters)

Solution to Cruise Crossword

boxes where each word begins. The definitions should be as terse as you can make them. Your crossword (or regular) dictionary will help you construct them. Don't make your definitions any harder than those used in crosswords previously published by the magazine. Likewise, follow those guidelines as to the mix of easy and difficult questions.

DOUBLE-ACROSTICS

Double-acrostics are easier to work than crosswords but among the more difficult puzzles to create. They consist of clues, with each letter in the answer assigned a number. These numbers correspond to those on a crossword-type grid into which the appropriate letters are written when an answer is deduced. The words formed by the letters in the diagram make up a quotation or message.

The first order of business in designing a double-acrostic is to choose your quote and make a crossword diagram to fit it (it's permissible for words to continue onto the following line). Number the letters consecutively. Next, count how many of each letter are in the message. If you have anagram or Scrabble tiles, your next task—forming words using all of the letters in the quote—will be much easier. If you don't have tiles, write letters on pieces of cardboard. Take these tiles (or pieces of cardboard) and maneuver them until you have formed other words and have no tiles left. Start by making words with the least commonly used of your letters: *z, x, v,* and *y.* Quotes with a good number of vowels in the words are easier to manipulate than those loaded with consonants. Here's an abbreviated example:

Quote: All's fair in love and war.
Words made from quote letters:
Evil
Now
Darn
Fala
Liars

Compose definitions for each of the words. Number each answer letter to correspond with its counterpart in the diagram and mark the diagram with the letters preceding the definitions/answers (A, B, C, D, and so on). This "Double Cross" from *Games* is presented in the classic double-acrostic format.

UNSCRAMBLING THE SCRAMBLES
Word scrambles are the simplest form of anagram. They're groups of letters that spell words relating to a theme. You'll most often find them in children's magazines (see Chapter 17), but editors of adult publications also use them occasionally.

A variation of the word scramble consists of short phrases whose letters can be transformed into words and other phrases. This puzzle from *Dell Pencil Puzzles and Word Games* is typical of the type:

Scrambled Places

There may be more sense to the phrases listed below than you think; each of the ten is the scrambled name of a place in California. All you have to do is rearrange (anagram) the letters in each of the phrases to find each one. Use each letter one time only.

1. Man To Scare
2. As Long Eels
3. Do Holy Low
4. As Con In Scarf
5. O.K., Lana D

6. Gain Does
7. A Sand Pea
8. Vetoes Red Jam
9. A River and Sea
10. A Livery Palm Lei

Double Cross by Michael Ashley

Answer the clues for words to be entered on the numbered dashes. Then transfer the letters on the dashes to the correspondingly numbered squares in the puzzle grid to spell a quotation reading from left to right. Black squares separate words in the quotation. Work back and forth between grid and word list to complete the puzzle. When you are done, the initial letters of the words in the word list will spell the name of the author and the source of the quotation.

■	1P	2A	3H	■	4E	5Q	6H	7F	8L	9S	10B	11M	12R	13I	14D	15U	16C	■	17Q	18E	19L	■	20J	21H
22W	23C	24T	25F	26M	27I	28O	29D	30S	31A	32R	33G	■	34P	35N	36F	37S	38H	39D	40G	■	41U	42O	43E	44H
45K	46C	47M	48G	49A	■	50D	51K	52C	53V	■	54M	55T	56E	■	57L	58J	59F	60Q	61U	62D	■	63L	64G	■
65Q	66W	67E	■	68B	69I	70P	71J	72G	73W	74K	75R	■	76D	77U	78T	79S	80I	81O	82H	■	83I	84W	■	85C
86N	87J	■	88L	89I	90T	■	91W	92T	■	93A	94Q	95F	96N	97G	98L	■	99G	100V	101R	■	102U	103W	104A	105E
106L	107S	108K	109C	110V	■	111O	112U	113M	114D	■	115P	116G	117T	118S	119Q	120M	121O	122F	■	123U	124T	125L	126S	127I
128A	129E	130W	131M	■	132G	133C	134E	135Q	■	136H	137Q	138F	■	139V	140L	141R	142D	143N	■	144N	145W	146O	147D	■
148R	149I	■	150R	151J	152H	■	153P	154D	155O	156K	157V	158B	■	159B	160I	■	161P	162L	■	163U	164K	165C	166S	■
167K	168L	169S	170Q	171C	■	172T	173I	174M	■	175K	176M	■	177I	178G	179E	■	180I	181K	182D	183N	■	184S	185U	186D
187P	188K	189T	190R	191Q	192E	193O	194D	■	195M	196K	■	197T	198Q	199P	200S	201G	■	202G	203J	204N	205R	206F	■	

A. Storage loft in a barn

2 31 49 93 104 128

B. Latvian native

10 158 68 159

C. Without an equal (or a light?)

85 23 165 171 133 109 52 46 16

D. Compiler of reference works

142 186 182 114 29 39 50 76 62
194 154 14 147

E. Embroidery on canvas

192 67 56 43 105 134 4 197 129 18 179

F. Movable properties, in law

7 25 36 59 95 122 138 206

G. Awkward situation (3 wds.)

72 40 132 201 48 97 178 64 202 116 33 99

H. Monocle

3 6 21 38 44 136 82 152

I. Food, sustenance

173 160 89 127 13 27 69 180 80 177 149

J. Tomorrow (Sp.)

20 58 71 203 87 151

K. By instinct

164 74 156 181 175 108 188 51 45 167 196

L. Area around one's home

57 106 83 140 8 88 168 98 125 162 63 19

M. Places where some mollusks are raised (2 wds.)

11 26 47 54 113 120 195 131 174 176

N. Toothed mechanism

35 86 96 204 183 143 144

O. Lacking the will?

28 42 65 121 81 111 146 155 193

P. Spun, as one's thumbs

1 34 70 115 161 153 199 187

Q. Tito's land

135 60 119 191 5 137 94 198 170 17

R. Conservative, reactionary (hyph.)

141 148 12 150 205 101 190 32 75

S. Trespassing, intruding

126 107 184 200 9 118 79 166 30 37 169

T. Copy of a document

24 55 78 90 92 117 124 172 189

U. Stage a *coup d'etat*

123 102 41 61 15 112 77 185 163

V. The R in RAF

53 100 110 139 157

W. Rather slender

22 66 73 84 91 103 130 145

Double Cross

A. Haymow; B. Lett; C. Matchless; D. Encyclopedist; E. Needle-point; F. Chattels; G. Kettle of Fish; H. Eyeglass; I. Nourishment; J. Manana; K. Intuitively; L. Neighborhood; M. Oyster Beds; N. Ratchet; O. Interstate; P. Twiddled; Q. Yugoslavia; R. Right-Wing; S. Encroaching; T. Photostat; U. Overthrow; V. Royal; W. Thinnish.

Scrambled Places

1. Sacramento; 2. Los Angeles; 3. Hollywood; 4. San Francisco; 5. Oakland; 6. San Diego; 7. Pasadena; 8. Mojave Desert; 9. Sierra Nevada; 10. Imperial Valley.

In constructing these anagrams, the first step is to settle on a theme, using the same idea sources as for word finds. Then draw up a list of answers, such as the place names, and work backward to make up the scrambles. In the single-word scrambles, that's a cinch—just mix up the letters. Phrase scrambles take more doing, but since the phrases don't have to make a lot of sense, it's not as hard as you may think.

There are many other kinds of puzzles: anagrams that rearrange actual words to form others (*sate, teas, eats, seat, east; pale, peal, plea, leap; patcher, chapter, repatch; design, deigns, signed*) and puzzles that combine letters and mathematics (cryptographs and the like). To structure these brainteasers, examine previously published examples for patterns and use the answers-first method.

Although many editors are looking for the same kinds of puzzles they have used in the past, heads of the magazines devoted to puzzles don't necessarily buy the types you see in their publications from freelancers. Rosalind Moore, editor of *Dell Pencil Puzzles and Word Games*, advises contributors not to submit any kinds of puzzles that appear regularly. These are done by a stable of puzzle makers who have been groomed by the Dell people over the years. Instead, she suggests that they send in "anything we're not already using." She adds that "some people have built-in editorial judgment and by reading back issues can get a feel for what we like. We pay a great deal of attention to over-the-transom submissions as we're always looking for new ideas." Dell puts out dozens of puzzle publications—92 in 1983.

At *Games* (among the highest-paying puzzle markets at from $75 to $120 a page), Senior Editor Will Shortz is looking for the standard kinds of puzzles as well as any others that are visually interesting, humorous, or novel. Shortz maintains that many puzzle makers fail because "they get so wrapped up in making the puzzle that they don't look at it from the solver's point of view." When promising submissions arrive at *Games* (they receive about a hundred per week), the staff tries to solve them and chooses those that are interesting and amusing.

WHAT DO YOU KNOW?

It is estimated that 50 million Americans pore over puzzles now and then. I'd hazard a guess that just as many people are hooked on quizzes. Though most of us groaned when mini-tests were announced in school, we can't resist grabbing the nearest ballpoint when we come upon them in magazines.

There are two basic kinds of quizzes: those that test the reader's knowledge and those aimed at giving the reader greater personal insight. The first category can be built around a virtually limitless number of topics, from foreign phrases to the patron saints of various cities and countries. Through quizzes of the "know thyself" variety, readers can find out if they're too trusting, where their stress areas lie, or whether they are compatible with their mates.

Salable quizzes must meet the following requirements:

1. *The questions must be clear and concise.* Make each word convey exactly the meaning intended. "Do you eat a lot?" is neither clear nor concise. It's not clear if the question refers to the amount one eats during a specific period of time or if one eats frequently. It is not concise, since the definition of "a lot" hasn't been established either in terms of frequency or amount.

2. *The theme must play on the reader's curiosity.* Your theme must be one that people find challenging. They have to be curious about the subject itself or how well their knowledge about it measures up. Rosalind Moore says that the kinds of quizzes she is looking for at Dell fall into two categories: the "see how smart you are" and the "you should know the answers." In the latter case, "the answers are in the back of your mind, but you don't really remember them," Moore says, "and you're dying to know the answers so you turn to where they are in the back of the book."

3. *The subject must appeal to a wide range of readers.* The quiz can't succeed if it interests only a small segment of the magazine's total readership. The subject has to be one to which most readers are able to relate.

4. *The theme must fit the publication's personality.* Write quizzes on boat safety for boating publications, on famous gunfights for Western magazines, on flowers in history for gardening magazines.

5. *The quiz must have a game quality,* i.e., be more like play than work, be fun and/or interesting. If your quiz resembles the final exam for Biology I, it will flunk in salability. Use the light touch. Try to inject a bit of humor, an element of intrigue, a dash of excitement.

6. *It must fit the reader's skill levels.* As a general rule, the larger a magazine's circulation, the lower the educational level of the average reader. The best way to zero in on these ability/knowledge levels, as well as the reader's interests, is to read the magazine. Only a small percentage of those who buy *Reader's Digest* are political science or math majors, so quizzes based on landmark Supreme Court decisions or mathematical equations just aren't going to make it. They would be not only too specialized, but also too difficult for most readers to complete with even a small measure of success. When writing anything for most big-circulation magazines, you should aim at readers with an eighth- or ninth-grade education.

7. *The length must be appropriate to the intended publication.* Study back issues to see how much space the average quiz takes and craft yours accordingly.

The True-False/Yes-No quiz usually consists of one to three paragraphs of introduction, followed by consecutively numbered statements or questions (usually 8 to 20) that can be answered by yes or no. The following quiz—"Are You Growing Old Gracefully?"—is typical:

It's not fun to grow old, but as they say, it sure beats the alternative. Psychologists tell us that the process is less painful if we accept the changes that the years bring, both in ourselves and our surroundings.

If you've ever wondered whether you are growing old gracefully, here's your chance to find out. Answer the questions, then check the scoring and analysis at the end of the quiz.

1. Do you think the clothing styles of 20 years ago were more attractive than those of today? (A) Yes; (B) No.
2. Do you make an effort to keep up with current fads and fashions? (A) Yes; (B) No.
3. When you're asked your age, do you shave off a few years? (A) Yes; (B) No.
4. Have you changed your hair style in the past ten years? (A) Yes; (B) No.
5. Do you prefer talking about things that happened in the good old days rather than events that are happening now? (A) Yes; (B) No.
6. Given the choice, would you want to live exclusively with people of your own age group? (A) Yes; (B) No.
7. Do you think most young people are less considerate/ ambitious than they were when you were in your twenties? (A) Yes; (B) No.
8. Do you think you have a right to certain courtesies simply because of your age? (A) Yes; (B) No.
9. If a younger person expresses an opinion with which you don't agree, do you feel compelled to set him/her straight? (A) Yes; (B) No.

SCORING: For each answer you selected, score yourself as follows—

Question 1: (A) 0 points; (B) 1 point.
Question 2: (A) 1 point; (B) 0 points.
Question 3: (A) 1 point; (B) 0 points.
Question 4: (A) 1 point; (B) 0 points.
Question 5: (A) 0 points; (B) 1 point.
Question 6: (A) 0 points; (B) 1 point.
Question 7: (A) 0 points; (B) 1 point.
Question 8: (A) 0 points; (B) 1 point.
Question 9: (A) 0 points; (B) 1 point.

ANALYSIS: If you scored from 0 to 3 points, you may be too inflexible and/or clinging to the past. Try to understand that time brings change and make an effort to adapt to it.

If you scored from 4 to 6 points, you have a well-balanced approach to aging. You are not overly resistant to change, nor are you trying too hard to remain young.

If you scored from 7 to 9 points, perhaps you are going overboard in trying to be with it. Whereas you don't want to be branded as an old crank, the years have entitled you to confidence in your convictions.

Often in creating these quizzes, you don't even have to make up the questions. Just find authorities willing to share little tests they have devised, write a few words introducing the subject, and put the scoring information from those experts into prose form.

Multiple-choice quizzes require the reader to check the letter or number of the most appropriate answer to each question. There are usually two, three, or four choices for each question. This one, called "How Involved Are You?" by Larry Smith, was printed in *Woman's World*.

Involvement means different things to different people. Here's a test of your reactions to a variety of situations. Check your responses to each of these photographs and then add up your total score in order to discover just how eager you really are to leap into the fray.

1. Burning Car on the Road [picture of car with hood up, engine smoking, and driver standing nearby]
    a. I'd drive on by.
    b. I'd ask if I could help.
    c. I'd stop and try to help out.
2. Mother with Crying Child [picture of mother holding crying baby]
    a. I'd encourage her to silence the child.
    b. I'd smile compassionately.
    c. I'd try to soothe the child.
3. Man Sneaking in Window [picture of man on a roof, crawling into a window]
    a. I'd intervene immediately before it's too late.
    b. I'd call the police.
    c. I wouldn't do anything.
4. Blind Man [picture of middle-aged man in suit with white cane crossing a street]
    a. I'd ask him if he needs any help.
    b. I wouldn't interfere.
    c. I'd help escort him.
5. Woman Loaded Down [picture of young woman with arms loaded, looking like she's about to drop something]
    a. I'd pass her by.
    b. I'd walk her home.
    c. I'd help her out if I weren't in a hurry.

The quiz is followed by a scoring chart and analysis.

The following quiz, "Funny Business," is in typical mix-and-match style. It appeared in *Games* and was created by Bill Camarda. If big businesses lived up to the "promise" of their company names, you might expect Sunkist to make tanning lotion. Here are some other goods and services that companies might provide if their names were a literal indication of their business. Can you match each hypothetical product with a real corporation?

1. Jump ropes	a. Goodyear
2. Calendars	b. Pan American
3. Home cookware	c. Sears
4. Bottled gasses	d. National Semiconductor
5. Birdcages	e. Wham-O
6. Providing part-time trainmen	f. Weyerhaeuser
7. Boxing gloves	g. U.S. Air
8. Outdoor grills	h. Swingline

Funny Business Answers

1. h, Swingline (jump ropes)
2. a, Goodyear (calendars)
3. b, Pan American (home cookware)
4. g, U.S. Air (bottled gasses)
5. f, Weyerhaeuser (bird cages)
6. d, National Semiconductor (part-time trainmen)
7. e, Wham-O (boxing gloves)
8. c, Sears (outdoor grills)

Fill-in-the-blanks quizzes are always of the test-your-knowledge type and aren't as common as yes-no, multiple-choice, or mix-and-match quizzes. They may consist of a list of lettered or numbered questions for the reader to answer. Blanks can be either at the end of each question or inserted somewhere inside the question, as in this "Catholic Quiz" from the *Annals of St. Anne de Beaupré*, by O.J. Robertson.

Groups of workers protected by a Patron Saint along with the town or place with which the Saint was closely associated are given. Can you name the proper Saint for each number?

1. Alpinists:
   St. _____ of Menthon
2. Canonists:
   St. _____ of Pennafort
3. Brides:
   St. _____ of Myra
4. Bakers:
   St. _____ of Hungary
5. Florists:
   St. _____ of Lisieux
6. Funeral Directors:
   St. _____ of Arimathea
7. Merchants:
   St. _____ of Assisi
8. Hatters:
   St. _____ of Ravenna
9. Soldiers:
   St. _____ of Tours
10. Advertisers:
    St. _____ of Siena

Catholic Quiz Answers

1. Bernard
2. Raymond
3. Nicholas
4. Elisabeth
5. Therese
6. Joseph
7. Francis
8. Severus
9. Martin
10. Bernadine

Combination quizzes include questions that are of two or three types, usually yes-no plus multiple-choice. Answers must be included with any quiz you submit; often an analysis of scoring will also be required.

You'll learn from your studies of quizzes in back issues that, like puzzles, most of them have themes. While little tests in specialized magazines always focus on topics of interest to their audiences, quizzes in general interest publications are almost always built around a theme, too, such as women in history, movie stars of the 1940s, or islands of the South Pacific.

Your best sources of idea inspiration will more than likely be the reference stacks of the public library and its card catalog. You will find your research materials there, too. Spend some time browsing through the shelves of books and you will come up with dozens of ideas. The following baseball quiz took just thirty minutes to put together, using a baseball encyclopedia:

It's in the Record Book

Games are played to be won and records made to be broken. Some of them produce baseball's heroes. Others, its goats. To test your baseball knowledge, choose the answers from the choices following each question.

1. What major league pitcher won the highest percentage of games during a season? (A) ElRoy Face; (B) Lou Gehrig; (C) Juan Marichal.
2. What team committed the largest number of errors during an inning? (A) St. Louis Cardinals; (B) Cleveland Indians; (C) Oakland Athletics.
3. Who holds the record for lifetime appearances at the plate? (A) Henry Aaron; (B) Babe Ruth; (C) Harmon Killebrew.
4. What batter appeared at the plate the most times during a season? (A) Pete Rose; (B) Brooks Robinson; (C) Orlando Cepeda.
5. Name the pitcher who made the most balks during a season. (A) Don Drysdale; (B) Steve Carlton; (C) Jim Hunter.
6. Who holds the lifetime home run record? (A) Babe Ruth; (B) Mickey Mantle; (C) Henry Aaron.
7. Who holds the season base stealing record? (A) Bert Campaneris; (B) Rickey Henderson; (C) Luis Aparicio.
8. What player holds the lifetime record for pitching one-hitters? (A) Whitey Ford; (B) Bob Feller; (C) Mike Cuellar.

Answers to "It's in the Record Book":

1. (A)	5. (B)
2. (B)	6. (C)
3. (A)	7. (B)
4. (A)	8. (B)

Since I got the answers from the same source as the questions, the job was child's play. You can do the same with almost any subject you choose and come up with a salable quiz if that subject is aimed at the right editor.

The easiest way to originate themes for know-thyself quizzes is through association. Editors of magazines that have used the "how trusting" or "how involved" themes, for example, might be interested in:

How

Cautious, Confident, Sympathetic, Enthusiastic, Self-Centered, Adaptable, Creative, Assertive, Self-Motivated, Impulsive, Realistic, Happy, or Innovative

Are you?

There's a second method for generating personal-insight quiz material. Take a theme that has been used by one magazine, change the title, devise new questions on the same theme, and submit the piece to a different publication. Though it doesn't require as much originality as the first technique, you'll nonetheless find markets for such pieces if the topic—such as stress or assertiveness—is one that's currently of widespread interest.

Most of these know-thyself quizzes will require the input of an expert and study of quizzes previously published in the magazine. You'll find those experts giving seminars and lectures, teaching at nearby colleges and universities, and conducting practices in family counseling, stress management, or weight control. The previously published quizzes will reveal the sorts of questions you must ask and how the editor likes them phrased.

Quiz with Variations

Similar to the know-thyself is the "evaluate your surroundings" quiz: "Can Your Car Pass the Safety Test?" "How Safe Is Your Water Supply?" "Does Your Child's School Measure Up?" Ideas for these pieces are generated in the same way as for personal-insight quizzes, and their formats are identical.

As in puzzle construction, it's easier to work backward from the answers. Get your information on the subject either from an expert in the field or from reading articles and books. Decide on the appropriate number of questions and state the important points you've uncovered in your research in the magazine's preferred form, followed by lettered choices (yes, no, or multiple). For example, in doing an "Are You Getting All the Vitamins You Need?" quiz, you might take this sentence from *Vitamin Bible*—"The vitamin content of good frozen green beans will be higher than those fresh ones you've kept in your refrigerator for a week"—and turn it around to read, "The fresh green beans stored in your refrigerator for a week contain higher vitamin content than good frozen ones. (A) Yes; (B) No."

Analysis of the magazine's previous quizzes will let you know just how difficult your questions ought to be. One point to keep in mind in creating almost any quiz is that a few questions should be easier than the others. The examples you study will also show how the quizzes are customarily scored; e.g., 20-18, exceptional; 17-12, excellent; 11-9, very good.

And now for the $64,000 question: Do you want to cash in on the puzzle and quiz market? (A) Yes; (B) No.

Analysis: If you've answered yes, you have chosen a winner. The field is open and unexplored by most writers. If your answer is no, there are still five more chapters in the book.

CHAPTER THIRTEEN

AND THE WINNER IS . . .

The immediate rewards of contesting are obvious.
There is the joy of creating and the thrill of win-
ning. There are the many luxuries you might never
have come by, but even if, for example, you could
buy your own dishwasher, winning it because you
know how to win it is . . . well, look at it this
way: Writing an entry is much more gratifying
than writing a check.

Gloria Rosenthal, In 25 Words or Less

Years ago, I had a neighbor who entered contests. Though the prizes she won weren't too impressive—a $10 merchandise certificate, a billfold, and a potted palm—she had an awfully good time dreaming up entries and fantasizing about winning a trip around the world.

Since that time, I've met contesters whose fantasies come true with astonishing regularity. One of them has been a three-time finalist in the Pillsbury Bake-Off, went to Hawaii as a finalist in the Pineapple Cook-Off, won the National Beef Cook-Off, and has accumulated so many electric skillets and microwave ovens she could open an appliance store. Others have won cars, recreational vehicles, trips to Paris or London, and lots of cash.

Most of the people who win big win often. There's nothing rigged about it. They have simply developed a knack for knowing what will please the judges.

My own experiences with contesting began because I wanted a change of pace while writing my first book. Mulling over hobby possibilities, I thought of my neighbor and her potted palm. I checked out a book on contesting from the library. It gave the address of a contest bulletin, and I sent in my check for a year's subscription.

Three months later I received an elegant carving set in the mail, one of 120 fourth prizes in a national sandwich contest. Six months after that I found myself in a middle school kitchen in Maryland, cooking up a concoction in the Oyster Cook-Off. I knew I hadn't a hope of winning. After all, at least six of the twelve finalists were old hands at bringing home the bacon from major cook-offs. But I kept on stirring Oyster Stewpendous and won the grand prize.

Since that time I've won a first in a national pizza contest and several smaller prizes. Not bad, considering the total time I've spent on my hobby has averaged four hours a month. (You don't have too much time for hobbies when you're writing books.)

There's no reason you can't be in the winner's circle, too. Contesting is a natural for writers. No matter what we may think at times, it *is* easier for us to come up with ideas and titles and to put words together because we've had more practice doing it.

Writers have the benefit of other experiences, too. They've learned that the first idea to flit across the mind has probably popped into lots of other heads as well—the "simultaneous invention" phenomenon. They are able to refine that idea, change it, make it truly original and therefore more likely to be a winner. Writers also have had more experience with evaluating their own work and know which efforts are their best and which are only so-so. Analyzing winning entries requires the same skills as analyzing articles or stories.

FINDING THE COMPETITION

But to win contests you have to know where to find out about them. You'll want to subscribe to one or more contest bulletins. Most of them are monthlies. These newsletters give information on current contests and provide help in putting together your entries for some of them (winning entries from previous years, idea-triggering lists, and the like). Among the better-known bulletins are:

Contest News-Letter Roger Tyndall P.O. Box 1059 Fernandina Beach, FL 32034	$12/year Free sample copy for SASE (business size)
Eggleston Enterprize P.O. Box 2732 Milford, NY 13807	$6.50/12 issues Free sample copy for SASE (business size)
Golden Chances Tom Lindell P.O. Box 655 South Pasadena, CA 91030	$10/year Sample copy for SASE plus $.50

Ideas, Techniques and Secrets (ITS) $8.50/12 issues
Box 3134
New Milford, CT 06776

The Prizewinner $10/year
P.O. Box 10596
St. Petersburg, FL 33733

Shepard Confidential Contest Bulletin $9.50/12 issues
P.O. Box 366   Sample copy $1
Willingboro, NJ 08046

The bulk of the information in most of these publications is about sweepstakes, but each issue contains data on at least two or three skill contests. Though there are techniques to entering sweepstakes, we'll concentrate on skill contests in this chapter, since they're the only kind that give the writer an edge.

Whereas a decade or so ago, statement and jingle contests were the most popular competitions, the majority of today's skill contests listed in these bulletins center on recipes. Top prizes in the major recipe competitions are big. In the 1982 Pillsbury Bake-Off more than $100,000 in prizes was awarded, including the grand prize of $40,000, four $15,000 category prizes, and twelve prizes of $2,000 each. The National Chicken Cook-Off for 1982 offered a $10,000 first prize; $4,000, second; $3,000, third; $2,000, fourth; $1,000, fifth; and all-expense-paid trips to Dallas for a finalist from each state and the District of Columbia. Grand prize in the Karo Go Chinese Recipe Contest was a fourteen-day trip to China for two plus $1,000 in cash. Grand prize among the 451 prizes in the Chef Boyardee Pizza Mix Cook-Off was a $20,000 kitchen or $20,000 in cash.

Though there are fewer statement, jingle, and naming contests, their prizes are equally worth winning. Bic's Flick My Bic Limerick Contest in 1982 offered $50,000 in prizes. The 1981 Gleem Toothpaste Statement Contest awarded a total of 1,030 prizes, including a grand prize of an expense-paid trip to Hollywood or $5,800 in cash.

Many magazines—from *Harper's* to the *New York Antique Almanac* to the *National Enquirer*—also sponsor contests, often on a regular basis.

Woman's Day is a great magazine for writer-contesters. They run the monthly Silver Spoon Award recipe contest (see Chapter 4) and various other contests throughout the year. One recently called for 75 to 750 words about "My Most Moving Holiday Tradition." Another, "My Most Versatile Outfit," required a full-length photo of the entrant in the outfit (with accessories, plus up to 500 words telling why the outfit was versatile, how it could be adapted to different uses, and where and how often it was worn.

Occasionally, magazine contests are listed in contest bulletins, but the only way you can find out about most of them is by looking through lots of magazines—again, a spin-off from your marketing research. Be on the lookout, too, for local contests. Business-sponsored contests are usually announced in newspapers, and newspapers themselves often conduct various competitions.

COOKING UP A WINNER

Since you'll most often have chances to enter *recipe contests*, let's talk about the ingredients that go into their prizewinners. Most recipe contests are sponsored by food companies and by groups whose purpose is to advertise and encourage the use of a specific brand or a kind of food, such as beef, chicken, or pineapple. Many of the winning recipes are used in advertising (on the product's packages or labels, in booklets and magazine ads, and so on).

Highlight the Featured Ingredient

In creating your recipes, the main point to remember is that the sponsor is putting on the contest to promote its product. According to Marilyn Latham of the Maryland State Department of Agriculture, who has helped organize several recipe contests, emphasis should be placed on enhancement if the sponsor is promoting a generic food. If you enter a contest calling for recipes using fish, for example, choose one that emphasizes the fish flavor. Perhaps your favorite recipe does disguise the fish taste and therefore appeals to your fish-resistant family, but that's not the recipe to send in.

Too Many Steps Spoil the Spoils

Simplify procedures as much as you can without sacrificing taste. Recipes that are too complex rarely win prizes. Be creative and original, but don't be too innovative. Take a good basic recipe and give it a new twist. The judges are looking for recipes that purchasers of the product will want to duplicate in their own kitchens, so combinations of ingredients can't be too exotic. And by all means, try the recipe out in your kitchen before you submit it. The way to a judge's heart is not through heartburn.

If the finished product is a success, you need try the recipe only once. There's no need to seek reactions from people other than your family (friends, through politeness, are usually not reliable) unless your food preferences are not those of most people.

Aim for ease of preparation. Your recipe should be one that can be made by an average cook in a reasonable length of time. Use only ingredients that are easy to obtain and appropriate to the contest's theme. If the sponsor calls for budget dishes, don't enter one that calls for steak or escargots.

Fitting Recipes to Recipients

Find recipes the sponsor has liked in the past, such as those printed on the product's package. They will give not only an idea of the kinds of recipes to submit, but also a ballpark figure for the number of ingredients and amount of space used for the method of preparation.

Submit recipes appropriate to the contest's focus. Don't send in a recipe for salad when the rules list the categories as hot breads, casseroles, and desserts. One of the judging criteria is often appropriateness to the category.

Make sure that your recipe complies with the contest's ingredient rules. If you must use at least a cup of the sponsor's product, don't submit a recipe that calls for only three-fourths of a cup.

Check your eligibility to enter. Only people over 18 years of age (or under 18) can enter some contests. If you have owned beef cattle within a certain period of time, you cannot be a National Beef Cook-Off contestant. People in various occupations, such as chefs, food service professionals, or those who work for certain companies, are ineligible to enter other contests.

Don't submit a cookbook recipe without changing it in some way. Adding or subtracting one ingredient is generally sufficient. If you win a big prize, you will be required to sign a statement saying that your recipe has never been published. If inclusion of a short statement about the recipe is not contrary to the rules and you can come up with a grabber, include it. Your blurb might be about the recipe's origin, versatility, thriftiness, or nutritional value.

Thousands of entries are received in the major recipe contests, so you'll want to attract the judges' attention to set your recipe apart from the common submission. The most effective way to do so is to give your recipe a winning name. Be clever and upbeat, but never obscure. The name should tell something about the dish and make readers (judges) want to try it. Here are the names of some winners in a recent Kraft Marshmallow Creme contest: Razzle Dazzle Raspberry Pie, Mochalaska Pie, Capuccino Candy, Marshmallow Cloud Mousse, Peanutty Kookie Fingers, and Mallow Rice Cake 'n Orange Sauce.

Putting the Ingredients Together (on Paper)

Follow the contest rules exactly. If no directions for typing (or printing) the recipe are given, put your name and address, single-spaced, in the upper left-hand corner. Center the recipe's title about four inches down on a page of $8^1/_2$x11-inch plain white typing paper. Then list all the ingredients in the order they will be used. (I usually double-space this part of the recipe.)

When commercial sponsors specify that a certain ingredient (or ingredients) must appear in the recipe, include the product, with its full brand name, in capital letters. In a contest sponsored by Karo, for example, you must identify dark corn syrup as KARO DARK CORN SYRUP. Products other than those manufactured by the sponsor are listed by their generic names (e.g., 2 cups milk, 3 tablespoons margarine). If the sponsor makes other ingredients used in your recipe, call them by their brand names, even if they aren't the ingredient the contest is pushing. If you need proof that this technique helps, just read the entries published by companies (such as Kraft and Pillsbury) in any book of recipe contest winners.

I try to find a recipe previously published by the sponsor to use as a model when I'm typing the preparation directions. However you type yours, keep them as clear and concise as you can and in the proper sequence. If the oven should be preheated, mention that at the beginning of the directions. Include appropriate pan, kettle, or casserole sizes.

Don't forget to include all the necessary steps. In fact, it's a good idea to note down the directions at the same time as you're actually preparing the dish. Following the directions, you might add information about a possible garnish: "Garnish with tomato slices and avocado wedges, if desired," for example. Close by giving the number of servings: Serves 8-10.

WINNING WORDS

Though the way you work your words—in titles, blurbs, and concise directions—will put your recipe entries at the head of the competition, words *alone* can win statement, limerick, and naming contests (the three other popular types).

Since there are several devices that can be employed in all of these contest categories, let's talk about them before we discuss the contest types individually.

Acrostics. The first letter of each word or line spells another word, or, as in the following example, selected letters from the last line of a statement spell out the product's name:

> I like finesse because "the old gray hair ain't what it used to be" until concentrated FINESSE "brings it back alive" naturally to *FINE* Silkiness, Sheen and youthful Elasticity.

Alliteration. The use of two or more words beginning with the same letter, such as this winning last line of a rhyme in a national hosiery contest: "Their smooth hug, smartly snug, stays sagfree."

Analogy. The adaptation of familiar terms from one field or subject to describe another. You might, for instance, use football terms in describing a breakfast cereal or movie jargon to sing the praises of a toothpaste.

Contrast. Using words with opposite meanings, as illustrated by this winning entry in a last-line contest sponsored by Simoniz:

> The new SIMONIZ method is slick
> Gives you 6 months' protection—but quick!
> Liquid Kleener's the clue
> That cuts work-time for you
> Why put-off when put-on is "no trick"?

Coined Words. Creating new words by combining, dividing, respelling, or otherwise changing traditional words. One contestant won $20,000 by saying that the sponsor's hotdogs were "bunderful." An antifreeze contest winner described a motorist's bad-weather headaches as "winterference."

Mystic Three. A phrase coined by Wilmer S. Shepherd, founder of the Shepherd School of Contesting, to define any interesting trio of words or phrases. We hear them every day, especially in songs and common expressions: baubles, bangles, and beads; calm, cool, and collected; ready, willing, and able.

Parody/paraphrase. Changing a well-known song, saying, quotation, or the like, as in the "old gray hair" phrase in the foregoing acrostic example.

Repetition. Repeating the same or similar sounds, words, or phrases: "More stylage, more mileage, more smileage."

Visual Tricks. The use of unusual punctuation, initials, abbreviations, or upside-down words and phrases to catch the eye.

Other devices you might use are puns/plays on words, or words with double meanings, all of which have been discussed in other chapters of this book. If you decide to go all out as a contester, I suggest you read every book on contesting that you can find (see bibliography for suggestions) and perhaps subscribe to a correspondence course. The Shepherd School of Contesting, once dubbed "the Harvard of the boxtop universities," offers a twelve-month home study course that's considered tops by its legions of prizewinning graduates.

In 25 Words or More

Statement contests go to almost any length to extol the virtues of a sponsor's product. The most common length requirement is for 25 words or less, but you will read occasional entry rules asking for 50, 500, or even 750.

If a 25- or 50-word statement is required, you'll no doubt wish you could use a few more. In 500- or 750-word statement contest, you may have shot your wad of hype when you've used only 400.

While using only 400 words in a 500- or 750-word statement contest won't disqualify you (you might even win if they are *very* well written), your advantage increases with the number of words praising the sponsor's product.

The relationship between the specified length and what you want to say is a lot like that between stationery and envelopes: You never seem to have enough of one or the other.

Nevertheless, you *can* even things out—compose sincere, sparkling entries within the word limits—if you know the product. You don't have to use the product regularly to compete in a contest, but you do have to become familiar with the uses, ingredients, and features touted in its ads.

Before you begin composing your entries, list words and phrases describing the product. For example, suppose you want to enter a statement contest focusing on a particular brand of shampoo. Your list might look something like this:

rich lather	works in hard water
soft pink color	comes in easy-to-hold bottle

less expensive than
  other brands
smells like carnations
feels like lotion
gives hair body
gets rid of dandruff
makes hair: gleaming
          shiny
          healthy-looking
          shimmering
          silky
          soft
          manageable
          alive-looking

bottle has pouring spout
bottle is plastic
easy on hair
untangles snarls
nonallergenic

It's important during this part of your research to note as much as you can about the product's smell, texture, appearance, and taste (if applicable, of course).

Next, copy down the ingredients, underlining any that are unusual or that set the product apart from its competitors and might be considered selling points: natural flavorings, rare fragrances, added nutrition. Sometimes you'll want to note ingredients that are missing: preservatives, salt, abrasives, and other undesirables.

Then, study the product's advertisements in newspapers and magazines or on television and radio. Read everything written on the container to promote the product. What aspects of the product are the sponsors or ad agencies promoting? Are any of the words or phrases candidates for wordplays? Who are the potential purchasers—homemakers, children, the general public, athletes? Can you think of clever, alternative uses for the product? List phrases the advertisers have chosen to herald the product's attributes. Also study any bulletins or contest newsletters that contain tips on the contest or others somewhat like it.

Start writing only when you have analyzed your subject thoroughly. Don't worry about word length until later. If you have done your homework well, you will have more material than you can possibly use—and plenty of ammunition if you want to fire off more than one entry.

After you have spent twenty or thirty minutes consciously matching up information with ideas and devices, push everything into your subconscious and go about some other task. It's amazing when inspiration surfaces: while you're weeding the garden, putting new spark plugs in the car, feeding the cat, or working on another writing project.

Your statements needn't be in prose. Verse is also popular with statement-contest judges. Here are four statements that won prizes. Notice the variety of devices and forms their contributors used. The first two were winners in Rath's 90th Anniversary Statement Contest.

A lifebuoy at mealtime, you're never at
sea, unwavering goodness, Rath guarantee
Perfection protected by famed guarantee
Mealtime standby when mom's absentee.

🦴 🦴 🦴

For nine decades my "Tribe of Rath"
has provided premium products that
"PORK UP" menus to "PERK UP" appetites
in your wigwam, without wasting wampum.

The next two are among the several $25 winners in the Gleem Hollywood Extravaganza Contest. The statement to be completed in 25 words or less was, "If I win a trip to Hollywood, I will pack Gleem Toothpaste for Adults in my suitcase because . . ."

Wherever we travel, including Califoriginal Hollywood, provident Gleem keeps teeth and gums cleanly stimulated, as we enjoy its friendly bubblicity and welcome charm.

🦴 🦴 🦴

GLEEM—the bacteria-censoring "X" pert—keeps my mouth "G"-rated clean, my teeth looking like "superstars," my breath from spoiling an otherwise "Picture"-Perfect Smile!

Once you have several ideas for entries, put conscious effort to work again, shaping the statements and polishing them. After that, it's only a matter of typing your entries according to the rules and popping them in the mail.

ITTY-BITTY FIVE-LINE DITTIES

In *limerick contests*, the first one, two, or four lines are provided. It's up to the contestant to supply the rest. The limerick form has a standard rhyming pattern with no variations. There are always five lines, with the first, second, and fifth lines rhyming with each other. The third and fourth lines (which are shorter than the others and indented) also rhyme with each other. The two-lines-provided limerick looks like this:

> While flicking my Bic Christmas eve
> I dreamed of the things I'd receive.

Each of the following entrees won $1,000 cash prizes in the Flick My Bic Limerick Contest:

> No gift-budget suffers
> When Bic stocking stuffers
> Such glowing response will achieve.
>   ✌   ✌·   ✌
> And the Bics in my "sleigh"
> Delivered 'long the way
> Would be "Claus" for much joy, I believe.

In composing your limerick entries, analyze the product as for statement contests. Then make a list of rhyming words. Since at least the first line will have been given and lines two and five *must* rhyme with it, you have one guiding rhyme word (in the two-lines-given Bic contest, entrants knew that they had to rhyme the final line with *Eve* and *receive*). When the first four lines are given, both words with which you must rhyme yours have been established.

With the help of a rhyming dictionary, write down all the possible rhyme words. If the third and fourth lines are not given, you can supply any rhyming words you choose for those lines. Then look at those words in relation to the information you've gathered about the product. Use the conscious effort-subconscious thought method in putting it all together.

What's in a Name

The winning entries in naming contests (naming a new product or the product's mascot are the usual tasks involved) are almost always coined words. Winners in various puppy-naming contests were Heeliotrooper, Sir Droopalot, Funocchio, Pawper, Hurricanine, Rovercoat, Whiffenpooch, and Wag Mop.

Winners in cake-naming contests have come up with such coined words as Buttercup Budgetade, Fragilily, Jasminbrosia, and Peaka-beauty Cake. Some of the contestants who won prizes in an Occident Flour Name the Kitchen contest called it Chef's Captivilla, The Elbow Room, Merry Menumill, and Dineamic.

To create your entries, do the same product research you would for a statement or limerick contest. If a mascot or some other item is to be named, write down all applicable characteristics. Manipulate the words, adding, subtracting, or changing letters, keeping in mind the fact that your entries will be judged not only on how clever they are, but on their appropriateness as well.

Magazine Mail-Ins

Magazine contests are a mixed bag. Some publications run them regularly; others, on an ad hoc basis. *Harper's,* for example, conducts monthly contests that for most of us would not be cost-efficient to enter. They involve crossword-type diagrams that must be filled in with words deduced from clues that are obscure, to say the least. But if you like challenges and the chance to win a year's subscription to the magazine, you might want to enter.

The *New York Antique Almanac,* in its "People Puzzler" department, recently asked readers to match each of fourteen first ladies with one of fourteen lettered phrases describing accomplishments and areas of dedication while in the White House. Other contests have included one asking for photos of husband and wife look-alikes (sponsored by the *National Enquirer*) and one for photos of comical cats (*Woman's Day*). The *Woman's Day* prize was $5,000.

To decide which contests to enter, assess your interests and skills, the amount of time you will have to spend, and whether or not you consider the prize worthwhile. Frankly, I'd rather win a lifetime supply of ballpoint pens than a mink coat.

THE CONTESTER'S LITERARY COMPANIONS

Many of the reference books you will want for contesting are those you already have in your writing library: a dictionary, a thesaurus, a rhyming dictionary, and a book of quotations. You'll also find that books of limericks, jokes, proverbs, famous poems, and even nursery rhymes are useful. An oldie as far as contest books are concerned—but a goodie when it comes to thousands of homonyms, rhyming, and double-meaning words—is *Prize Winning Jingles*, by William Sunners.

You can sometimes obtain copies of a contest's winning entries by sending an SASE to the address provided in a contest's rules. Serious contesters send for this information whenever it is available. Winning entries are great for starting the associative process when you're entering similar contests. They're even more worthwhile when you enter a subsequent contest by the same sponsor.

Although it isn't unusual for some contestants to send as many as 100 entries to the big-prize contests, this strikes me as contest overkill. If you do submit multiple entries, experienced contesters suggest that you use a different version of your name on each of them so that you can identify your winning entries. In most cases, judging agencies will inform you only that you have won a prize, without alluding to the content of the entry itself.

PASSING JUDGMENT

All contest entries are picked up in mail sacks from the post office to which they are addressed and are then transported to the judging agency. Clerks pass the entries through envelope-slitting machines and check them for qualifiers (box tops, labels, or whatever proof of purchase has been specified in the contest rules). Entries without qualifiers are thrown out. So are illegible submissions and those postmarked after the contest's closing date.

There are other rule violations: typed or written entries when hand-printing has been specified; failing to include one's name and address (or the dealer's name if that is required); exceeding the number of words allowed. In short, adding or deleting anything not specified in the rules can result in disqualification. It has been estimated that 60 to 70 percent of all contest entries are thrown away unread because rules have been broken.

The survivors go to preliminary readers who do more winnowing, casting out entries that are profane, obscene, or just don't make sense. Then the lower-echelon judges take over and rate the remaining entries according to criteria established for the contest. Originality and creativity, appropriateness, sincerity, and clarity are the usual judging criteria in statement, limerick, and naming contests. Typical for recipe contests are originality, availability of ingredients, appropriateness, appearance, taste, and ease of preparation. Although how various criteria are weighted differs with each contest, originality is almost always one of the most important considerations.

At this stage, duplicate (or very similar) entries hit the wastebaskets. The remaining entries, with the junior judges' scores attached to them, go on to the judging agency's top executives for final judging.

Your entry can get past most of its competition if you simply follow the rules. I always underline them so I won't miss any. The following checklist will help you, too:

1. Is the entry to be typed, printed, or written?
2. What size paper is called for?
3. Must an official entry blank be included?
4. Should the completed entry form be attached to the entry or not?
5. What qualifiers should be enclosed?
6. Is the way qualifiers should be attached specified?
7. Is your name and address to go on the same sheet as the entry, or on a separate piece of paper?
8. Is the envelope the size specified? (If no size is indicated, use a business envelope.)
9. Is your entry folded so there is a bit of extra room between it and the edges of the envelope? (Entries must survive mutilation by the envelope-slitting monster.)
10. Is the envelope addressed correctly? If, for example, rules give the following address:

    Fannie's "Fancy Fudge" Contest
    P.O. Box 182, Dept. EZ
    Hershey PA 17033

Don't forget the quotation marks and don't spell out words that are abbreviated. Be sure the post office box and zip code numbers are correct, and don't leave out the department letters. If the envelope's information varies *in any way* from that specified, your entry may not even be opened before it is discarded.

One final word: It's important to keep track of your winnings. The IRS does. Prizes are taxable, so consult your accountant. Here's hoping you'll have to consult him often.

CHAPTER FOURTEEN

THE ART OF RANTING OR RAVING (FOR PAY)

No opinion is worth any more than the reason or reasons proffered in its support.

P. Albert Duhamel,
"The Structuring of a Book Review," 1978

 ired of the second balcony at the symphony and peering around pillars at the ballet? Do you yearn for hardcover volumes with crackly fresh pages rather than dog-eared paperbacks from the book exchange? Want to expand your record library?

Perhaps you ought to consider writing reviews and experience the arts with paid-as-you-go pleasure. In addition to the money you'll receive, free books, records, and tickets to performances you review are often part of the bargain.

Though the books and records are the same you could buy at the store, I've found the complimentary performance seats are almost always better than any I could pay for at the box office. That's because the best seats in the house are either sold in advance to subscribers or kept available for people the sponsor wants to impress—the critics.

Clifton Fadiman once said, "True literary criticism is a venerable art. You can number the top-notchers on your fingers and toes." What Fadiman didn't say was that no top-notch reviewer is born a master of the venerable art. The first-rate critics rose to the top by taking advantage of their opportunities and serving a period of apprenticeship.

Reviewing is not for everyone. It is a demanding pursuit and one that leaves the reviewer open to a lot of slings and arrows. Everyone loves to critique the critic. Payment for reviews is generally less than for articles of equal length, and writing them often requires more time. On the plus side, tickets to performances, books, records, and other fringe benefits are considerable. And there's a certain prestige to having your by-line on reviews.

Of course, to become a successful reviewer, you have to know what you're talking about. In order to do a good job, your knowledge must be more than superficial. In fact, you must know a great deal more about your subject than the general public. You have to either already be an expert on whatever you're reviewing or must truly love (and study) your chosen area so that you acquire the necessary expertise.

Rock reviewers who have studied guitar, opera reviewers who've taken voice lessons, and drama critics with theater background do a more competent job than they would have without those experiences. People with a longtime interest in dance, books, or artistic disciplines will find reviewing a gratifying blend of business and pleasure.

If you can't tell a jeté from a pas de deux, you had better learn or else let someone else cover the ballet. Likewise, you had better have a thorough understanding of opera before you attempt to critique *Faust*.

Reviews aren't limited to the classical forms. As you do your market research, you will find that there's a demand for commentary on contemporary music recordings, showroom and cabaret acts, movies, and television shows in addition to art exhibits, books, theater, musical comedy, and other stage performances. But contemporary forms require no less background knowledge and homework than classical.

As a reviewer, you have an enormous responsibility. An unfavorable newspaper review of a fledgling string quartet may mean that its first concert will be the last. Big-city critics can make the difference between standing room only and an empty house. Careers often hang in the balance of the reviewer's pen. The reviewer, like it or not, must at times play God.

That responsibility extends beyond the footlights to each potential member of the audience. After all, it's $25 the reviewer is asking him to spend to see the revival of *Tobacco Road*—or is telling him to save instead of going to *La Traviata*. The potential audience member looks to the critic's good judgment in deciding how to spend that hard-earned money, and that trust must never be taken lightly.

GETTING THE PART
Breaking into review writing is easiest at the local level. Bob Ritter, Executive Editor of the Gannett-owned Reno newspapers, advises writers who are looking for assignments to approach an editor with

copies of reviews they've written along with information on their credits and background: a college major in fine arts, theater experience, and the like. Ritter says he is more impressed by well-crafted reviews that have appeared in small publications than those published in large ones. "Big papers have large enough staffs for lots of editing," he says. "Small ones don't, so chances are the writer's work is his own and hasn't been heavily edited."

To find out what editors to contact, look at the newspaper's masthead or telephone their offices to ask for the name of the person in charge of reviews.

If you've never had work published, write two or three sample reviews to show the editor. Once you have established a working relationship, ask for a supply of the newspaper's stationery on which you can write future requests for performance tickets, records, and review copies from publishers. Keep in mind that whatever items you receive should be used for their intended purpose and never sold or given as gifts.

REVIEWING THE MARKETS

Since most magazine reviews are written on assignment, send copies of your published newspaper reviews along with your qualifications to the editors you have in mind. If they like your presentation, the editors will either ask you to review specified works or suggest that you provide them with information on possible review subjects.

Surveying the magazine market will reveal a vast number of review possibilities, from *Small Boat Journal* to *Consumer's Digest* to *Cats Magazine* and *American History*. It's easy to analyze what the editors of these specialty magazines are looking for, since they use only commentaries on works directly related to their areas of specialization: feminist books for *Ms.*, books by or about people of Scandinavian descent for *Scandinavian Review*, records and performances featuring contemporary pop music for *Rolling Stone*.

There are publications, such as *The Review of Books and Religion*, whose content consists primarily of reviews. They are good markets for the writer who is also an expert in a field. Perhaps you're an authority on astronomy or have a Ph.D. in economics. Maybe you're a world-class gymnast or a livestock show judge. Whatever your area of expertise, contact the publication's editor, listing your credentials and offering to review books in your field.

BOOK REVIEW BASICS

Although reviews of movies and live performances often out-number those of books in newspapers, the majority of reviews in magazines focus on the printed page. Like reviews of all art forms, book reviews can be classified as (1) objective and (2) subjective. An objective review emphasizes the work—its aim and scope—and the special qualifications of the writer to write the book, as in this review published in the *United Methodist Reporter*.

The Mystery of the Ordinary
by Charles Cummings, Harper & Row,
San Francisco, 133 pages, $9.95

by Mary Brooke Casad

Perhaps no other can speak to us more clearly about the meaning of everyday existence than one who has lived the monastic life. Trappist monk Charles Cummings draws from twenty years of contemplative living to extend "an invitation to slow down for a reflective look at our simplest actions" in *The Mystery of the Ordinary*.

The ordinary experiences that Dr. Cummings selects as chapter titles include hearing, seeing, walking, resting, standing up, eating and drinking, and hurting.

"Ordinary things have a great power to reveal the mysterious near-ness of a caring, liberating God," he writes. "Unfortunately, the sameness and repetition of everyday activities can numb our aware-ness to the point that these ordinary realities no long speak to us with power."

Each chapter begins with a description of the physical actions in-volved in performing these functions, which become miracles in and of themselves under Dr. Cummings' keen observation.

"To discover the mystery of the ordinary, it is not enough merely to go through the motions of rising, walking, eating, resting, as we have done every day of our life," he writes. "What is helpful is to be gently, attentively present to the full reality of our human experiences here and now. Then these ordinary happenings can become vehicles that carry us toward the mystery of God."

Most reviews used by the higher-paying magazines fall into the subjective group. These pieces require a good deal more work to write, since the emphasis is on the reviewer's reaction to and evaluation of the book. These excerpts are from a subjective review which appeared in *Easy Living*:

A Biography of Montgomery Clift.
by Robert LaGuardia. (Arbor House, $12.95.)

Movie fans remember Montgomery Clift as the classically hand-some, Byronic figure who died at the tragically early age of 45. The real "Monty" was very different—"collapsing over and over, in a state of drugged drunkenness . . . waking up in a semi-coma from drugs and liquor . . . being picked up bodily by his male nurse and put under a cold shower . . . a thyroid condition had made him pop-eyed . . . he would not eat . . . he made tearful, desperate calls, but his best friends had left him."

Clift is a textbook case of a gifted actor from a good family whose sexual ambivalence and weakness of will launched him on a self-destructive course that ultimately cost him his life. A good case can be made out for the presumption that Clift's life is more interesting as a psychiatric study than as an acting career.

Any biographer of Montgomery Clift is thus faced with the task of exploring his psychological traumas and their origin besides record-ing his successes and failures as an actor. In this first of two Clift bio-graphies to appear this year, Robert LaGuardia is only partly success-ful. His reportorial style, heavily sprinkled with anecdotes and inter-views, gives his text the tone of an extended magazine treatment rather than a true biography. The insights and interpretations that a biographer should bring to his subject, doubly important in Clift's case, are absent. "Monty" is an account of the *how*, not the *why*.

Three paragraphs telling about Clift's life follow, synopsizing the book's content without subjective commentary. The final paragraph again brings the subjective into play:

It could have been a long and brilliant career, but the demons that pursued Montgomery Clift finally possessed him body and soul. It will need a more searching psychological probe than LaGuardia has given us to track down the baleful influences that shaped Clift's haunted, hagridden life.

Experts advise that to maintain your integrity, never read the jacket copy, publishers' handouts, or other reviews of the book before you write your own. Always read the entire work, they say, and *nev-*

er ever review a book you haven't understood.

When writing reviews of fictional works, indicate the kind of book (gothic, mystery, science fiction) and give the time of the story and the setting. Supply information about the characters, but under no circumstances reveal a surprise ending. You may hint that is unexpected, but say no more.

Questions you should answer in the nonfiction review concern the author's premise, the intrinsic significance of the work, unique qualities (if any) and the book's accuracy.

In subjectively reviewing both fiction and nonfiction, compare the book with others in the genre or on the same subject as well as previous books by the same author. Beware of the halo effect. Just because the writer's last book was a mainstream masterpiece doesn't necessarily mean that every book he writes will measure up. Point out strengths and weaknesses of style and content, giving reasons for both positive and negative criticisms.

Whatever type of review the publication calls for, don't neglect to mention the title of the book, its author's name, price, and number of pages. When applicable, include translators' names and all the editors of anthologies. Be sure that all of this information is accurate.

DISSECTING THE DISCS

Record reviews are generally shorter than those of books and are almost always subjective. The typical format contains description and evaluation of the music, including instrumentation and arrangements, musicianship, and comparison with previous recordings by the same artist(s) or those of other performers, as in this review by Steven X. Rea, which appeared in *High Fidelity*.

Chas Jankel: Questionnaire
Chas Jankel, Philip Bagnal, & Pete Van-Hooke, producers
A&M SP 4885

I hear that the title track of Chas Jankel's second solo album is all the rage on the dance floors of trendy New York nightspots. *Questionnaire* is a rowdy beats-per-minute salsa send-up, rife with blasting trumpets, crashing percussion, steel drums, and a walloping, rocksteady backbeat. But while it may be easy to dance to, *Questionnaire*—along with the seven other cuts on the singer/songwriter/multi-instrumentalist's LP—is puffy and lightweight, rendered all the more so by Jankel's bland, breathy, very-very-English vocals.

Jankel first came to attention as Ian Dury and the Blockheads' mainstay collaborator, cowriting such hits as *Sex & Drugs & Rock & Roll*, *Hit Me with Your Rhythm Stick*, and *Sweet Gene Vincent*. Though the same spirited brand of pop/funk runs through his solo work, one sorely misses the eccentric, grizzly charm that Dury brought to the music. Basically, *Questionnarie* is a collection of highly danceable, thoroughly inane tunes.

Now You're Dancing and *Magic of Music* typify the approach: Both are energetic paeans to the power of song. On the former, Jankel demonstrates his prowess as a lyricist, creating such unusual rhymes as "prune" with "moon" and "June." What plucks *Magic of Music* from the depths of mediocrity is Jamaican trombonist Rico Rodriquez, whose eloquent, loping notes permeate the reggae-ized composition.

Musically *Questionnaire* is hard to fault. Jankel plays just about anything and everything (keyboards, guitars, synthesizers, percussion) with polish and skill, and he is joined by the likes of Rico, the very able drummer Pete Van-Hooke, and backup vocalists Janie Romer and Laura (sister of Tina) Weymouth. For dance-crazy advocates of ultraslick funk-guitar riffs, slam-bam drumming, and battle-ax bass patterns, Jankel's disc will be fairly satisfying. But if content and vocal ability still have any effect on record buyers' tastes, *Questionnaire* should prove to be a commercial bomb.

It's imperative that the reviewer be familiar with the artist's other works and the genre in general if she is to write a quality review. Although you don't have to possess a great deal of musical ability to be a record critic, you must be well versed in the idiom you're writing about.

The best way to get review records is by contacting the record companies. You can request specific records at first, then send the resulting reviews back to the companies' public relations people. After they have received a few reviews from you (confirming the profitability of investing a certain amount of inventory in you), the record people will probably start deluging you with discs. The easiest way to get the names and addresses of the record companies is by going to the nearest record store and asking to see their "phonolog." This book also contains listings of recordings currently available.

Another way to do the job is by making friends with a disc jockey. DJs are bombarded with complimentary records and should be agreeable to letting you borrow albums for a day or two at a time. Although many libraries lend records as well as books, by the time they acquire the records it's almost always well after their release dates.

SNEAK PREVIEWING

Also predominantly subjective, the most popular form of movie review emphasizes plot, performances, and overall production. A critique of cinematography and special effects, as well as background information on where the film was shot and any special problems that had to be overcome, should be included when relevant. (You can get this info from press packets provided by the studio's public relations department.)

This well-written review of *Quest for Fire* by John Stickney was printed in *Discover* and fulfills all the requirements. It is atypical, however, in that less than the usual amount of emphasis is placed on individual performances.

Quest for Fire
directed by Jean-Jacques Annaud

As science fiction epics go, *Quest for Fire* does for prehistory what *Star Wars* did for the future. Mankind's struggle for survival 80,000 years ago becomes earthily, plausibly alive, not least because the imaginary world on the screen is informed by sound application of paleoanthropology. Life for early man may have been nasty, brutish, and short, but it was not dull.

Quest for Fire, a Canadian and French co-production, combines a thrilling script (based on the turn-of-the-century French science fiction classic *La Guerre du Feu*, by J.H. Rosny, Sr.), an array of zingy special effects, a cast of talented unknowns, and, most important, an inspired director, the Frenchman Jean-Jacques Annaud, whose *Black and White in Color* won an Academy Award for the best foreign language film produced in 1976. This movie was shot in Kenya, Canada, and Scotland. The spectacular locations dramatically convey Annaud's vision of the awesome space and silence surrounding isolated, vulnerable, primitive people.

At first sight the Ulam, a tribe of some thirty hunter-gatherers, seem anything but vulnerable. Men and women alike are heavy-set, beetle-browed, and lantern jawed. The film, like present-day paleoanthropology, depicts a Neanderthal better favored in brainpower, appearance, and agility than the old stereotype of a shambling, stoop-shouldered lummox. But the hide-clad Ulam look and behave in an eerily simian manner—a portrayal that may not be inappropriate to Stone Age man. The zoologist and writer Desmond Morris (*The Naked Ape*) coached the actors in body movement, and author Anthony Burgess (*A Clockwork Orange*) devised a laconic dialect after researching the roots of Indo-European languages.

Among the Ulam's few civilized conveniences is fire, which they can tend but not create. One day, after a terrifying attack by the Wagabou, ape-like marauders several rungs below the Ulam on the evolutionary ladder, the fire is snuffed out. Naoh (Everett McGill) and two other young Ulam warriors are sent out for a light, an adventurous mission. Homeward with them comes the lithe young Ika (Rae Dawn Chong), a mate for Naoh from a much advanced tribe, the Ivaka. Ika, whose people have long since learned to rub two sticks together, amazes the Ulam with the secret of fire.

The plot, usually thoughtful in its conjecture, sometimes overreaches. Once, when the Ulam are beset by the Kzamm, a tribe of cannibals, Naoh rallies a handy herd of woolly mammoths for a kind of cavalry charge against the enemy. Naoh is also such a quick study with Ika, getting the hang of a new sex position, and of javelin-throwing, that he seems ready to evolve into *Homo sapiens sapiens* overnight. The affection and allegiance among Ika, Naoh, and friends are too modern, skeptics might argue. But Annaud's point is that some sentiments are immutable.

The point is convincingly made. Courageous in his choice of subject, Annaud has delivered superb, penetrating entertainment. For ambition and impact, most movies cannot hold a candle to *Quest for Fire*.

PERFECTING YOUR PERFORMANCE

Though you can reread books and listen to records over and over without it costing you money, you'll only be given one ticket for each live performance in most cases. In order to write a quality review, therefore, you will need to prepare for the performance.

If possible, become familiar with the performance facility—concert hall, amphitheater, nightclub—in advance. Make yourself aware of any areas which may be acoustically poor, where viewing is impaired, so you can alert potential ticket buyers to the problem.

Learn whatever you can about the star performers' previous experience: where the prima ballerina got her training, under whom the conductor studied, and so forth. If you can, get background information on minor performers, too. One of them might steal the show and your advance planning will save you scurrying around for info while battling a deadline.

Read the play, study the libretto, listen to recordings of the music before you go to a performance. Skimming the program notes during intermission won't be adequate—nor will it be fair to the performers or your readers.

Make a checklist of things you'll want to note during the actual performance and memorize it. If you're reviewing a play, opera, ballet, or musical comedy, include on your list such items as lighting, sets and special effects, leaving room for evaluations of individual artist's performances as well.

When the production involves music, whether it be a symphony or a country-western concert, list such criteria as choice of material, pacing, and quality of musicianship. Ask yourself whether the program is balanced, the various selections complement one another, and their sequence is pleasing.

Since most performances are presented in darkened theaters, scribble key words on the individual sheets of a scratch pad so that you won't write over something you've already written. These memory-joggers will help you expand on your ideas after the last curtain call.

One of the questions currently undergoing hot debate is whether it is fair to use the same standards of judgment for a little-theater production in, say, Fargo, North Dakota, as for a play on Broadway. Before you embark on a reviewing career, decide whether your standards will be absolute or relative.

PICTURES AT AN EXHIBITION

Before you visit an art exhibit you plan to review, you'll save time and frustration if you make a list. A clipboard is handy, I've found, for this sort of review viewing. If brochures listing the exhibited works are available, arrange to obtain one for advance study. Here are some of the questions you will want to ask yourself when you're on the scene.

1. Is the quality consistent?
2. Which of the works are most outstanding?

3. Has the purpose of the exhibit been accomplished (e.g., chronicling the artist's artistic progression, providing a representational sampling of work in the genre, complementing the exhibit's theme)?
4. Are any unusual media involved?
5. During what time period were the works completed?
6. Is the exhibit worth traveling an hour or paying money to see? Why? Why not?

PLAYING TO THE AUDIENCE

The cardinal rule for any kind of reviewing is always to keep your readers in mind. Almost all fall into three groups: people who use reviews as guides to their book, record, movie, TV program, or live entertainment choices; people who want to know what's going on in the arts; and those who, having read a book, listened to a record, watched a TV show, or attended a movie, art exhibit, or performance, want to know what others have to say about it.

Built into your role as reviewer are certain obligations to these readers. Although imaginative writing enhances a review, if you're too clever you will obscure the purpose of the piece. By the same token, even though you have an extensive background in the genre, don't be esoteric or highbrow. You may impress readers with your knowledge, but you won't be fulfilling your function as a reviewer.

Don't let personal feelings get in your way. You may disagree with the author's point of view, but that is not in itself sufficient reason to warrant condemnation of a work. Never let your prejudices color your conclusions. Don't quote out of context, misrepresent, or omit material because of a personal bias.

The hallmark of a first-rate reviewer is credibility. You'll want readers to know that when they see your by-line they can believe what they read; that you won't give them bad advice on spending their entertainment dollars. So don't exaggerate. Be precise and honest.

When a performance is top-drawer, say so. But if the play is cliché-ridden, its plot hackneyed, and the actors all seem to have overdosed with Valium, tell it like it is, even if the producer is your brother-in-law. However, before you scathe, do become knowledgeable about the "fair comment" provisions of press law. You'll find that while you can call a work of art or a single performance unredeemable trash, your comment that the artist is incapable of producing anything of value can land you in court. Even brothers-in-law can sue.

To hone your critiquing skills, study the reviews in such publications as the *New York Times*, *Christian Science Monitor*, *Atlantic Monthly*, and the *New Yorker*. You'll note that well-crafted reviews have verve and punch, often attained by the use of similes and carefully chosen adjectives. They also achieve a good balance between description and evaluation of content and style. Their authors are specific, avoiding overused words like *brilliant*, *boring*, *pleasant*, *pretty*, *interesting*, and *nice*.

You'll score editorial curtain calls if you are scrupulous about submitting reviews of the required length. If word limits aren't spelled out, count words in a half-dozen previously printed reviews in the publication and work within that range. Be sure the review arrives at the publication in good condition, on time, and directed to the proper person. If for some reason you cannot handle an assignment, notify the editor at once.

Reviewing the arts is perhaps the least lucrative of the short forms if you calculate gain as the ratio between time spent and payment. But if you look at reviewing in terms of the enjoyment it offers, the contacts you will make, and the stimulation of being center-stage in the cultural scene, it can be one of the most rewarding forms of professional writing.

CHAPTER FIFTEEN

EAT AND TELL

A gourmet can tell from the flavor whether a wood-cock's leg is the one on which the bird is accustomed to roost.

Lucius Beebe

henever I hear of struggling writers who live in garrets and warm their soup over camp stoves, I shake my head in dismay. Why in the name of Craig Claiborne aren't they dining on nectar and ambrosia at that charming cafe two blocks down the street and writing a review about it?

One writer, Karen MacNeil, did just that. "I was renting in a poor Puerto Rican neighborhood—a ghettoey area of Manhattan," says MacNeil. "I saw an ad in the paper for a restaurant reviewer. I decided to apply: It was solely to eat."

The editor was discouraging. Why should he hire her when many of the applicants were well-known reviewers, he asked. But MacNeil was hungry, so she talked him into giving her one day to prove herself.

Since MacNeil didn't have money to spare for dinner, she headed to the bar at her favorite restaurant for information.

After she had deluged the bartender with questions and requests for recipes, the chef came out of the kitchen. "But wait, Madam," he said. "Come in and have dinner."

"All kinds of dishes floated out of the kitchen," says MacNeil. "Some I'd never seen before. At 2 a.m., full and satisfied on the best meal of my life, I got home and wrote." She landed the job, and her career—which has included food-focused pieces for *Travel & Leisure*, *Bon Appetit*, and a book on nutrition and cuisine—was launched.

You don't have to be starving to become a restaurant reviewer. Any writer with a taste for good food can develop the skills necessary to sell culinary comments. Of course, it will also help if you're familiar with all kinds of foods and not timid about trying the unfamiliar. You should have (or acquire) a good knowledge of cooking techniques, too, so that you can tell whether the salmon was poached or baked.

BEFORE SITTING DOWN AT TABLE

In order to tell about your gastronomic adventures, you have to know what exactly it is that you have eaten, so you'll also want to invest in some cookbooks if you don't already have a lifetime supply. My reference library includes the *New York Times* cookbooks, Julia Child's *Mastering the Art of French Cooking*, and that marvelous kitchen standby, *The Joy of Cooking*, as well as those published by *Gourmet* and an assortment of specialty cookbooks. I also collect paperbacks of restaurant reviews when I'm traveling and cut out the best of the magazine reviews for my files. It will also help (and perhaps provide material for other articles) to take some gourmet cooking courses. Watch for those offered by kitchenware shops, utility companies, and appliance stores, since they're often free. If you can, arrange to spend an hour or so in the kitchen of any good-sized restaurant, observing the chopping, stirring, saucing, and garnishing. Read books about foods and wine. They are great bedtime reading and will add to your body of culinary knowledge. The more you know about food preparation, the better reviews you will write.

Pleasing the Publisher's Palate

Once again, you'll need to sharpen your marketing skills, for even the best-crafted review doesn't have a chance unless it's paired with the right publication.

In addition to the many newspapers that feature food and restaurant reviews, there are a variety of magazines that print them regularly. You'll want to become familiar with as many of them as you can.

City and regional magazines are where you'll find the most opportunities. Some of them use reviews of single restaurants. Others like reviews to compare three or four of a particular kind of eatery: elegant cafes, pizza parlors, Chinese restaurants, or delis, for instance.

Since the offices of city and regional magazines are usually not too far from where you live, phone the editor for an appointment. Then, armed with a sample review (or clips of reviews you have published elsewhere), meet with her to talk about restaurants. Have several in mind and tell her about them. Even if your city or regional publication doesn't usually run restaurant reviews, your visit to the editor might prove productive. Perhaps she has considered them but hasn't yet found the person for the job. If she hasn't thought about using reviews, your conversation may prompt her to do so.

Airline in-flights are another potential market. Most of them use some form of review, either subjective or brief, objective pieces, about dining places in their route cities.

Auto club publications are good markets, too. For example, *Discovery*, the Allstate Motor Club magazine, carries a regular "Food for the Traveler" department that features reviews of restaurants around the country. In order to get an assignment, you must query first, enclosing a copy of the menu with your letter.

Newspapers and city/regional magazines are the easiest of these markets to break into. Payment for a review can range from a free meal and a few dollars to $100 or more.

Editors have definite ideas what they want in the reviews they buy. *Discovery's* editor, Sarah Hoban, says, "What makes me want to read a restaurant review is, first of all, a description of the food itself. Then I want a good feel of the restaurant. The purpose of the review is to sell the reader on going there, so the writer should do his or her best to describe the food and atmosphere."

Susan Hermance of *Utah Holiday* agrees that a description of the food is most important, "not just writing down what's on the menu." Then, in addition to the restaurant's decor and ambience, Hermance likes to know about entertainment—whether it's any good (or annoying and distracting). It's also important to note whether servings are generous or skimpy (i.e., worth the price), whether parking is tight or costs, and whether anything detracts from the overall service.

It's often difficult to tell by reading reviews whether they are written by freelancers, staffers, or writers assigned to do them on a regular basis. Therefore, in almost all cases it's a good idea to query the editor, listing the restaurants you wish to review.

Choose restaurants that complement those featured by the publication in the past, whether sophisticated, family-style, or funky. The restaurant should be worth reviewing; i.e., it should serve well-prepared food and should not be on the verge of having its health department permit revoked. You'll get ideas about potential candidates from friends, ads in newspapers, phone books, and local tourist publications.

Get Ready for Supper

Your reviewing job will be easier if you devise a worksheet to take with you to the restaurant. You may feel conspicuous (not to mention gauche) taking notes in white-linen-and-candlelight establishments, but this problem can be solved by a couple of well-timed trips to the powder room for intensive scribbling.

In less posh surroundings, I usually fold my review form (printed side out) in the pages of an oversize paperback. That way, from time to time I can open the book, jot down a phrase or two, and resume eating.

The form I've devised looks like this. I write additional comments on the reverse side, which is blank.

READY, SET, EAT

I prefer to dine alone when I am reviewing. Distractions are minimal, I can take complete notes without being rushed, and there is plenty of room on the table for my book. The advantage of group dining—being able to sample more of the menu choices—is outweighed for me by these considerations unless my dinner companions are gourmets who delight in spending the mealtime discussing the food.

If you're being paid well enough to afford it (or someone else is picking up the tab), visit the restaurant twice—the first time alone; the second, with one to three gourmet friends who will share their reactions and let you sample what they've ordered. John Brady, former editor of *Writer's Digest* who currently edits *Boston Magazine*, likes to take his young daughter to appropriate restaurants to gauge the restaurant's treatment of youngsters.

If your one-time experience at the restaurant is solo, order house specialties, including one item from each category of courses. Never order a food you detest. No matter how well it is prepared, odds are you won't like it.

When your meal is really bad, you might want to give the restaurant a second chance—if your wallet and stomach can absorb the cost. Perhaps it was the chef's night off, his stand-in got sick, and the cooking was done by the proprietor's two 15-year-old nieces. If a return visit is out of the question, try to learn whether the regular chef was in the kitchen or if there were other extenuating circumstances. When you can't find out, you might want to write something like, "It's possible that I was there on an off night" to be as fair as you can. Anyone who has ever cooked knows that there can be times when the mayonnaise curdles and the custard won't set. As a reviewer, you will want to be sure your evaluations are accurate.

NAME OF RESTAURANT _____
ADDRESS _____
PHONE NUMBER _____ HOURS OPEN _____
DAYS CLOSED _____

CREDIT CARDS ACCEPTED (CHECK THOSE APPLICABLE)
    VISA ☐   MASTERCARD ☐   AMERICAN EXPRESS ☐
    DINERS CLUB ☐   CARTE BLANCHE ☐   OTHER _____

DECOR/AMBIENCE (e.g., wall coverings, flocked wallpaper, photos
of old lumber mills, cabinets of china and cut glass, piano player who
does show tunes) _____
_____
_____

CLIENTELE (e.g., young professionals, dockworkers _____
_____
_____

SEATING: TABLES, BOOTHS, BANQUETTES, COUNTERS (e.g.,
What color scheme and materials are used?) _____
_____
_____

TABLE SETTINGS: DISHES, GLASSWARE, LINEN, PLACE MATS,
FLOWERS, OR OTHER DECORATION (e.g., What colors are they?
what materials? ironstone dishes, silk flowers?) _____
_____
_____
_____

WAITER/WAITRESS ATTIRE, IF OUT OF THE ORDINARY (e.g.,
peasant blouses, black bodices and pastel dirndl skirts, artist's
smocks and berets) _____
_____
_____

HOUSE SPECIALTIES (brief description of each) _____
_____
_____
_____
_____
_____

SPECIAL TOUCHES (e.g., individual loaves of bread, pots of pâté, fingerbowls, special menus for children, complimentary liqueurs, red roses presented to ladies on leaving) _____
_____
_____

PRICE RANGE (specify whether complete dinner or à la carte) ___
_____
_____

WINE LIST: EXAMPLES AND PRICES (e.g., extensive selection, rare vintages, wide assortment of Californian, French, or German) ___
_____

BAR/DRINK FEATURES (e.g., drinks garnished with paper umbrellas and fresh fruits, unusual glassware, exotic drinks) _____
_____

HIGHLIGHTS (e.g., dessert cart, singing waiters, excellent salads)
_____

WEAKNESSES (e.g., slow service, cold food, dishes too highly/lightly seasoned) _____
_____

ADDITIONAL COMMENTS _____
_____
_____
_____

After-Dinner Hints

Though I make it a practice to visit restaurant review candidates unannounced, as I leave I always present my card and request a copy of the menu (with a promise to return it).

If necessary, I also make an appointment to interview the manager or owner within a day or two. These interviews are usually brief. During the fifteen or twenty minutes I allocate for this facet of my research, I find out who the owners are, how they got into the restaurant business, and when they began. I also obtain background information on the head chef and the manager: where they were trained, where they worked in the past. This information is vital for reviews like, "Imported Perfection" by Lee Perry, from *AirCal Magazine*, since they focus as much on the restaurant's ownership/management as they do on the cuisine. The following excerpts illustrate that focus:

> La Brasserie, located in Orange, is a five-room restaurant in its fifth year of operation. La Brasserie's owners, Paul Rossi and Joseph Vieillemaringe, are natives of France and believe that the best restaurant is one in which the ownership is in front and back: Joseph is head chef, and Paul graciously attends to the expanding roster of devoted clientele.
>
> Vieillemaringe is from the town of Limoges in south central France, where he began his culinary career peeling vegetables at age 12. "I was in the generation of post-war kids," says Joseph. "After the war you had to make a living and we had seven kids at home."
>
> Joseph feels strongly that anyone going into the restaurant business should apprentice in order to refine the craft. "Nowadays we see people go to school to be a chef but to apprentice is the most important. You would study three months with vegetables, three months with the soup, then the fish, and the pastry, and the sauces. The head chef, he always tells you: 'go here, go there.' "
>
> Joseph is a demanding head chef, and by his own admission is "not an easy man." Easy or not, the offerings at La Brasserie reflect a dedication to careful preparation. "The key to good food," he says, "is to keep it simple—you need a system that you stick to. When you have something good, it is better to say to the customer 'wait one minute more,' so you can give just the right touch."

The article continues with seven more paragraphs about food and ambience, then closes with this paragraph:

La Brasserie is open Monday through Friday from 11:30 to 2 p.m. for lunch, Monday through Saturday from 5 to 10 p.m. for dinner; and is closed on Sunday. The restaurant is located at 202 South Main Street in Orange. Reservations may be made by calling (714) 978-6161. Visa, MasterCard, American Express, and "even cash," says Paul Rossi, are accepted.

Occasionally, I also speak to the chef—to find out what he did to give the chocolate mousse such a flawless texture or what she put into the vichyssoise to achieve that distinctive flavor. Some reviews are accompanied by recipes and the chef is the person to get them from (get the manager's permission to print the restaurant's recipes first).

This is an ideal place to reinforce what was said earlier about querying an editor rather than sending a completed manuscript. In the three months between the time the *AirCal* excerpts were chosen for this book and the manuscript was completed, the magazine changed publishers (from McFadden Publishing Company to Halsey Publishing). Editor Steve Winston at Halsey reports that the new *AirCal* won't be using restaurant reviews.

If you send a manuscript to any magazine without querying first, you run the risk of changes in the publishers and/or editors, placing your manuscript in a no-win situation. Whenever you are in doubt as to whether certain kinds of pieces in a publication are bought from freelancers, make a twenty-second phone call to ask before you write the query.

Picking Up the Tab

Since the pay for most restaurant reviews is at least $75 (and often a good deal more), paying for your meals won't hurt so much. There are times, too, when the publication will foot the bill or when you will be invited by a public relations firm or the restaurant itself to dine at a particular establishment. In the invitation situation, the pros recommend that you present the invitation *after* you have finished the meal to ensure that you'll get the same treatment your readers can expect.

SLAVING OVER A HOT TYPEWRITER

After you've read reams of restaurant reviews and have written a few of them, you'll acquire an extensive vocabulary of adjectives. If you have the foresight to include these key terms on the worksheet you use at the restaurant, you'll make the actual writing of the review much smoother. Noting the words that carry the exact nuances you wish to convey is especially important in restaurant reviewing, since they are among the most adjective-laden pieces you'll find. Take a *small* versus an *intimate* dining room, for example; or *attentive* versus *efficient* service. In each pair, one adjective conveys a meaning quite different from that of the other.

The reason for all these descriptive words is to give the reader a strong sense of ambience. Note the descriptive phrases in this review, "KK Tei," by Loryn Yim, which appeared in *Aloha*:

Restaurants remind me of entertainers. The good ones have a faithful following and earn a lasting name for themselves. The mediocre ones persevere, but never come close to hitting the mark of fame. And the rest fade away like many a Hollywood hopeful, to be replaced by others eager for a lucrative bite of the business.

KK Tei is into its fourteenth year of operation with no signs of retiring or falling into disfavor with its "fans." It has enjoyed star status in Hilo for a long time, its good food and reasonable prices outweighing what few negatives exist. True, the traffic that passes along busy Kamehameha Avenue often drowns out the restaurant's background music. Yes, the only air that circulates is from the breezes that blow (or don't blow) through opened sliding doors and windows. And yes, interior decorations are somewhat sparse (there are only a few fans and scrolls to perk up the walls). But it's a place where you can take the kids without worrying about what's going to be said or spilled, and where you can eat lunch in jeans and a tee-shirt without feeling the least bit apologetic. KK Tei is not only family-style, it is family-run—owned and managed by relatives of its founder, the late K.K. Kobata.

Japanese food is its forte, but there are also American choices on the menu for those who can't get over their terror of seaweed and *sashimi*. Lunch entrees such as *tonkatsu*, shrimp *tempura* and pork tofu may be ordered either with rice or mashed potatoes and vegetables, or Japanese-style with *miso* soup, rice, *tsukemono, namasu, sashimi* and tea. (To me, pork tofu goes with mashed potatoes as well as peanut butter goes with catsup—but at least diners have the option.) Prices average about a dollar more if you opt for the Japanese accompaniments. There are also sandwiches, salads and a nice variety of noodle dishes.

I've never been able to turn down the *teishoku* or combination meal whenever I see it on the menu. KK Tei's *teishoku* choices are beef *teriyaki*, *shoyu* pork, sweet/sour spareribs and grilled butterfish, served with shrimp *tempura*. It was easy to single out our favorites—I decided on the *teriyaki teishoku* and my companion zeroed in on the butterfish. Both were priced at about five dollars, and both came to the table very hot and generously portioned. I would've liked the *teriyaki* with a smidgin more ginger and a smidgin less of the salty *shoyu*, but it was a treat nonetheless when eaten with rice. The butterfish, upon sampling, was lightly seasoned and just cooked, so that the fish's natural flavor and moistness were preserved. To me, there's no greater culinary sin than overcooking or overwhelming a fish.

The *miso* soup was especially good, with slices of onion and squares of tofu in the broth. The *sashimi* was also excellent—very fresh and firm with not a trace of "fishiness." KK Tei obviously has a good thing going for it, being located near the harbor and the freshest catches of the day. I was disappointed, though, with the *tempura*, which my companion informed me was done local-style with a soft, very thick batter instead of light and crisp—the traditional Japanese way. But the shrimp (when I got to them) were juicy, and the *tempura* sauce was the way I like it best—warm with a hint of *daikon* flavor.

Dinners at KK Tei are also offered either Japanese or American-style. The entrees are the same, but the rest of the meal depends on whether you have a yen for rice or mashed potatoes, *tsukemono* or tossed greens. Prices are the same either way: The New York steak, for example, is $10.50; the *teriyaki* chicken, $6.00; and the shrimp butter-yaki (shrimp, mushrooms and vegetables sauteed in garlic butter and spices), $8.70. Most of the entrees fall in the six-dollar range—a pretty good deal for a pretty good meal.

KK Tei welcomes private parties and has rooms available that can accommodate from six to 190. Advance reservations are required, no matter how small or large your special group may be.

One of the highlights of a visit to KK Tei is not even on the menu. Beyond a wall of sliding wooden doors is a beautiful Japanese garden with pebble pathways, waterfalls, tranquil pool with carp, and an *ojisosama*. It's a nice place to pause and enjoy some time with a special friend. The gardens are lighted at night, and with light winds nudging drowsy orchids, golden carp playing in the water, and trees and shrubs dramatically silhouetted, a stroll is a splendid way to end an evening. Or begin one.

KK TEI
1550 Kamehameha Avenue
Hilo, island of Hawaii.
Phone: 961-3791
Free parking in restaurant lot.
Daily except Sunday
Lunch 11:00 A.M.-2:00 P.M.
Closed Christmas Day, New Year's
Day and Thanksgiving.
Reservations requested.
Major credit cards accepted.

Notice the differences in the format for nuts-and-bolts information about hours, credit cards, and the like, between the KK Tei and La Brasserie pieces. It's attention to details like these that whets an editor's appetite for your reviews.

To my way of thinking, the best review writing is relaxed, with clever turns of phrase—a style popular with most editors. I especially admire the reviews Ingrid Wilmot writes for a number of magazines, including several of the airline in-flights published by East/West Network, Inc., and *National Motorist.*

Wilmot's recipe for a well-crafted review includes "knowledge of preparation of food, fairness, an open mind, a curious palate, plus a touch of humor." She has put all those ingredients into this review, which appeared in the programs of several southern California theaters, including those of the Shubert Theatre and the Hollywood Bowl:

CENTURY CITY DINING & WINING

Century City is a mini model of L.A. with its high powered corporate offices, first class shops, famous theatre and entertainment complex, prestigious hotel and stylish town houses. And where can one digest all this glamor and excitement? That depends on your schedule.

Say, you're drained (physically) from the daily grind or (financially) from a shopping spree, THE CHAFING DISH in The Broadway, 10250 Santa Monica Blvd., 277-1234, is a good bet. Why did I think it was just a tea room for the ladies who lunch, when it's so much more? There's even a small salad bar, with fresh greens, potato salad, fruit, crackers and cheese ($3.95). The familiar "springtime veranda" theme, dominated by lime green, white latticework and live plants, is always jolly.

Nowhere on that menu does it say, but now you know, that dinners come with salad or soup. On my visit, the navy bean with ham was hearty and robust as a seaworthy sailor. You may also have to interrogate the waitress about the "special": entree, salad bar or soup, coffee and Broadway's renowned cheese cake, all for $7.95, probably your best deal of the week. Always available is Dover sole. You've paid a bundle for the tableside deboning of this fish, executed with surgical skill by a flamboyant captain. Trouble is, you can't charge it to Blue Cross. Here they do it behind the scenes and bring it out with sliced almonds and mushrooms for $5.50 and it's lovely. Also tasty, though a bit heavy on the gravy, is the London broil ($5.75), a big portion of tender sliced beef with a mound of yellow rice and, yes, frozen peas. They were well seasoned, so I won't fink to the truth-in-menu-man that it says thereon "served with *fresh* vegetables." Daily from 11 a.m. to 8 p.m., Saturday until 8:30 p.m. Free parking. AE and Broadway card. No reservations.

Just one of the things you'll love about THE HIGHWAYMAN, 10250 Santa Monica Blvd., 552-4505, is the wonderful idea of letting you choose dinner in three portions and price ranges. Why hasn't anybody thought of this before? Thus, even their luscious lamb rack, charred and crisp without, pink within, comes in small ($8.95), medium ($12.95) and large ($15.95) as well as all beef and fish items. Shark, which people have been devouring with a vengeance since *Jaws I*, has the texture of mahi-mahi and tastes great charbroiled. What doesn't? Their famous pork ribs have an almost Oriental ginger-clove scent and their steaks are really juicy, faithfully basted with Highwayman sauce, containing worcestershire, red wine and 25 other ingredients so secret only two persons, one living in South Africa, know the recipe. Pray for their health because that sauce must be preserved for posterity. Quality leaves nothing to be desired, judging by the filet mignon ($9.50, $14.25, $16.25). A la carte includes rice pilaf or baked potato and fruit garnish, which most of us would trade for a vegetable. You could start with their unusual artichoke pate, containing cream cheese and garlic, nicely set forth with bread rounds ($2.75); and because all's well that ends well, you don't want to miss the yummy Kahlua mousse pie ($2.50).

Having given the food its just dues usually paves the way for some constructive (I hope) criticism. I feel they lack finesse. Where, for example, are the finger bowls for the sticky pinkies? And, when the first wine ordered is unavailable and a more expensive one is suggested and brought, is it not proper etiquette to charge the price of the first choice by way of apology? In front, a cocktail bar buzzes with activity, but the calm circular dining room which centers around a mammoth Areca palm beneath a domed ceiling, a knotty pine wall hung with copper utensils has a very pleasant, friendly air, as have all members of the staff. Weekday lunch, dinner nightly, cocktails. Free parking. All credit cards. Closed Sunday.

Finally, for what qualifies as the Total Dining Experience, I refer you to THE VINEYARD, on the lower level of the Century Plaza Hotel, Avenue of the Stars, 277-2000. From the cordial welcome by Maitre d' Gulen, to the attentive busboy who passes the bread basket, a *real* bread basket as you will see, they treat you like the guest of honor at a testimonial—without getting on your nerves. A sommelier pours vintage wines from a tremendous list and your glass never runs dry.

The luxurious menu shows the imagination of the *nouvelle* while retaining the comfort of the familiar, but just so you shouldn't get bored, Chef Raimund Hofmeister supplants it with seasonal specials like pheasant, wild game, grouse and hare. Wow! Should you find the complimentary cheese dip a mite tart (I did), chart a different beginning. Perhaps the exquisite sweetbreads with fresh pfifferling mushrooms en vinaigrette? Don't tell me you're tired of that! Very well then, there's smoked goose breast, oyster bisque, chilled avocado soup or a scintillating Plantation Salad ($4.50), combining Japanese mushrooms in limestone lettuce cups, parchment crisp Belgian endive and a bouquet of watercress. Delightful! I would have loved to try the salmon in sorrel sauce and caviar ($15), scallops with dill ($14) or the beef filet with goose liver and pink peppercorns ($17.50) but finally settled on duckling in Madeira sauce with artichokes, sliced Spanish and black olives ($16) and thick, incredibly tender veal medallions in a fresh leek-cream sauce ($18). No regrets whatever. Everything arrives *sous cloche,* not losing a degree of temperature between stove and table and includes an array of vegetables. This night a cauliflowerette, baby carrot and a Brussels sprout. Were they *al dente?* You bet your asparagus! Oh, and a few stalks of those, too, and with the veal a wild rice mix. Even if you have the fortitude to wave the dessert cart past you, you'll never resist the petit fours. Those chocolatey little devils would make Pritikin himself lose his head. The center focus of the elegant room is an enormous basket of silk flowers;

the three smaller dining areas are lined with wine vitrines; tables are well spaced for conversational privacy and a harpist softly strums pretty melodies to complete the illusion of heaven. Your cloud awaits nightly at 6 p.m. Weekday lunch. Validated parking. Cocktails. All credit cards. Closed Sunday.

As you can see, first-rate reviewing involves detouring readers away from the soggy souffle as well as singing praise to the pella.

TRUTH IN RESTAURANT REVIEWING

Be aware of fair comment as it applies to press law. It's perfectly okay to criticize a restaurant's food, service, and decor. But if you say that the place is a total loss, that its personnel are incapable of producing a decent meal or providing adequate service, you had better be prepared to appear in court.

The reviews I feel most comfortable writing are those about restaurants I have chosen myself. Eating out is expensive, and under no circumstances do I want to lead unsuspecting diners to the local ptomaine tavern or give a bum steer to a steakhouse. When I select my own review restaurants, I've exercised quality control even before I begin writing.

Anne Mackenzie, whose restaurant reviews have appeared in the Baltimore *News American*, *Maryland Magazine*, and the Bel Air *Aegis*, likes to visit each restaurant twice in the company of her husband or a photographer, ordering the establishment's most requested dishes. Although Mackenzie believes that "a little constructive criticism" is part of the reviewer's job, she will never "truly pan" a restaurant, as she has seen a number of them fail as the result of a critic's comments. In addition to remarking on ambience, food, service, and the wine list and giving particulars about location and such, Mackenzie suggests that writers also include information on what services for the handicapped are available.

But there are times when restaurant write-ups are assigned by editors of hotel in-room visitors' guides or magazines such as weekly tourist publications. These markets don't allow the reviewer the freedom to comment candidly that non-public relations magazines do, since reviews are usually about restaurants that advertise in the publications.

It is possible, however, to be honest without writing a negative word, especially if you're called upon to do a number of short reviews. Wax enthusiastic with mouth-watering adjectives about the eateries that are really memorable, and confine your remarks on the unrecommendables to "House specialties include . . .," "Among the less expensive entrees are . . .," or "A half dozen desserts are offered, including Jell-O, fruit cocktail and chocolate sundaes." If the decor is tacky, you don't have to say so. Just describe it objectively. Readers will opt in most cases for the cafes you've written about in glowing terms, and you needn't worry about having led them astray. Beside, some people may like orange formica with cerise velvet drapes.

In writing, one experience always seems to lead to another. Perhaps, like Karen MacNeil, you'll go on to books on nutrition and cuisine. Or you may become so *enormously* successful reviewing restaurants that you'll be able to write diet books with great authority.

CHAPTER SIXTEEN

PINT-SIZE PIECES

Mankind owes to the child the best it has to give.
United Nations Charter

ust because you were a kid once doesn't automatically qualify you as a writer of children's articles. But if there's a part of you that never quite grew up, that looks at the world with the wonder of new eyes; if you can recall your childhood pathos and pleasures, intrigues and interests, you have the makings of a children's writer.

Children go for the gusto. They're enthusiastic, aware, alive. They haven't had time to become jaded, blasé, or disillusioned. And they don't want to read pieces by writers who have.

There's another capacity you must have: that for translating the feelings and curiosities you had as a youngster into those of today's children. Although children who grew up before the advent of space shuttles and test-tube babies had the same basic emotions youngsters have today, they grew up in different environments and therefore had different experiences.

My mother pointed this out to me some years ago when her grandsons were worrying aloud about the threat of nuclear war. "When I was little," Mom said, "we worried about the horse running away with the buggy. That could mean death, too." Yesterday's child cried over a broken china doll. Today's child, with an unbreakable doll, cries when the mechanism that makes the doll talk won't work anymore. But they shed the same tears.

Writing for children's publications won't make you an instant millionaire. Average pay is two to four cents a word. Only a few magazines pay as much as $300 and more for 900-word features. But if you also write for adult publications, writing for children can be more profitable than you might imagine. An idea can often work for both juvenile and adult articles; so your research can do double duty.

Say, for example, that on your travels you come in contact with an aboriginal tribe in the South Seas who make marvelous carvings out of soapstone-like a substance and whose daily life is filled with intriguing customs. You've already sold a story on their carvings to an art publication and one about the area's scenic attractions to a travel magazine. If you write children's articles, you have at least two more article possibilities: how to make carvings from soap and what day-to-day life in Tonbagongacoola is like.

THE YOUNG SET

To get off to the right start in your marketing campaign, study the listings under "Juveniles" in *Writer's Market*. Each specifies the age group for which the magazine is intended. These vary widely (2-12, 6-12, and 9-12 years, for instance). Select twenty or thirty of the magazines that sound most promising and obtain copies. Your own children may receive some of them. Ask friends whose children regularly read different publications to save old issues for you. You will be able to find still others at your local library, the libraries of colleges that have teaching programs, or on the newsstands.

Send for sample copies of the rest, along with guidelines for writers. Some of the sample copies will cost you a dollar or two; others are free or can be obtained by sending a self-addressed, stamped envelope. Later, when you receive an assignment or go-ahead on speculation, you can ask the editor for three or four back issues so that you can study the magazine's style.

Other sources of information on children's publications are *Children's Media Marketplace*, *Children's Magazine Guide*, *The Writer*, and *Writer's Digest*.

When you have become well acquainted with the kiddies' publications, you will note that some companies put out a number of them. The Children's Better Health Institute of the Benjamin Franklin Literary & Medical Society, Inc., publishes *Children's Digest*, *Jack & Jill*, *Humpty Dumpty's Magazine*, *Children's Playmate*, *Child Life*, *Turtle Magazine for Preschool Kids*, *Health Explorer*, and *Jr. Medical Detective*. This can be an advantage when submitting a query or manuscript. If your idea or article is a good one but isn't quite right for the magazine to which you've sent it, the editor will pass it along to editors of affiliated publications.

On studying your collected magazines, you will find that many of the weekly Sunday school publications use few nonfiction articles. Most of them print a short story and several activities in each issue, and only occasionally a nonfiction piece. A few of these weekly magazines, however, do run articles regularly, so let your sample copies be your guide. Monthly church-sponsored and secular magazines, though they come out less frequently, are bigger nonfiction markets.

Competition is fiercest at the highest-profile (and often highest-paying) magazines, such as *Highlights for Children*, where editor Kent L. Brown reports that he receives 100 queries and 1,000 manuscripts each month. At not-so-well-known magazines like *Our Little Friends* and *Primary Treasure* (published by the same company), the acceptance odds are much better.

This by no means exhaustive list will help you to size up your chances:

Publication	Number of Queries/ Manuscripts Received Monthly	Number of Manuscripts Purchased Monthly
Alive for Young Teens	100+	10
Christian Adventurer	100	13 (per quarter)
Ebony Jr.	80-100	10
The Friend	625	not available
Highlights for Children	1,000	100
Junior Trails	80-100	5-10
Odyssey	50-100	1-2
Our Little Friend, Primary Treasure	400	40
Ranger Rick's Nature Magazine	100-200	10-20
Story Friends	75-100	5-7
Teens Today	120-130	4-6
Trails	50-75	3-5
Wonder Time	108	7-13
Young Judean	not available	18-20/year

WHY THEY SAY NAY

Don't let these figures keep you from your typewriter. First listen to a few editors' reasons for rejecting submissions. Brown says that rejected material "is not of interest to our readers—too specialized or too mature" and "the author does not know anything special about his or her topic." Louis Schutter of *Our Little Friend* and *Primary Treasure* says rejected material "does not meet our specialized needs." Most of *Odyssey* editor Nancy Mack's articles come from a stable of regular writers. Her reasons for rejection—bad research, poor organization, too technical or boring—are those that any competent writer should be able to overcome. Mike Dixon, editor of *Alive for Young Teens*, says that one of the main reasons for his rejection of manuscripts is that they're not slanted toward the right age group (12-15). John Maempa, *Junior Trails* editor, says much of the material he receives is "not relevant to the junior-age readers [10-11] as pertaining to social trends, interests, hobbies, peer pressure, etc." Marcia V. Roebuck, managing editor of *Ebony Jr!*, says, "Most of the manuscripts that we receive do not meet the interest needs or level for our reading audience."

So it goes, with a recurring theme. Contributors have not taken the time to get to know their intended publications.

Apparently, they haven't become acquainted with their intended readers either. If you're writing for eight- to ten-year-olds (or any other age group), it's vital that you understand what people of those ages think is important—what's interesting enough to make them read your magazine article instead of watching television.

Topics that grown-ups find interesting often leave kids cold. So you cannot assume that just because you find bioethics or sixteenth-century philosophy fascinating, they'll make terrific subjects for children's articles.

If you don't have children of the age you're writing for, borrow one or two (or three). Take a friend's children on a day's outing. Ask questions: "What do you like to read about?" "What's the most interesting thing you can think of?" "What's your favorite thing to do?" "What are you going to be when you grow up?" Then listen. *Really* listen.

WRITING FOR A CHILD'S AGE

The same little friends you "borrowed" will come in handy again when your article is written. Watch their reactions as they read your manuscript. Are they enthusiastic, perplexed, bored? Ask if there's anything more they would like to know about the subject. Also ask, point blank, "What parts did you think were boring?" Kids are generally very frank. They'll tell you.

If for any reason you suspect you're getting the appearing-to-be-interested-to-be-polite reaction, say something like "I didn't like the part about the _____ too well." When you initiate the criticism, most children will stop being polite and start being honest.

Not only should you know your readers' likes and dislikes. You must also have a good idea of their abilities. But how do you know how well a seven- or ten- or eleven-year-old can read? There is a wide variation in reading ability among children of the same age group. Therefore, you will want to aim at the average reader.

According to Alice Taylor of the Washoe County, Nevada, Department of Education, basic spelling books for the various grades will give a good idea of what words a child can (or should be able to) read at a given level. If you are writing for six- to eight-year-olds, build your article around words the average second-grader can read.

You might want to read some nonfiction books on your subject to get an idea of what a particular age group is expected to know as well as how to deal with the subject.

Another technique is to use words no more difficult than those appearing in back copies of the magazine. Articles for younger children (who will be read to) can often contain harder words than those meant to be read by children themselves.

It's not only what you say, but how you say it. Have you ever noticed the kind of people who turn kids off? They're patronizing, gushy, dictatorial, preachy, grouchy. Those are pretty much the same qualities you would find in a pile of rejected children's articles. Pieces that talk down to youngsters, tell them what to do without giving reasons, or treat them as babies aren't going to captivate young people, much less slip by a competent editor.

In any case, using basic vocabulary shouldn't be a limiting factor. Almost every subject can be explained in simple language. But it takes a good deal of thought to find the right words. After you've rough-drafted the piece, grab your thesaurus and tackle rewriting with an eye to simplification. Divide long sentences and paragraphs, too.

Lisa Rossbacher, who writes science-related articles for both children and adults, says, "I feel strongly that writing nonfiction for children requires at *least* as much understanding of the subject as writing for adults—and sometimes more. Because I cannot assume the reader will have any basic background, I must be particularly careful that my writing is clear, precise, and as simple as possible.

Writing for adults and then revising to shorter words and simpler sentences just won't work. The whole organization and texture of the article needs to provide all the necessary information to help the reader understand."

TOP TOPICS

Children's pieces usually fall into three recognizable categories: biography/profile, how-to, and informational, with the latter predominating.

Biographies and Profiles

You'll see by studying the magazines that most *biographies* are about famous historical characters who have made outstanding contributions to society: Abraham Lincoln, Florence Nightingale, Albert Schweitzer. *Profiles* usually are about children who have accomplished something out of the ordinary or adults whose exploits, inventions, or jobs are of interest to youngsters, such as Abebe Bikila who was featured in this *Highlights for Children* piece. Jenny Beck wrote it.

Winning a marathon is one of the hardest things an athlete can do. A marathon is 42.2 kilometers (26 miles, 385 yards) of nonstop running. No one can run that distance well without the courage and the determination that it takes to convince a panting, aching body to keep going.

The marathon is named in honor of Pheidippides (fi Dip ih dees), a soldier in ancient Greece who knew how to keep going. After having traveled almost 500 kilometers on foot to get help in a battle at Marathon, Pheidippides then had to carry news of the victory to Athens, 35 kilometers away. He started his run exhausted, reached Athens, gasped out the news, and fell dead.

The most extraordinary of modern marathon runners was also a soldier. As the son of an Ethiopian shepherd, Abebe Bikila (ah BAY BAY buh KEE luh) spent many hours running in the mountains near his home. Later, when he became one of the emperor's palace guards, he kept on running regularly. He enjoyed it, and running was a good way to stay in shape.

Outside of Addis Ababa, the capital city of Ethiopia, not many people had ever heard of Bikila when he entered the 1960 summer Olympics in Rome, Italy. But two hours and fifteen minutes after the marathon began, he burst through the tape and into the circle of international superstars.

The marathon began in the Olympic stadium. After a lap around the track, the runners filed out onto the streets of Rome. Part of the race would be run along the Appian Way, a road that Ethiopians had been driven down as Roman slaves thousands of years before.

Bikila started the race in a new pair of running shoes. They soon began to hurt his feet. After only a few kilometers he pulled them off. He was used to running barefoot, and that was the way he ran the rest of the race! As he entered the stadium two hours later, Bikila was 25 seconds ahead of the next runner. The crowd rose to its feet cheering. No one they had ever heard of could run such a race barefoot, and Bikila had just run it faster than anyone else in history.

After the race Bikila turned down the cool drinks and blankets that were offered. Instead he trotted another lap around the track to cool down. Later he told reporters that Ethiopians were poor people, not used to cars and trucks. "We run everywhere," Bikila said simply.

Four years later Abebe Bikila hoped to win a second Olympic marathon. No one had ever won two. A month before the race he had to have an operation. Experts said that there was no way that he could win, but Bikila did not believe them.

With his smooth, steady running style that looked so easy, Bikila started out with the pack. This time the course would take him through the streets of Tokyo. When he entered the stadium at the end of the race, he was four minutes ahead of the next runner.

Long before most of the other runners had even finished the race, Bikila was on the infield grass doing sit-ups and push-ups. Many people in the stands thought that he was showing off. Those who had watched him run before knew better. Later he explained, "It's routine with me. If I don't exercise after an exhausting run, I get cramps."

He had run the race in Tokyo in two hours, twelve minutes, and eleven seconds. He had beaten his time of four years earlier, and once again no one had ever run a faster Olympic marathon. (Since marathon courses differ so much, no official records are kept, but runners and fans enjoy comparing times even so.)

Four years later Abebe Bikila hoped to win a third Olympic marathon, this time in Mexico City. Bikila was used to running in high altitudes, for his home in Addis Ababa, like Mexico City, is far above sea level. The thinner air (with less oxygen) would not be a problem to him as it would to most of the other runners. But at thirty-seven, he was old for an Olympic runner, was in poor health, and no one else seemed able to imagine his winning a third marathon.

Leaving the stadium this time, Bikila quickly got in front of the pack. He was a leader for the first third of the race, but his easy stride was gone. It was replaced by one that showed his pain. Before the halfway point, Bikila dropped out of the race, suffering from stomach cramps and a heavy cold.

After Mexico City people were sure that Bikila's days as an Olympian were over. A year later he was almost killed in a car accident. His spine was injuired and his legs were paralyzed. He would be in a wheelchair for the rest of his life. But Bikila was a true Olympian. He loved sports and decided that he would still be an athlete, even if he could never run again. In 1971 he won a medal in archery at the Paraplegic Olympics in London.

In 1972, two years before his death, Abebe Bikila went to the Olympics in Munich, West Germany. This time he went to watch as an official guest of the German government. Athletes from around the world came to greet him in the Olympic Village. They came to show respect for a true hero.

How-Tos

How-to subjects for children run the gamut from licking the blues to planning a Halloween party to catching a cricket for a pet. (Other children's how-tos are primarily for craft projects and will be discussed in the crafts section of the following chapter.) The following "Three Cheers for August," is an article by Ivey Harrington in *Trails* telling readers how to make up their own holidays.

"I'm exhausted," Jen July exclaimed. "If I hear one more firecracker. . ."

Andy August hung his head. "You're lucky, Jen. Look at me—31 days of boredom. I could put Rip Van Winkle back to sleep."

"Why, Andy," scolded Jen. "You're the luckiest month of the year!"

"I am?"

"Look at all the other months," said Jen firmly. "We're always stuck with the same holidays. December always has Christmas, February always has Valentine's Day . . ."

"But I'm the same, too," retorted Andy. "Always boring!"

"Well, do something about it!" ordered Jen. "You can make up your own holidays and celebrate them any way you want."

"Make up my own holidays?" Any scratched his chin. A smile slowly spread over his face; then he grabbed a pen and started to scribble.

Andy August didn't waste a minute that month . . . and neither should you. Grab your calendar and fill August with holiday fun. Follow Andy's hints or invent some holidays of your own to make August the best month of the year!

Ice Cream Crazy Day

What's the best taste of summer? Ice cream! Salute that delicious dish with an ice cream smorgasbord. Invite friends or families in your neighborhood to bring their favorite flavors. (Or better yet, have guests bring their own ice cream freezers for a Make Your Own Celebration.)

Because I Love You Day

Plan secret surprises for those special people in your life. Attach notes saying "because I love you" to the surprises you create. You'll have a holiday watching your friends and family try to figure out who the phantom surpriser is.

First Annual Barefoot Day

What makes summer beautiful? Why, bare feet, of course! Celebrate this great summer sensation with a Bare-Is-Beautiful Foot Pageant. The trick is to make your feet look fantastic without socks or shoes—ever seen polka-dotted toenails?

Or, if a foot pageant doesn't tickle your toes, try a Foot-a-Feel Celebration. Fill several pans with assorted "ooshie stuff" (mud, moss, banana peels, shaving cream). Blindfold your friends and have them take the foot test. See if they can guess what's oozing between their toes. (Make sure to have this party out of doors!)

Terrific T-Shirt Day

Celebrate the T-shirt season. Have a T-shirt party and give a prize for the most unusual T-shirt. For a treat, make T-shirt cut-out cookies.

Or have a T-shirt trade off. Each friend brings a T-shirt he or she is tired of (check with Mom or Dad first for permission). Swap and shop or have a T-shirt grab bag.

Nancy Drew Day

Salute that daring detective, Nancy Drew, by having a Solve-a-Mystery Celebration. Beforehand, plan a "mystery" for the Drew detectives to solve. Gather a group of Nancy Drew fans. Decide who will be Nancy, Bess, and George. Don't forget Carson Drew, Ned Nickerson, and the villains.

First Annual Dripping Dog Day

Have fun freshening up your favorite dog. Plan a dog washing party with a couple friends. Have buckets, brushes, soap, water, and a couple of dirty dogs! Dress to get wet. Even if Rover doesn't like for you to wash behind his ears, you'll have a dripping good time.

Remember to plan a few quiet holidays, too. Keep a *Reading Holiday* ready—it's the best way to make a rainy day fun.

And to keep your parents smiling, plan a *Dare-to-Look-Under-Your-Bed Day.* You may find a long lost treasure—or at least some dust that needs attention.

Do you have August all planned? Andy is depending on you to make his month a happy one.

Informationals

The most popular subjects for *informationals* are related to science (both natural and physical), health, and people in other lands. When writing any informational piece, keep the journalist's who, where, when, what, why, and how firmly in mind. *Especially* the why. Kids ask a lot of questions, and you will want to anticipate all of them.

Asking *yourself* questions is one of the best ways of coming up with article ideas. How do salmon find the streams where they were hatched? Why does bread rise? Where do clowns get their clothes?

Laurence Pringle, whose articles have appeared in *Highlights for Children*, advises:

Find out what ideas are special to you. Your excitement or curiosity about the subject will come through in your writing, and other people will get interested, too. A woman friend of mine is fascinated by dogsled racing, which is hardly a well-known sport. Because of her strong interest, she has published several magazine articles and a book on the subject.

Some of the ideas I have written about can be traced back to interests or experiences I had while growing up in the country. I used to pick and eat wild raspberries; later I wrote a book about wild edible plants. There were no ponds or rivers close to my boyhood home, so the only fish I caught—with a hook made of a bent pin—were little chubs and other minnows from small creeks. I wanted to know more about these little fish, and eventually I studied the whole minnow family and wrote about it. . . . So, think about your own "ordinary" life. What are you curious about? Somewhere among your hobbies, friendships, troubles, dreams, and even your nightmares there are wonderful things to write about.

To be sure that your ideas are salable, study the guidelines for writers and magazine copies thoroughly before you write a word of your query or manuscript. How else can you find out that virtually all the articles in the *Children's Playmate—Humpty Dumpty* group deal with health, safety, exercise or nutritionally oriented themes? Or that *Odyssey* pieces must have some relation to astronomy or outer space?

In religious magazine articles, the denomination's beliefs or adjuncts of its programs are often tied into their messages. A piece in the LDS-sponsored *The Friend*, for example, might dovetail with the Mormon's emphasis on genealogy.

It's also important to get a feel for the magazine's underlying philosophies and taboos. Many of them are put out under church auspices, and though no reputable kiddies' publication uses blue material, that published by fundamentalist churches is absolutely lily-white. No *gees* and *darns* can slip into the dialogue. Movies, lipstick, pop records, dancing, and dozens of other subjects non-fundamentalists don't give a second thought to writing about are never mentioned—except in rare cases when they're alluded to in a negative way with no hint of approbation.

RESEARCH REMINDERS
You can't spin children's pieces off the top of your head. Research is as important for children's pieces as for adults.

Although Linda Linnard Andre specializes in biographies of artists, her comments on research can be applied to any kind of biography:

> I read a great deal before I begin to write. First I read to get the general feel of an artist's life and outlook. I sort out what's important.

Then I go hunting for very specific anecdotes and quotes that will bring my artist to life and set him apart from other artists. I never invent dialogue for my subject because I am always suspicious of that kind of writing. How does the author know what George Washington said to his mother at breakfast?

I generally try to stay away from dates, lists of where an artist studied, and names of other artists who influenced him. These are topics that are important to art historians, but I don't think they grab the imagination of a child. In fact, they don't really grab my imagination either.

Unlike skeptical adults, children tend to believe everything they read. Therefore, writers of informational articles for youngsters have to be particularly scrupulous about the accuracy of their facts. NASA Publications Specialist Gregory Vogt, who writes science articles for *Odyssey*, says:

I believe that writing science articles for children puts a special responsibility on the part of the writer to assure accuracy in factual content and understanding basic scientific principles. I realize that all non-fiction writers should strive for accuracy and understanding but science writing requires a special emphasis in this area. In many subject areas facts can be well-established and indisputable. It is the interpretation of those facts that is open for discussion. However, in science, facts can change. Unless a reference book is very new, the old "facts" will be presented as the most up-to-date. The responsibility of the writer is to know what facts are most recent and what facts are obsolete. The writer cannot count on the publisher to catch any mistakes.

Vogt's advice to writers of children's science articles to "get a good foundation and do their homework well" applies to writers of other informational articles as well. He also suggests that writers unsure of their sources should find someone who is well-versed in the subject to review the manuscript before it's sent to the publisher.

When interviewing a subject for a profile, children's writers use many of the same techniques that writers of adult personality pieces do (see Chapter 8). But there's an additional ingredient that good writers look for: their subject's humanness. If our subject had a hard time with arithmetic in school, if his father has to remind him to do his chores, if she frets because she has freckles and wears glasses, tell your readers. Don't portray your personality as perfect. The child must be able to identify in some way with the person written about—to see that person as someone who, despite accomplishments, is human rather than a god or goddess they can never hope to emulate.

When you write a how-to, be sure that the instructions are clear and in sequence. You might want to follow the directions as you've written them to be sure they're going to deliver the promised results. Even better is having a young friend test the project. Generally, the tips on writing how-tos for adults (see Chapter 5) apply to children's how-tos as well.

CLUES TO CONSTRUCTION

Though occasionally you will find longer articles, most children's pieces fall into the 300-800 word range.

Focus is generally much broader than for adult pieces of the same length. The reason is basic: children just haven't had as much time to learn as grown-ups, and one begins learning with surveys, not specifics.

Although there are definite techniques involved in writing children's pieces, they aren't difficult to master. Imagery must be kept simple. Quotes should be uncomplicated. The writing style must be lively. Adults will often read an article—dull or not—because they feel the need to have the information it contains. Kids won't.

Sentences are straightforward, the majority of them declarative. Transitions are usually natural ones, relying on sequential arrangement of material to keep the piece flowing. The style in good children's articles is clean; there is no attempt at dazzling writing. This excerpt from a piece in *Junior Trails* by Nancy M. Armstrong illustrates typical style:

> Coyotes have lived in the western part of North America for centuries. However, while more coyotes are still found in the Southwest than any other place, they can now be seen in almost every state. Coyotes have traveled north to Alaska and eastward to the New England states. The coyote has learned to live in almost any kind of country, although he prefers open plains.
>
> The coyote looks like a small German shepherd dog and seldom weighs more than 40 pounds. He runs very fast. His speed has been clocked at 45 miles per hour. The coyote has a pointed face and ears that stand erect. His teeth are made for biting and tearing. He has

long, thin legs and clawed feet which help him dig. His fur is gray or yellowish-brown in color with a long bushy tail tipped in black.

Any references you make without accompanyng explanations must be to people, places, and things your readers can relate to and have knowledge of. If you write about rumble seats, victrolas, and other relics of the past, you must tell your readers what they are.

TEEN TOPICS

Articles for teenagers are very much like those for adults as far as length, scope, and structure are concerned. Subject matter is the only area in which you will recognize a difference. Adults enjoy reading about people of all ages. Teenagers usually prefer reading about people their own age or a little older. That is why so many teen magazines profiles are about teenage TV and movie stars, and teenagers with outstanding accomplishments, unconventional jobs, or unusual hobbies.

If you will recall either your own or your offspring's adolescence, the thing you and they wanted most of all was to be accepted, to be like the other kids. It's the same with today's teenagers, even though they may act more sophisticated. More often than not, therefore, teen how-tos are aimed at self-improvement or projects they can undertake to enhance their images: how to have clearer skin, make a halter top, decorate their rooms with pillows.

Though children's publications are aimed at both sexes as a rule, most teenage publications are written for girls, and the majority of their readers are just entering or in their early teens.

FOR LOVE OR MONEY

Writing for the younger generation may not bring you riches, but it will give you the satisfaction of knowing that you've given children something to think about, strengthened their values, provided them with constructive projects. Perhaps you'll make time pass more quickly for a boy who's sick in bed or awaken an interest in a teenage girl that will lead to a fulfilling career. You'll know that you have given the children you write for your best. That's payment money can't buy.

CHAPTER SEVENTEEN

KEEPING LITTLE BODIES BUSY

Too often we give children answers to remember rather than problems to solve.

Roger Lewin

magine a cozy room with kiddies sprawled on the rug, pencils in hand. One of them is drawing what looks like a dinosaur by following the dots. Another is making a list of objects hidden in a picture. The third has just finished a mini-cross-word and is wondering which puzzle to try next.

It's a scene to gladden the heart of a children's magazine editor. Magazines with activities kids really go for are the ones that attract subscribers. But a good children's activity is hard to find. Editors moan that they always get those that call for inappropriate skill levels or duplicate worn-out ideas—material unsuited to their publications. These editors say that the majority of contributors fail to study their publications carefully. Therefore, the few writers who do study them get all the paychecks.

There's no reason you can't share in the by-lines, too. Gather together back issues of ten or twelve magazines (you can borrow some of them from the children's section of the library). Take a separate sheet of paper for each publication and list on it the kinds of activities used as well as any dominant themes—health, religion, nature, and so on.

You'll find that most activities fall into seven categories: puzzles, quizzes, jokes, riddles, recipes, experiments, and crafts.

Ideas for children's activities come easiest to people whose own activities include doing puzzles and working on crafts. But even if your days are too busy for these pastimes, you can generate ideas by browsing through puzzle and craft books. Adapt those that children would be capable of completing, changing them so that they center on subjects or items that interest youngsters. By simplifying adult-item craft projects, you'll devise "How to Make ＿＿＿＿ for Mother's Day [or Father's Day]" articles. You might also call such craft projects "Gifts for Grown-Ups You Like." Children also love to make items they can use to decorate their bikes, their books, their rooms, or themselves.

Since children's publications pay a great deal of attention to the seasons, you might want to list special days or times of year, noting activities and objects associated with each. Under "Winter" your list of possibilities could include:

Word scramble based on winter sports and activities (skis, sleds, etc.)

Craft project: making pom-poms for ice skates

Recipe: variation of hot chocolate or other cold weather drink: cake or ice cream dessert shaped like snowballs.

Mini-crossword themed around winter words (icycles, snow-shoes, etc.)

PUZZLES APLENTY

Among the puzzles, the most common are word scrambles, word finds, hidden pictures, mazes, dot-to-dots, mini-crosswords, missing letters, coded messages, number problems, and visual mind-stretchers. Some of them—word scrambles, word finds, and mini-crosswords, for instance—are simplified versions of the adult puzzles described in Chapter 12. You can get the basic details of their construction from that chapter.

Word scrambles (often called hidden words in children's magazines), like their adult counterparts, are either a jumble of letters or an actual word out of which other words can be made. This one from *Wee Wisdom*, by Dee Lillegard, is typical:

Sprung from Spring

The letters that make up the words below can all be found in SPRING.

1. A barnyard animal __ __ __
2. To tear __ __ __
3. To drink slowly __ __ __
4. Something worn on a finger __ __ __ __
5. To smile __ __ __ __
6. To whirl or twirl __ __ __ __
7. To hold tightly __ __ __ __
8. To cut or clip __ __ __ __

Sprung from Spring

1. pig		5. grin	
2. rip		6. spin	
3. sip		7. grip	
4. ring		8. snip	

To create word scrambles for juveniles, take a simple word (those with one or two vowels and several consonants work best) and list the words you can form from it. Compose simple definitions for each word, give the little piece a snappy title, type it neatly (double-spaced) on a sheet of typing paper with your name and address, and send it off.

Kiddies' *word find* puzzles are just like those for adults, except that there are fewer words in relation to the total number of letters and often some simple artwork is involved. In a *Child Life* "Vegetable Stew Word Search," names of twenty vegetables were printed on a simply drawn bunch of broccoli, an ear of corn, a green pepper, and a zucchini. The letters of the word find, instead of being enclosed by a box, were printed in a big soup kettle.

Hidden pictures and *mazes* require some artistic skill, but not a whole lot. If you can think of clever ideas, it is possible to produce salable work by tracing items from magazines or books and combining them with a little freehand drawing of your own (or get a friend who can draw to collaborate). Most hidden pictures contain ten to fifteen objects listed above the puzzle and integrated into the drawing in such a way that they aren't apparent to youngsters at first glance. A guitar can be drawn as part of a gnarled tree; a pear can be worked into the pattern of a man's coat. The picture itself should be lively and should depict a scene that will capture children's imaginations.

Mazes involve following the path that leads to a pictured object or objects. A Valentine maze in *Child Life*, for example, consisted of a heart, inside of which were four children's names on envelopes at the top and four little houses about halfway down the heart. Squiggly lines led from each of the envelopes (with several dead-end offshoots) to one of the houses. Instructions said: "Johnny and Nancy are delivering valentines to their friends. Please help them by following the lines from each name to a house. When you reach each house, print the first letter of the name that is connected to the house. You will have a valentine, too!"

Dinosaur Dot-to-Dot

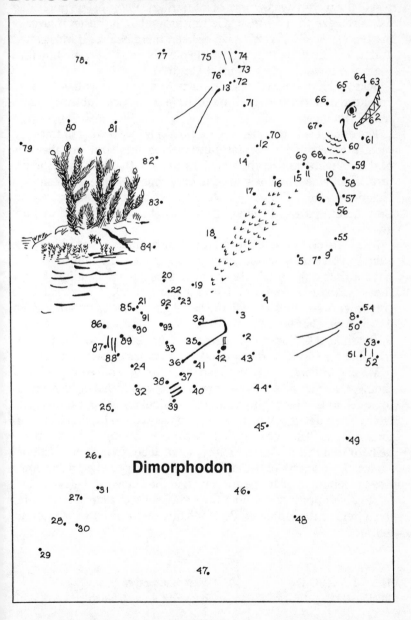

Dimorphodon

A maze in *Jack and Jill* called "Whose Kite Am I?" had sketches of three little boys at the bottom of the page and a kite at the top. The rest of the picture was a maze of kite strings. *Young Judean* published a desert maze with the text: "Getting around in the desert is no easy matter, especially if you've never been there before. If Moses had gotten lost, do you think you would have been able to help him find the route towards the Promised Land?"

Seasonal hidden pictures and mazes are popular with editors, as are those tied to the magazine's focus (e.g., biblical subjects, health-related themes).

The easiest way to construct a *dot-to-dot* is by drawing or tracing a picture (it needn't be elaborate) and placing numbers along the lines of the drawing so that the pencil can follow them to draw the picture. Then erase the lines, leaving only those that are impossible to include in your 1-2-3-4 sequence. The dot-to-dot from *Playmate* on the preceding page will give you an idea of how simple the drawings are.

Mini-crosswords usually call for no more than 45 words, but occasionally you will come upon one that uses more. They almost always have a theme (a vertebrate crossword puzzle appeared in *Ranger Rick's Nature Magazine;* one with biblical clues, in *Junior Trails*). To construct these puzzles, use the same guidelines as for adult crosswords (see Chapter 12).

For smaller children (age seven and under), crossword puzzles may call for filling in the squares with names of pictured objects.

Missing letters are easy to construct. After you have decided on a theme, make up a list of words related to it and a list of corresponding questions (keeping in mind the vocabulary of your target audience). Then delete letters from the answer words, leaving blanks in their places. This one, called "Alphabet Soup," by Phillip Redelheim, was printed in the *Young Judean*. It began with instructions: "A lot of the letters of the alphabet are in the pot of alphabet soup. Use the letters to fill in the 26 blanks, in the ten words below according to the definitions." Under the directions was a circle containing the letters of the alphabet. Below that were these letter words and definitions.

Alphabet Soup

1) __ I Z __ O R   Memorial prayer
2) E __ O __ U S   Book of the Pentateuch

3) S __ O __ A R   Ram's horn
4) __ E G E __   Southern part of Israel
5) __ E __ U __ A __ E __   Capital of Israel
6) M __ Z U __ __ H   Placed on doorpost
7) __ E A __ E   Shalom
8) __ O __ E R   Made Babel famous
9) __ __ E E N   Esther
10) __ E N __ __ U R __ __ N   First Prime Minister of Israel (last name, two words)"

1) Yizkor; 2) Exodus; 3) Shofar; 4) Negev; 5) Jerusalem; 6) Mezuzah; 7) Peace; 8) Tower; 9) Queen; 10) Ben-Gurion.

Coded messages are a cinch to devise, too. First you must establish your code, assigning a number, a symbol, or another letter to each letter of the alphabet (e.g., a = 15, b = 7, c = 26; a = , b = , c = + ; a = i; b = d; c = s). Then think of an appropriate message. Short scripture verses are popular among church-sponsored publications; proverbs and other sayings are often used in secular magazines. Make blank lines for each word of the message, with the number/symbol/letter for each letter of the word below the line. This example by Verna Sherman, from *Junior Trails*, on the following page illustrates a common form of coded puzzle.

I have a feeling that kids who hate arithmetic don't do the **number problems** in magazines, which accounts for the fact, perhaps, that you won't find many of them used. As you will notice, both of the puzzles below have catchy titles but actually aren't much different from the written problems in grammar school arithmetic books. The first one, by Ruth Schiefen, was used by *Friends;* and the second by *Highlights for Children.*

For the Birds

Lisa had $3.50 to spend on supplies for her bird feeder. She bought a box of oatmeal for seventy cents, sunflower seeds at eighty cents a pound and two dollars' worth of suet from the butcher. When she got home she still had forty cents. How can that be?

For those of you who, like me, couldn't figure out the answer, it's because she bought only a half pound of sunflower seeds.

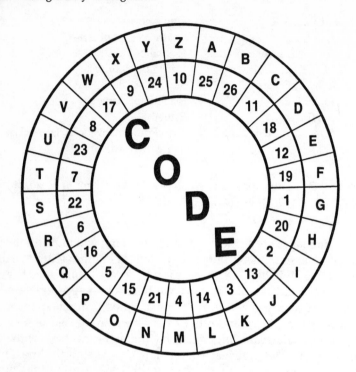

Use the code and find the Scripture verse.

_____

14 12 7   12 8 12 6 24

_____

4 25 21   26 12   22 17 2 19 7   7 15

_____

20 12 25 6,   22 14 15 17   7 15   22 5 12 25 3,

_____

22 14 15 17   7 15

_____

17 6 25 7 20.

Clues Add Up

OK, Sherlock, here are the clues. Can you solve all three of these problems?

Tough

- Both numbers are even.
- One number is less than four.
- Zero is not one of the answers.
- They add up to twelve.

Tougher

- Each number is even.
- There are three numbers.
- They add up to thirty.
- No number is used more than once.
- No number is more than twelve.

Toughest

- Each number is odd.
- Each number is less than ten.
- There are three numbers.
- They add up to twenty-one.
- There is more than one right answer.

Clues Add Up
  Tough - 2 and 10
  Tougher - 12, 10, 8
  Toughest - 9, 7, 5, and 9, 9, 3

If you come up with new wrinkles to old problems—I've seen several variations of the "If Mike is older than Matt who is younger than Mark who is . . ."—by all means submit them. Or try contemporizing the old divide-and-subtract theme. Here's my own example: Annie went to visit the President. He gave her 24 jelly beans. Annie gave half of them to Daddy Warbucks who fed half of his jelly beans to Sandy. How many did Sandy eat?"

If number problems don't add up for you, consider the *visual mind-stretcher*. These puzzles usually consist of a simple diagram and instructions to rearrange the objects in the diagram in a certain way. Variations on this theme—using circles or objects—for example, have been printed in dozens of publications. This puzzle is my adaptation of a very old, very common visual mind stretcher.

Ten apples are arranged like this:

Can you make this arrangement by only moving three apples?

Answer:

MORE KIDDIE PLEASERS

Children's quizzes are essentially of the fill-in-the-blanks, true-false, and mix-and-match varieties. You construct them in the same manner as adult quizzes (see Chapter 12), always keeping in mind your readers' abilities. These two, by S.H. Kreng and Laura Sargent, from *Trails'* "Funstuff" department, illustrate two different types of fill-in-the-blanks quizzes:

A Pride of Lions

Have you ever seen a pride of lions? This is the correct way to talk about a group of lions.

See if you know what to call these groups of animals. Fill in each blank with one of the words given below.

CLUTTER	TROOP
CLOUD	SMACK
BAND	PADDLING
BED	KNOT
LEAP	GAGGLE
TRIP	PEEP

1. A _____ of gorillas
2. A _____ of cats
3. A _____ of chicks
4. A _____ of goats
5. A _____ of toads
6. A _____ of clams
7. A _____ of leopards
8. A _____ of gnats
9. A _____ of geese
10. A _____ of jellyfish
11. A _____ of kangaroos
12. A _____ of ducks

A Pride of Lions

1. band	7. leap
2. clutter	8. cloud
3. peep	9. gaggle
4. trip	10. smack
5. knot	11. troop
6. bed	12. paddling

Animal Doings

Fill in the spaces with animal names that describe the actions.

1. You — — — — your food down when you gulp it in a hurry.
2. You — — — — a burden when you carry something heavy.
3. You'd better — — — — when a ball comes flying through the air!
4. When you hit a ball, you — — — it.
5. You — — — — for compliments when you want to hear nice things.
6. You — — — people's footsteps when you follow right behind them.

Animal Doings

1. wolf	4. bat
2. bear	5. fish
3. duck	6. dog

Although quizzes in religious publications usually center on biblical references, you will also find general knowledge quizzes like this mix-and-match from the *Annals of St. Anne de Beaupré's* "Kiddie Korner," a page especially for children.

Plants Around the World

The first column lists fifteen commercial plants. The plants grow in various countries, but one major producer of each is listed in column two. Which plant and which land would you match?

1. Coffee	A. France
2. Tea	B. Cuba
3. Rice	C. Philippines
4. Pineapples	D. Honduras

5. Rubber		E.	Japan
6. Tulips		F.	The Netherlands
7. Potatoes		G.	Brazil
8. Grapes		H.	Jamaica
9. Vanilla Beans		I.	Algeria
10. Bananas		J.	Malaysia
11. Ginger		K.	Mexico
12. Cigar Tobacco		L.	Spain
13. Olives		M.	Ireland
14. Cinnamon		N.	China
15. Cork Trees		O.	Sri Lanka

Plants Around the World

1.G,2.E,3.N,4.C,5.J,6.F,7.M,
8.A,9.K,10.D,11.H,12.B,13.L,
14.O,15.I

Although most *jokes* and *riddles* in juvenile publications are submitted by children, you'll occasionally find a market for groups of riddles or jokes based on a theme, such as this "Tick-Talk," published by *Ranger Rick* and heavily illustrated with ticks doing outrageous things like "tick or treating."

What does a tick bank robber say? This is a tick-up.

Where do ticks live in the Far North? The Arctic.

How does a tick clean its teeth? With a tooth-tick.

What kind of tick lives on the moon? A lunatic.

How do ticks tell time? With a tick-tock.

What game do ticks like to play? Tic-tac-toe.

What do a lot ticks die from? Heart Atticks.

What do ticks say on Halloween night? Tick or treat!

What do you call a tick that can draw and paint? Artistic.

What happens when a tick falls into a jar of vinegar? It turns into a tickle.

What subject do ticks hate in school? Arithmetic.

What happens when a tick drinks too fast? It gets tick-ups.

Ticks that do flips, cartwheels, and handstands are good at what? Acrobatics.

What do you call ticks named Romeo and Juliet? Romantics.

Recipes must be for foods that most kids like and that are easy to prepare. Get ideas from foods offered on restaurant kiddie menus, or poll the neighborhood youngsters to determine their favorites. Then look through your cookbooks for similar foods that you can adapt, with an eye toward dishes that are easy and quick to prepare. Avoid those with many ingredients (six to eight at most; fewer, if possible).

Catchy names for children's recipes are even more important than for those aimed at adults. Incorporating names of storybook, movie, and TV characters or popular games and places will add appeal: E.T. Cookies, Circus Cupcakes, Checkerboard Sandwiches. In creating recipes for children, follow the same pattern as for adult recipes (see Chapter 4), keeping directions simple. This recipe for Leprechaun Soup appeared in *Playmate:*

You will need:

1 can tomato soup	4 stalks celery
2 cans water	1 small onion
5 beef bouillon cubes	¼ cup chopped cabbage
2 carrots	1 cup peas
2 small potatoes	1 cup corn

Directions:
1. Wash and peel carrots and potatoes.
2. Have a grown-up help you cut the carrots, potatoes, celery, and onion into small pieces.
3. Let a grown-up heat the soup, water, and bouillon cubes.
4. Add all the vegetables.
5. Cover and simmer for about one hour.

Analyzing the recipe, we see that it is essentially a regular soup recipe with a clever title. You can do the same thing with any simple recipe, be it for cookies, candy, hamburgers, casseroles, or cool drinks.

When creating your recipes for children, explain any cooking terms with which they may not be familiar. (I wonder if most kids would understand *simmer* in the recipe above.) When writing recipes for candy or other edibles that involve viscous liquids at high heat, advise that it would be good to have adult supervision.

Experiments, in order to be salable, must be both instructional and fun to do. They should be safe to perform without adult supervision. If you have a scientific bent, think of basic principles and entertaining, easy-to-understand ways they can be presented. Keep the instructions simple. Use readily available and inexpensive supplies. Remember, too, that mothers will bless you if mess can be kept to a minimum. This experiment from *Ranger Rick* meets all these requirements.

Make a Weather Station

You wake up on a bright, sunny morning with nothing to do. The sky is blue, with puffy white clouds. It's a perfect day for a club picnic!

After packing a tasty lunch, you and the other club members hop on your bikes and ride along your favorite trail. Soon you come to a shady spot and stop to eat. But suddenly the clouds darken and a bolt of lightning crackles across the sky. The rumble of thunder fills the air. You look up to find the sky full of dark clouds . . . and a big raindrop splashes right in your eye.

By the time you pedal home you're soaked to the skin. Worst of all, the clouds have disappeared and the sun's come out again!

But don't let crazy weather get the best of you. Your nature club can make a "mini" weather station and be ready for stormy surprises!

With just a few materials, your club can make simple instruments that help forecast the weather. Two of the easiest ones to make are a tin can barometer (ba-ROM-uh-ter) and a feather wind vane.

Tin Can Barometer

A barometer measures air pressure—the weight of air pushing against the earth. When the air begins to push hard (weather forecasters say the air pressure is rising), fair weather is usually ahead. When the air begins to push down less hard (the air pressure is falling), bad weather may be on its way.

To make a tin can barometer you'll need: a coffee can, a piece of plastic wrap, a rubber band, a piece of cardboard, a soda or broom straw, some glue, and tape.

1. Cut the plastic wrap to fit over the top of the can. Hold it tightly in place with a rubber band.
2. Tape the cardboard to the outside of the can.
3. Glue or tape the straw to the center of the plastic.
4. Make a mark on the cardboard where the straw now points. Then mark the words "high" and "low" about 1 inch (2.5 cm) above and below this mark.

Pick an area outside to test the barometer. As the air pressure changes the end of the straw should move up or down. If it rises, go on a picnic. But if it starts to fall, watch out! A storm may be on its way.

Feather Wind Vane

A wind vane points to the direction the wind is coming from. And the wind's direction can be a good clue to what the weather will be like.

All you need to make a feather wind vane is: a large feather, a large eyedropper without the rubber top, a thin 3½-inch nail, a 1-inch nail, an arrow-shaped piece of cardboard, a Styrofoam® ball, some wire, and a 1x3x3-inch wood base. (If you don't have a large feather, cut a piece of thin cardboard in the shape of one.)

1. Hammer the 3½-inch nail through the center of the base.
2. Carefully bore a small hole into the center of the Styrofoam ball. Then push the pointed end of the eyedropper into the hole.
3. Stick the quill of the feather into one side of the ball.
4. Tape or glue the cardboard arrow to the head of the 1-inch nail.
5. Push the 1-inch nail into the other side of the ball. (This will help balance the vane.)
6. Slide the open end of the eyedropper over the large nail so that it swings around freely.
7. If needed, wrap a piece of wire around the small nail to balance the vane perfectly.
8. Label the sides of the base North, East, South, and West.

Put the vane outside with the barometer. Point the side of the base marked "North" in that direction. (If you're not sure where north is, ask someone or use a compass to find it.)

Once your wind vane stops whirling and twirling in the breeze, check to see which way the arrow is pointing. That's the direction the wind is coming from.

Using a Cloud Chart

How can your wind vane tell you what the weather will be? It's easy—if you have a good cloud chart. For only $1.00 you can get a chart with colorful pictures of each kind of cloud. Under almost every photo, the chart "predicts" what the weather may be, depending on the direction of the wind.

Of course, having a weather station doesn't mean that you'll be able to forecast the weather exactly. But at least your club will be ready for fun—in rain or snow or hail or sun!

Rangers: You can get a 17 inch x 22 inch cloud chart by sending $1.00 to Ranger Rick's Cloud Chart, National Wildlife Federation, 1412 16th St., NW Washington, D.C. 20036

Crafty Crafting

Like adults, children are interested in making things they can use. But whereas grown-ups have developed the patience to stick with a project for days (weeks or months, if need be), most youngsters want to complete a craft in one session or, at most, two.

Therefore, children's crafts are not very complicated. They are also copiously illustrated, either with photos or sketches. If you supply sketches with your submissions, they need not be of professional quality. They must, however, be clear enough that the illustrator can understand exactly what you mean.

Specialized children's magazines almost always use crafts related to the publication's central theme. Editor Nancy Mack of *Odyssey* (a magazine for youngsters that focuses on astronomy and outer space) likes projects such as "Build Your Own Rocket Launch System" and "Make Our Great Odyssey Starcruiser" (a rocket). Trudy D. Farrand, editorial director of *Ranger Rick's Nature Magazine,* goes for crafts emphasizing the natural sciences. One she especially likes is "Bat Mobile," by Tony Albert—an illustrated one-pager with the twist that its directions are presented in rhyme:

This flock of fiendish creatures
Is just right for Halloween,
Or for a spooky party,
And always in between.

Tie thread around a sweet-gum ball,
Then knot it good and tight.
Add acorn caps for hollow eyes—
Your friends will faint from fright!

With black construction paper wings,
Your bats will dangle there,
Hanging from two crisscrossed sticks,
And flying through the air.

Rangers: If sweetgum trees don't grow in your part of the country, make your bats' bodies from any dried, round plant parts you can find. (Teasel heads, small pine cones, or wads of cockleburs work great!) Then glue on the eyes and wings.

Another very simple but effective craft idea Farrand bought consisted of five birdhouses from trash: a "coffee can cottage," a "detergent dream house," a "margarine tub mansion," and two models of "milk carton cabins."

Crafts for general interest juvenile magazines, such as *Wee Wisdom*, *Child Life*, and Sunday school publications, are based on ideas that appeal to most children, whatever their special interests might be: food treats for birds, a soup-can racing car, plaques made with dried vegetables, paper bead necklaces. Editor Kent L. Brown of *Highlights for Children* chooses a wide variety of imaginative projects for his crafts pages: a mouse hand puppet made from two plastic cups; a lamb fashioned from a tongue depressor, two clip clothespins and cotton; a wind-sled kite from a plastic garbage bag and drinking straws.

The most important thing to keep in mind while designing craft projects for youngsters is that they haven't had a great deal of experience making things. You can't take their knowledge of even the most basic processes for granted. When a piece of paper is to be folded lengthwise, not only words but also a diagram should show how. Testing by children will ensure that your directions are complete. Leave nothing to the imagination as far as directions are concerned.

But the best craft projects, according to experts, do leave room for creativity and self-expression. The basic instruction, according to Bobbie Armstrong, has to be given in order for the child to be able to branch out. Armstrong, who has taught crafts for an arts-and-crafts store chain and for recreation departments, says that the most successful crafts for children under high school age are those that are "pretty speedily done." The reason some craft projects fail, she says, is that they are too ambitious for the child's abilities.

Sally Nail, whose experience has included teaching deaf children as well as those without disabilities, agrees that projects should be simple enough to be completed in one sitting. "If a child makes something and never sees it completed, that's kind of a disaster," she says. Nail advises writers to alert their readers to have plenty of supplies available before they begin; running out of glue or other materials in the middle of a project is sure to be frustrating. She also feels that tools should really work. Using a blunt-pointed primary scissors is like trying to cut with two fingers, she points out. It's better to have the child use scissors that work, under adult supervision.

The writer who is interested in crafts should have no trouble finding ideas for children's projects. People who run hobby and craft stores are good sources of information, as are elementary school teachers and crafts people at recreation departments.

Since scrap crafts are so popular, you'll get salable ideas by assembling an assortment of throwaways: spools, odd-shaped metal and plastic containers, boxes, empty bottles, jars and covers, wallpaper remnants, and the like. Experiment with them. The physical act of handling the objects will often stimulate ideas.

Whenever you see a new craft, note how it's done. Then start thinking about ways of altering it. If it is an adult craft, work on ways of simplifying procedures, if necessary, and adapting the finished product to a child's world.

Children's activities look deceptively simple, as though they would be a cinch to create. On the contrary, they may prove to be one of the biggest challenges you'll encounter in your career. But challenges are what make this writing game so exciting.

SO, ON YOUR WAY

In these seventeen chapters we've talked about a smorgasbord of sales opportunities. All of them call on your creativity—your ability to come up with fresh ideas and angles. But none of them call for writing that anyone with the desire to succeed and the willingness to work toward that goal can't produce.

I hope at this point you're impatient to put the book aside and start writing. With all the options for both adult and juvenile material, and with intelligent marketing, you'll find opportunities galore to write less for more—more possibilities for publication and more money for the time you spend. Best of all, you'll discover the excitement and joy that is part of the writer's life.

✦ ✦ ✦ ✦ ✦ BIBLIOGRAPHY

Bernstein, Theodore M. *The Careful Writer.* New York: Atheneum, 1977.

Borland, Hal. *How to Write and Sell Non Fiction.* New York: Ronald Press Company, 1973.

Brady, John. *The Craft of Interviewing.* Cincinnati: Writer's Digest Books, 1976.

Cassill, Kay. *The Complete Handbook for Freelance Writers.* Cincinnati: Writer's Digest Books, 1981.

Crawford, Tad. *The Writer's Legal Guide.* New York: E.P. Dutton, 1978.

Duncan, Lois. *How to Write and Sell Your Personal Experiences.* Cincinnati: Writer's Digest Books, 1979.

Giles, Carl. *Writing Right—To Sell.* New York: A.S. Barnes and Company, 1970 (queries).

Gunther, Max. *Writing the Modern Magazine Article.* Boston: The Writer, Inc., 1973.

Hull, Raymond. *How to Write "How-To" Books and Articles.* Cincinnati: Writer's Digest Books, 1981.

Jacobs, Hayes B. *Writing and Selling Non-Fiction.* Cincinnati: Writer's Digest Books, 1967.

Jerome, Judson. *The Poet's Handbook.* Cincinnati: Writer's Digest Books, 1980.

Lewis, Claudia. *Writing for Young Children.* Garden City, New York: Anchor Press/Doubleday, 1981.

Markow, Jack. *Cartoonist's & Gag Writer's Handbook.* Cincinnati: Writer's Digest Books, 1967.

Merriam-Webster staff, ed. *6,000 Words.* Springfield, Mass.: G. & C. Merriam Co., 1976. (Words that have come into the English language since 1962.)

Perret, Gene. *How to Write and Sell (Your Sense of) Humor.* Cincinnati: Writer's Digest books, 1980.

Polking, Kirk, ed. *The Beginning Writer's Answer Book.* Cincinnati: Writer's Digest Books, 1977.

Provost, Gary. *Make Every Word Count.* Cincinnati: Writer's Digest Books, 1980.

Rockwell, F.A. *How to Write Nonfiction That Sells.* New York: Regnery, 1975.

Rosenthal, Gloria. *In 25 Words or Less.* New York: Simon and Schuster, 1980.

Schemenaur, P.J., ed. *1983 Writer's Market.* Cincinnati: Writer's Digest Books, 1982.

Stenbock, Evelyn A. Teach Yourself to Write. Cincinnati: Writer's Digest Books, 1982.

Strunk, William, Jr., and White, E.B. *The Elements of Style.* 2nd ed. New york: Macmillan Publishing Co., Inc., 1972.

University of Chicago Press. *A Manual of Style.* 12th ed. 1967.

Weisbord, Marvin, ed. *A Treasury of Tips for Writers.* By the American Society of Journalists and Authors. Cincinnati: Writer's Digest Books, 1981.

Winkler, G.P., ed. *Associated Press Stylebook.* New York: The Associated Press, 1970.

Wyndham, Lee., revised by Arnold Madison. *Writing for Children and Teenagers,* 2nd revised edition. Cincinnati: Writer's Digest Books, 1980.

✦ ✦ ✦ ✦ ✦ INDEX

H

Hallmark Books, 132

Hallmark Cards, 134, 135, 136, 138, 141, 145

Halsey Publishing, 212

Harper's, 181, 190

Hart, Lorenz, 152

"Hats Are Back and Guess Who Hasn't Got One?," 156

Health, 96

Health articles, 96, 99, 229, 230

Health Explorer, 221

Hearsay, 78

"Hearts Are Trumps," 37

Heloise, 42, 54

"Helping Keep Neighborhoods Safe," 75

Hidden pictures, 236

High Adventure, 24

High Fidelity, 198

Highlander, The, 124

Highlights for Children, 222, 225, 229, 239, 250

Hints, 42. *See also* Tips, marketing of, 44; refining of ideas for, 45; sources for, 42

Historical characters, 225

Historical societies, 82

History as source of quotes and quips, 20

Hobbies, 118, 279, 180, 233; as source for project how-tos, 56; stores for, 251

Hollywood Bowl, 215

Home Cooking, 148

"Home Is Where the Chili Is," 115

"Home on the Range," 156

Home as source for project how-tos, 56

Homonyms, 191

Honolulu Advertiser, 22

Horizon, 124

"Horoscope Hangup," 157

Horse & Horseman, 86

House magazines, 7

"How to Accept Favors Without Feeling Guilty," 65

"How to Change Your Life to Make It More Interesting," 66

"How I Fight Insomnia," 65

How to Make and Sell Original Crosswords and Other Puzzles, 164

How-tos, 55, 94, 232, 233; for children, 227; community problem, 74;

 organization problem-solution, 78; personal enhancement. *See* Personal enhancement how-tos procedure. *See* Procedure how-tos; project, 56; types of, 55

How to Write and Sell Your Personal Experiences, 82

How to Write and Sell (Your Sense of) Humor, 21

Humor, 16, 86, 133, 135, 137, 143, 170; in anecdotes, 30, 35; in greeting cards, 136, 138; marketing of, 24; in quips, 23

Humpty Dumpty, 221, 230

I

Iambic, defined, 151

Iambic foot, defined, 149

Ideas, 98. *See also* Sources: adaptation method of generation of, 65; for anecdotes, 29; for children's activities, 234; for greeting cards, 140; for hints and tips, 45; for light verse, 152; for mini-informationals, 88; for personal experience articles, 81; for personal opinion articles, 70; for procedure how-tos, 65; for projects, 56

Ideas, Techniques and Secrets (ITS), 181

Illustrations, 61, 87, 249. *See also* Artwork; Photographs for studio greeting cards, 137

Imagery, 39, 41, 93, 232; for anecdote, 36; defined, 36

Imperative verbs, 62; for recipes, 50

"Imported Perfection," 211

Industry. *See* Business

Inflight, 111, 112

Informationals, 231. *See also* Mini-informationals, for children, 229

Information Report, The, 103

Inspirational, defined, 139

Inspirational publications. *See* Religious publications

"Instant experts," 87

Instant Word Finder, 163

Interesting facts, 23, 98

Interests, 8

Internal rhyme, 151

Interviews, 68, 101, 106, 113, 114, 116,

✿✿✿✿✿PERMISSIONS ACKNOWLEDGMENTS

"The Blue Door," by Mary Louise Kitsen. From *Seek* magazine © 1981. The Standard Publishing Company, Cincinnati, Ohio. Division of Standex International Corporation. Reprinted by permission.

"Don Kir Van Collects Barns," Copyright 1981 by Joel Schwarz. Reprinted with permission from the H.M. Gousha Company, from the July/August 1981 *Odyssey*.

"Cut Meal Costs with Florida Diner's Club" from *Travel Advisor* of *Travel Holiday Magazine*, Floral Park, NY 11001, December 1977. Reprinted by permission.

"Extravagant Granola" and excerpt from "Successful Swaps" by Diane Huneke from *The Mother Earth News*, September/October 1981. Reprinted with permission from *The Mother Earth News*® , copyright 1981 by The Mother Earth News, Inc., P.O. Box 70, Hendersonville, NC 28791.

"Significa" article, "The Baboon Who Ran a Railroad" by Irving Wallace, David Wallechinsky and Amy Wallace from *Parade*, July 11, 1982. Reprinted by permission.

Excerpts from "Imported Perfection" by Lee Perry from *AirCal*, March 1982. Reprinted by permission.

Excerpt from "Go fly a kite!" by Freda Jacobs from *Capper's Weekly*, October 28, 1980. Reprinted by permission.

"Hearts Are Trumps" from *Catholic Digest*, April 1982, reprinted with permission of Ruth M. Hube of Cincinnati, Ohio.

"Leaf It Be" by Forester in *Chicago Tribune*, reprinted in *Reader's Digest*, October 1981. Reprinted by permission.

"Cruise Crossword" puzzle and answers by Jack Luzzatto from *Cruise Travel*, September/October 1981. Reprinted by permission.

Anecdote by Irene Valenti Kucinski from *Expecting*, Fall 1981. Copyright by Parents' Magazine Enterprises, a division of Gruner + Jahr, U.S.A., Inc. Reprinted by permission.

"Double Cross" puzzle reprinted from *Games* Magazine (515 Madison Ave., New York, NY 10022), March/April 1982. Copyright © 1982 Playboy Enterprises, Inc. Reprinted by permission.

"Viewpoint" by Mary Alice Kellogg from *Glamour*, February 1982. Copyright © 1982 by The Condé Nast Publications, Inc. Reprinted by permission.

"A Memo to the Chef of the United Nations Cafeteria" from *Gourmet*. Copyright © 1978 by Dan Carlinsky. Reprinted by permission.

Anecdote by Smiley Anders from *The Morning Advocate*, Baton Rouge, Louisiana. Reprinted by permission.

"Slump of the Secure Player"—Newsline, reprinted from *Psychology Today Magazine*. Copyright © 1982 Ziff-Davis Publishing Company.

"The Real Mystery" by Jackee McNitt-Watson from *Savvy*, January 1982. © 1982 *Savvy* Magazine, N.Y. Reprinted by permission.

"Woodpeckers Lured by Plastic Trees" by Karen Braeder from *Science Digest*, April 1982. Reprinted by permission.

Excerpts from "A Special Island" by Dorothy Becker and from "Woodcarver" by Monte Hansen reprinted from *Small World*, a publication of Volkswagen of America, Inc., Winter 1981-82 and Spring, 1980 issues respectively.

Excerpts from "Tips on buying real bargains at yard sales, flea markets and auctions" from *The Star*, July 6, 1982. Reprinted by permission.

"Tell us about your worst moment and win $25" by Virginia Banghart from *The Star*, July 20, 1982. Reprinted by permission.

"Things Kids Say" by Felice Belcher from *The Star*, July 20, 1982. Reprinted by permission.

"Three Cheers for August" by Ivey Harrington from *Trails*, July/August. Reprinted by permission from *Trails*, © 1981, Pioneer Girls® Inc., Box 788, Wheaton, IL 60187.

Other Writer's Digest Books

General Writing Books
  Beginning Writer's Answer Book, edited by Polking, et al $9.95
  How to Get Started in Writing, by Peggy Teeters $10.95
  International Writers' & Artists' Yearbook, (paper) $10.95
  Law and the Writer, edited by Polking and Meranus (paper) $7.95
  Make Every Word Count, by Gary Provost (paper) $6.95
  Teach Yourself to Write, by Evelyn A. Stenbock $12.95
  Treasury of Tips for Writers, edited by Marvin Weisbord (paper) $6.95
  Writer's Encyclopedia, edited by Kirk Polking $19.95
  Writer's Market, edited by P.J. Schemenaur $18.95
  Writer's Resource Guide, edited by Bernadine Clark $16.95
  Writing for the Joy of It, by Leonard Knott $11.95

Magazine/News Writing
  Complete Guide to Marketing Magazine Articles, by Duane Newcomb $9.95
  Craft of Interviewing, by John Brady $9.95
  Magazine Writing: The Inside Angle, by Art Spikol $12.95
  Magazine Writing Today, by Jerome E. Kelley $10.95
  Newsthinking: The Secret of Great Newswriting, by Bob Baker $11.95
  1001 Article Ideas, by Frank A. Dickson $10.95
  Stalking the Feature Story, by William Ruehlmann $9.95
  Write On Target, by Connie Emerson $12.95
  Writing and Selling Non-Fiction, by Hayes B. Jacobs $12.95

Fiction Writing
  Creating Short Fiction, by Damon Knight $11.95
  Fiction Writer's Help Book, by Maxine Rock $12.95
  Fiction Writer's Market, edited by Jean Fredette $17.95
  Handbook of Short Story Writing, by Dickson and Smythe (paper) $6.95
  How to Write Best-Selling Fiction, by Dean R. Koontz $13.95
  How to Write Short Stories that Sell, by Louise Boggess $9.95
  One Way to Write Your Novel, by Dick Perry (paper) $6.95
  Secrets of Successful Fiction, by Robert Newton Peck $8.95
  Writing Romance Fiction—For Love And Money, by Helene Schellenberg Barnhart $14.95
  Writing the Novel: From Plot to Print, by Lawrence Block $10.95

Special Interest Writing Books
  Cartoonist's & Gag Writer's Handbook, by Jack Markow (paper) $9.95
  The Children's Picture Book: How to Write It, How to Sell It, by Ellen E. M. Roberts $17.95
  Complete Book of Scriptwriting, by J. Michael Straczynski $14.95
  How to Make Money Writing . . . Fillers, by Connie Emerson $12.95
  Confession Writer's Handbook, by Florence K. Palmer. Revised by Marguerite McClain $9.95
  Guide to Greeting Card Writing, edited by Larry Sandman $10.95
  Guide to Writing History, by Doris Ricker Marston $9.95
  How to Write and Sell Your Personal Experiences, by Lois Duncan $10.95
  How to Write and Sell (Your Sense of) Humor, by Gene Perret $12.95
  How to Write "How-To" Books and Articles, by Raymond Hull (paper) $8.95
  Mystery Writer's Handbook, edited by Lawrence Treat (paper) $8.95
  Poet and the Poem, revised edition by Judson Jerome $13.95

Poet's Handbook, by Judson Jerome $11.95
Sell Copy, by Webster Kuswa $11.95
Successful Outdoor Writing, by Jack Samson $11.95
TV Scriptwriter's Handbook, by Alfred Brenner $12.95
Travel Writer's Handbook, by Louise Purwin Zobel $13.95
Writing and Selling Science Fiction, by Science Fiction Writers of America (paper) $7.95
Writing for Children & Teenagers, by Lee Wyndham. Revised by Arnold Madison $10.95
Writing for Regional Publications, by Brian Vachon $11.95
Writing to Inspire, by Gentz, Roddy, et al $14.95

The Writing Business

Complete Handbook for Freelance Writers, by Kay Cassill $14.95
How to Be a Successful Housewife/Writer, by Elaine Fantle Shimberg $10.95
How You Can Make $20,000 a Year Writing, by Nancy Hanson (paper) $6.95
Jobs for Writers, edited by Kirk Polking $11.95
Profitable Part-time/Full-time Freelancing, by Clair Rees $10.95
The Writer's Survival Guide: How to Cope with Rejection, Success and 99 Other Hang-Ups of the Writing Life, by Jean and Veryl Rosenbaum $12.95

To order directly from the publisher, include $1.50 postage and handling for 1 book and 50¢ for each additional book. Allow 30 days for delivery.

Writer's Digest Books, Department B
9933 Alliance Road, Cincinnati OH 45242
Prices subject to change without notice.